Central to the faith of early Friends was the present sense of the Second Coming of Christ and the bringing of heaven on earth. Friends around the world may still be able to unite around this vision of a transformed society but how and when heaven will be fully realised are questions which have underpinned three centuries of change and division. This book looks again at the letters of Paul, the experience of early Friends, and the history of Quakerism through the lens of the Second Coming and draws radical new connections which the authors believe have the potential to give Friends and others a clarity about the Quaker tradition and the power to offer a key component in the revitalisation of Quaker faith.

Timothy Peat (left) has been Bible Studies Tutor at Woodbrooke Quaker Study Centre since 1995 and, as Timothy Ashworth, has published Paul's Necessary Sin: the experience of liberation (Routledge 2006).

Douglas Gwyn (center) has authored several books on early Friends and on contemporary issues of Quaker faith.

Ben Pink Dandelion directs the work of the Centre for Research in Quaker Studies at Woodbrooke and is Professor of Quaker Studies at the University of Birmingham.

Original edition: 1998
Published by Woodbrooke College, Selly Oak, Birmingham, England
And Curlew Productions, Kelso, Scotland
(ISBN 1 900259 09 5)
out of print

Twentieth Anniversary Edition: 2018
Published by Plain Press, Philadelphia and Birmingham
ISBN: 1548452297
ISBN 13: 9781548452292

Heaven on Earth

Quakers and the Second Coming

Ben Pink Dandelion
Douglas Gwyn
Timothy Peat

with a foreword by John Punshon

Curlew Productions & Woodbrooke College

Foreword

John Punshon

The New Testament contains abundant evidence that the early Christians believed in the imminent Second Coming of Christ in a real, physical and historical sense. This understanding was plainly not a rationalisation or a spiritualisation of something else, but the necessary and inevitable corollary of Jesus' own words. The doctrine of the Second Coming is therefore a part of the Christian revelation rather than a theological reflection upon it.

It is none the less problematical, particularly because the Second Coming as described in Scripture seems to have been indefinitely postponed. Theological reflection is therefore inevitable, unless one goes outside historic Christianity and is satisfied with some kind of psychological, anthropological or mythological explanation of why people entertain such beliefs, as opposed to their inherent meaning or credibility.

Clarity is important here because there are many Friends not committed to historical Christianity for whom this is a perfectly permissible course to take. This book is in part written for them and offers a model, so to speak, of what a credible doctrine of the Second Coming would look like. It considers some of the sources and implications of the original Quaker variant of eschatological doctrine. The authors build on the proceedings of a Woodbrooke course in which Friends with a variety of points-of-view sought to come to terms with a little understood part of their doctrinal heritage. It is therefore earthed in the common search for meaning among a group of interested Friends.

The doctrine of the Second Coming is intrinsically interesting and difficult. Until the last century there was little discussion of it, but two developments have concentrated attention on it once more. The first was the rise of the prophetic movement in American evangelicalism which took seriously the prophecies in the New Testament as well as the Old. Quakers have a blind spot about charismatic phenomena while being perfectly happy to use Spirit language in general discourse, and they are also reluctant to enter a discussion of prophecy beyond a certain point. Thus, these developments passed many Friends by, though they are now an important part of the Evangelical scene.

The second development is associated with historical criticism of the New Testament, with which the liberal branch of Quakerism is more familiar and at home. At first, the Second Coming was regarded as belonging properly to a pre-scientific way of thinking and therefore to be regarded not as an essential part of Christian doctrine. About a hundred years ago it became clear on strictly critical grounds that one can only sever Jesus' ethics from his eschatology with considerable difficulty. This placed liberal theology in an impasse from which it has sought to escape in various ways.

This book represents an attempt to think out the problem again from first principles utilising scriptural evidence (mainly from Paul) and the thought of some leading early Friends, who do not say nearly as much about the matter as we would like. The writers propose a subtle and stimulating answer to the question of the Second Coming, and I hope that what they have to say will be widely noted and discussed among Friends.

Contents

Chapter One

Introduction

Ben Pink Dandelion

Central to early Friends' belief that they were working within God's time was the present sense of the Second Coming of Christ, as outlined in Scripture, and the bringing of heaven on earth. God's time, the realm of the mythic and the eternal, was coming to replace historical time to bring about the end of history and the beginning of a transformed humanity.

Friends around the world may still be able to unite around this vision of bringing heaven on earth but the questions of how heaven is to be drawn down onto the mundane plane of human geography, and when, underpin a history of change and division amongst Friends, and indeed the history of Christianity. As Schweitzer has written, 'the whole history of Christianity down to the present day, that is to say, the real inner history of it, is based on the delay of the *Parousia* [the risen Lord's return]' (1968:360). Amongst Christian groups and within Quakerism, the timing of 'heaven on earth' is unclear. It is a question whose answer has as many variations as there are theological nuances and yet it is central to an understanding of Quaker and church history.

This book looks at Quakerism through the lens of the Second Coming, and charts the varieties of this belief and its evolution across time from Paul the apostle to the present day. We argue that:

a) there is a coherence to the teachings of Paul which suggests an experience and theology of direct revelation and a renewed intimacy with God available to everyone at the time of the Second Coming;

b) early Friends can be seen to be fulfilling Pauline prophecy about the Second Coming and the final movement of humanity from a state of childhood to one of adulthood, these Friends believing they are working in a critical God-given moment in historical time;

c) this was a key separating factor from those Christian groups which were still rooted in the experience of the First Coming and whose structures and practices, such as the Lord's Supper, reflected this in an awareness that humanity still needed outward forms (ie. churches, priests, a Christian calendar, and sacraments) in this period of waiting;

d) the adoption of the pastoral system by programmed and Evangelical Friends as a partial reform of the Quaker Second Coming structures makes sense within the context of the changing nature of Quaker religious experience in the eighteenth and nineteenth centuries;

e) the change for Liberal Friends of interpreting their religious experience in terms of the Second Coming without a consequent change in structure leaves a way open for secularisation, which the structures and practices of other parts of Christianity are in place to guard against.

The first part of the book, 'Paul and the Promise of Transformation' (Chapters 2 - 7), is written by Timothy Peat. In it, he outlines his new and challenging scholarship on the coherence of Paul's message and on some of his understandings of what Paul was saying about the nature of faith and about the signs of the transformation of humanity which all could expect at the return of Christ. Tim also outlines the conditions Paul places on his prophecy and shows how 'the church' has responded to those conditions in its own theology of the interim.

In the second part of the book, 'Early Friends and the Second Coming' (Chapters 8 - 12), Douglas Gwyn finds the rise of early Friends amidst the contradictions and breakdown of English Puritanism in the seventeenth century. Radicals like the Levellers, Diggers, and Seekers all in various ways dreamed of an imminent Second Coming of Christ, a New Age of the Spirit, the Kingdom of God coming to replace the Stuart monarchy. But Puritan conservatism dashed such hopes by 1650. Early Friends revived those expectations, translating them into a present, unfolding reality, as they proclaimed the light of Christ within as the Second Coming of Christ. This was not merely a private apocalypse, an inward mysticism, but an earthquake that shook all sectors of English society in the 1650s. Tim draws the similarities between Paul's prophecy and the experience of early Friends, in particular showing how the early Friends claimed they had been effectively and permanently liberated from sin and brought into an intimacy with God where they continuously felt God's word guiding their actions. Doug charts the rise, defeat and eventual recontainment of the early Quaker Lamb's War as a Covenantal initiative for a new society where Christ reigns through the hearts of people. What we know of the Religious Society of Friends is a domesticated version of that early prophetic fire. Yet the apocalyptic resonances of early Quaker witness continue to disturb and inspire us down to this day.

The third part of the book, 'Quakers Through Time' (Chapters 13 - 18), begins with my interpretation of Tim and Doug's material. I go on to chart what has happened to Friends since the 1660s in relation to ideas of the Second Coming. The modification and later marginalisation of claims associated with George Fox's endtime theology begins with Robert Barclay (who first systematised Quaker theology) and continues through the Quietist period, reaching a culmination of rejection of these claims by an Evangelical Quakerism (re-founded in scriptural thinking and focused on the First Coming and the consequent meantime). Having lost the experience of the Second Coming, they logically follow the lead of 'the church' and adopt some of the outward forms felt helpful to a humanity in waiting. Liberal Quakerism does not adopt these outward forms, such as a pastoral system, and I question the degree to which explicit religion has been able to survive in such a context. Chapter 18 is a more personal chapter about my own struggles with faith.

There is a fourth part of the book, a section of conclusions. In 'Consequences and Possibilities', Chapter 19, I outline various optional positions as to how Friends relate today to Second Coming thinking and how this places them in relation to other Friends and ecumenically. The chapter ends with ideas on what the material can do for the life of Quakerism.

The book ends with an Epilogue from each of the three authors as we reflect on what our conclusions for Friends may be. There is additionally an Excursus, a chapter on the biblical understanding of time by Doug.

✣ ✣ ✣

Working with ideas of God's time, historical time, endtime, a particular biblical interpretation of Quakerism, and talk of the Second Coming will not be easy for all Friends. Indeed, many of the connections may be new, even for seasoned Quakers. As Schweitzer talks of a gradual de-eschatologising of Christianity (1968:360), so it can be said of Quakerism and the history of its history: if we have only learnt about Friends through the recent history books, we are unlikely to think about Quakerism as a Second Coming church. Doug's work has been almost unique in making these connections explicit.

This book is written in slightly different styles as a shared project rather than as a shared vision. Indeed the authors are not totally agreed on all points. However, a model does emerge, one likened to a Germanic sentence, in that it is only at the end that you hear the verb and can then make sense of all that has been said before. As in the cinema or the theatre, try to suspend your disbelief (or indeed your counter-belief) and sit with the arguments until the end so that you can better under stand the full picture. This is one understanding of the relationship between historical time and God's time, one reading of Paul and early Friends and the subsequent history of Quakerism. It may be challenging but this model has within it some critically important things for Friends to hear.

The suspension of disbelief

Within the world of theatre and cinema, audiences are invited to suspend their disbelief, to ignore the obvious constructions of performance, eg. the stage, make-up, lighting, and to enter fully into the fiction which the actors are attempting to create and interpret. The members of the audience enter that world, putting their own interpretations and judgements to one side for a while, suspending disbelief or counter-belief.

In reading this book, you are invited you to do the same, to put aside preconceptions about Paul or Scripture or talk of the Second Coming and read the book through, before stepping back into the world of analysis and judgement. This is not about trying to censor your critical faculties but is because the picture presented here only makes its fullest sense in its entirety. Only having read all three sections can we begin to ask what, if any, significance, this model or picture has for our own lives.

✣ ✣ ✣

This work has come together in a personally important way for all three of us, and Tim, Doug, and I are thankful for the year of being able to work alongside one another in Woodbrooke, and for the opportunity to run a course on this material together in January 1997. This book is based on the material for that course, generously commented on by the twenty students who took part, and to whom we dedicate this work.

In each of the first three parts of the book, there is a more personally reflective chapter. These formed part of the course in January 1997 and the place-ment of the chapters reflects where they fitted, at the time with such seeming synchronicity, into the wider programme. They are parts of the personal stories of three men, each finding themselves straddling two worlds (Quaker and Roman Catholic, Quaker and Quaker, Quaker and rationalist), each affected in his own way and in his own setting by the material presented here. For us this material has had strong personal and spiritual consequences as well as academic ones. The Epilogues also reflect this.

Those close to us, our families and friends, have already had to live with us living with this for some time. We are grateful for their patience, love and support. We have gained greatly from the careful reading of the text by Beth Allen, Paul Anderson, Christopher Holdsworth, John Punshon and Anne Thomas. We are indebted particularly to the thorough and loving editing of our work by Pam Lunn. We owe a debt of gratitude to Richard Sturm for further editorial suggestions.

However, this book is not the end of the story. As I say at the end of Chapter 18 about God, this material is no longer an option for me. It has come to inform the way I look at all aspects of Quakerism, the way I teach, the way I worship. Moreover, I believe it can point the way to a renewal of self-understanding amongst Friends worldwide.

Thomas Hamm (1991) has argued that today's accepted Quaker history belongs within a paradigm initiated in the 1850s. He argues that British evangelical Quaker history has informed and initiated the most part of what Liberals have later had to say about their heritage, including the critical 'how is heaven, and when?' questions.

This book charts and recharts the history of Quakerism through the questions about the Second Coming and the bringing of heaven on earth. In producing a complete model for understanding Quaker history afresh, the book is both a counter to received wisdom, and is able, if arrogantly, to comment on all notions of Quaker history. That is, the model of Quakerism presented here is, by default, yet another model, but it is also one which has within its internal logic, the ability to explore, explain, and analyse the whole of the history of Quaker thinking.

Note: Biblical translations

Except where otherwise noted, the Bible translation used is the New Revised Standard Version. Other English translations referred to are the Authorised Version (AV), Revised Version (RV), Revised Standard Version (RSV), New International Version (NIV), New Jerusalem Bible (NJB), Revised English Bible (REB) and the Good News Bible (TEV).

Part One:

Paul and the Promise of Transformation

Chapter Two

A biblical frame

Timothy Peat

History has a beginning and an end

The Bible begins with the story of Genesis - God's creation of all things - and ends with the book of Revelation, which climaxes in wonderful images of humankind in glorious intimacy with God:

> Then I saw a new heaven and a new earth; for the first heaven and the first earth had passed away and the sea was no more. And I saw the holy city, the new Jerusalem, coming down out of heaven from God, prepared as a bride adorned for her husband. And I heard a loud voice from the throne saying, "See, the home of God is among mortals. He will dwell with them as their God; they will be his peoples, and God himself will be with them; he will wipe every tear from their eyes. Death will be no more; mourning and crying and pain will be no more, for the first things have passed away" (Rev 21:1-4).

This is the biblical frame: in the beginning, God created all things and, at the end, there is to be a final transformation of all creation. This is not an easy frame to make sense of and in order to get the issue across as clearly as possible I would like to describe stages in the development of my own thinking.

When I first came to an adult decision about a spiritual direction in life, my decision was to learn how to meditate according to an eastern tradition with roots in Hinduism. This was a very important step for me and as I sought to practise meditation, I also sought to learn more about that tradition of meditation. In particular, I became familiar with the *Bhagavad-Gita*. I found it a practical guide in the spiritual life. Woven into the *Bhagavad-Gita* is a particular view of the spiritual life and how that relates to historical time:

> Lord Shri Krishna continued: 'Now I will reveal unto thee the Wisdom which is beyond knowledge, by attaining which the sages have reached Perfection. Dwelling in Wisdom and realising My Divinity, they are not born again when the universe is recreated at the beginning of every cycle, nor are they affected when it is dissolved.' *(Bhagavad-Gita,* ch.14 [Swāmi 1935:76]).

There are two things to note here:

(a) the picture of the universe in a repeating cycle of creation and dissolution;

(b) the image of the end of the spiritual life being a liberation from this cycle.

Within this tradition I discovered all kinds of helps for living the spiritual life - ways of finding peace in every aspect of life.

After I had been meditating for a couple of years I went into a Catholic church early one morning. What I found there surprised me. There was a real quality of peace. The priest spoke about the need to find peace in the everyday. I was very drawn to what I found. What was drawing me was the discovery that here in the church was support for the inner peace that I was looking for and trying to deepen in myself. My fundamental religious view was not at this stage under challenge, but as I got deeper into the Catholic Church it began to be. There are two things that an individual is faced with during every act of worship in church to which I want to draw attention:

1. *The reading of the Christian story.* The events that brought the Christian Church into being, and which make it what it is, are recalled week by week. These are understood as actual historical events: the exodus of the people of Israel from Egypt; the life and death of Jesus; the forming of the first Christian communities. What is presented is not primarily spiritual guidance like that which I had found in the *Bhagavad-Gita*.

2. *The participation in ritual.* These rituals are in a sense re-enactments of the key historical events joining the participants to these events in the past. These ritual acts are always outward or external and always communal.

These points provide a good focus for the shift that occurred in me. In my first contacts with the Church - and for some time afterwards - I saw the ritual actions as aids to coming to the same inner silence that I found in meditation. It was only after some time that I realised that a shift had occurred whereby I was now perceiving that the inner silence was an aid to participating more deeply in these ritual acts. The fact that these ritual acts were external and communal and were recalling real historical events was the absolutely central thing. They were not an aid to an inner state of peace. They were concerned with historical events which were deemed to have real historical effects. And then there was a final stage in coming to accept a biblical view of history. This came as I trained for the Catholic priesthood and had a chance to engage in some serious Bible study. I came to a recognition that the historical events relayed in the Bible and re-enacted in the rituals of the church are recalling those events in order to understand the involvement of God in history in the past, to strengthen a confidence both that God is acting in the present and, very importantly, that God will act in the future.

Perhaps the most telling change in understanding was in the shift that occurred in my idea of 'the kingdom of God'. The famous text: 'the kingdom of God is within you' (Lk 17:21) made good sense to me. It fitted comfortably with the search for an inner peace. But early in my biblical study I discovered that this interpretation of the kingdom of God as a present reality which has to be discovered 'within' could not be sustained. It was not the idea that the biblical authors were working with. The sense in Scripture was of the coming of the kingdom of God as a future event: a dramatic intervention of God to bring about a transformation in which the whole of creation was involved. I was not easy with this idea. But as I did more Bible study I had to acknowledge that this was the idea that Jesus was speaking of and was faithfully relayed in the other writings of the Christian Scriptures. Even that text 'the kingdom of God is within you' could not retain its old meaning for me. A different translation of these words of Jesus comes through seeing the verse in context and with an awareness of the likely Aramaic underneath the Greek that we have. I came to accept that 'the kingdom of God will suddenly be in your midst' is more likely to be an accurate expression of the words of Jesus (Jeremias 1971:101). I did try to cling on to my old view. The idea of future dramatic transformation for the whole of creation was much harder to take seriously, much harder to get any sense of. Yet I could not deny from my biblical study that this was the absolutely central theme, that God is acting in key events in history leading to the picture of transformation that we read in the book of Revelation: humankind in a renewed intimacy with God.

The technical word for the study of this idea of future transformation is 'eschatology'. (See box on p.106) To quote the German biblical scholar, Joachim Jeremias, speaking of the message of Jesus:

> The *basileia* (kingdom) is always and everywhere understood in eschatological terms; it denotes the time of salvation, the consummation of the world, the restoration of the disrupted communion between God and man [*sic*] (Jeremias 1971:102).

Paul and his letters

There are a number of ways in which the eschatological view of the kingdom of God could be presented. All the New Testament writings give evidence of it. In the chapters that follow it is the writings of Paul the apostle that will be the focus. Through giving close attention to the way his ideas relate to each other, combined with an exploration of some important details of translation, what emerges is a fresh and coherent picture which points up the nature of the experience underlying the early Christian movement. Once we have gained a sense of the nature of that experience, comparisons can be made with how early Friends spoke of their experience and how what emerges relates to our present situation.

Paul

First the person of Paul; who is he? If you wish to discover who Paul is - what kind of person, his psychological make-up, his religious and social background - you have a number of options. He gives various bits of personal information in the letters. Sometimes in the letters a more personal tone comes through, which can be revealing of what type of man he was. We have the Acts of the Apostles, written by Luke. This is an account of the days of the first Christian communities where the particular view of the writer is shaping what and how things are presented, but, while caution is required, there is still some useful and solid historical information to be found there (O'Connor 1996:vi). In recent years, there has been a significant amount of scholarly attention given to illuminating the historical, sociological and religious context of the first Christian communities (eg. O'Connor 1996; Meeks 1983). This has provided significant help in clarifying and assessing the appropriate weight to give to particular biographical details in Paul's life.

Having said that, in this presentation of Paul's thinking, almost no attention will be given to these ways of discovering the personality of Paul. What we have from Paul himself is a collection of letters. In this set of letters he claims to have been through a unique experience with universal historical importance: an encounter with God in which he feels himself called to be the apostle to the Gentiles, the one sent with a particular mission to the Gentile world. What will be presented in this section on Paul arises out of taking this claim to a unique calling seriously. What happened to Paul that made him speak as he did? What was the foundation for the extraordinary claims that he made? Is there coherence and consistency in what he says (Beker

1980:23-36)? In the chapters that follow we shall consider some of the extraordinary ideas that are central for him and explore their meaning.

The letters

In the Bible there are thirteen letters that carry Paul's name. The scholarly consensus is that seven can be confidently ascribed to him: Romans, 1 and 2 Corinthians, Galatians, Philippians, 1 Thessalonians, Philemon (Sanders 1977:431; Ziesler 1990:6f). For the purposes of this presentation, that consensus will be accepted. Of the other letters, Colossians has the most scholarly support for Pauline authorship. If Ephesians is not by Paul then it has been said that it is by his best disciple (Johnson 1986:372). 1 and 2 Timothy and Titus, known as the Pastoral Letters, have a different perspective; they are more concerned with an institutional framework for faith and they are seen as moving away from the radical presentation of faith that we find in Paul. However, even these are not without supporters for the view that they have a genuine Pauline authorship, albeit a Paul whose thought and style have changed (Johnson 1986:381-9).

There is doubt over the dating of the letters as there is over the chronology of Paul's life. This is just one set of possible dates: Conversion 34; 1 Thessalonians, the earliest, written about 50-1; Philippians 56-7; 1 and 2 Corinthians, 57; Galatians, Romans, 57-8; Philemon 61-3 (*New Jerusalem Bible* 1985:1853-1862). The dating of the particular letters becomes important if it is considered that Paul's thought changed significantly over time. However, this idea of significant change only follows if a lack of consistency is discerned in his thought. I hope to show that in the main areas of his thinking, there is an extraordinary consistency that runs through all the letters and that the accurate dating of the letters need not concern us in this presentation.

Why is it particularly helpful to turn to Paul to get an idea about the experience and thought of the early Christians? There are obvious answers. First, the writings of Paul are clearly a major part of the

Christian Scriptures. Secondly, they are the earliest of those Christian writings; the first letter to the Thessalonians was written less than twenty years after the death of Jesus. But there are more subtle and important reasons.

(a) *In his letters, Paul is concerned to win arguments.* They are controversial and argumentative pieces of writing; Paul has an axe to grind. Yes, it means that he is biased. But it is very revealing of the issues that were stake in those early communities and much more useful than a bland, idealised presentation of how things ought to have been. Here we have a taste of the reality. Paul considers that the debates that he is involved in are a matter of life or death for the communities, so he holds nothing back in arguing his case. We find insult and invective in them but, more importantly, the actual life of these communities is opened to us and we see how real human difficulties and divisions continued alongside the extraordinary claims.

(b) *Paul's letters are written to address particular situations.* The letters were written for particular groups at particular times to address particular needs. Paul expresses himself differently to the different groups on the different occasions; he uses different images to illuminate his teaching. He does not simply have a theory, a collection of statements that he trots out consistently; images arise out of his experience to enable him to speak powerfully and appropriately to the particular community situation he is addressing. And what we shall find is that these different images complement each other. This is very strong support for the basing of his teaching in real experience: his own and that of the communities to which he writes.

(c) *Paul's letters are written for 'insiders'.* Paul's letters are not 'evangelical' in the sense that they are not written to draw outsiders into the communities. Paul is writing to others who share many of the same assumptions. He can say: 'you remember how it was when I was with you; you had an experience of the Spirit coming among you.' And he can go on from that and say: 'you know what it is like to live by the Spirit, now carry on being led by the Spirit; do not go back to your old ways.' He does not spell out the detail of what happened because it is part of the history of the community that he is writing to, something he shared with them. If there was not some real dramatic experience that they shared then what he says would make little sense.

A new interpretation of Paul

How is the reader to test the validity of the new interpretation of the thinking of Paul that is presented here? Some suggestions may be useful.

1. *Issues of translation.* Translations reflect mainstream scholarly thinking on Paul's theology. Comparing translations is a way of bringing other views into the picture to place alongside the one presented here. At several important points in the presentation there will be discussion of details of translation. Although you may not have access to the Greek text, you can assess which translation makes coherent sense - which makes most sense of Paul's thinking and which makes most sense in your own experience.

2. *Read Paul's letters.* An obvious but easily forgotten point. Reading Paul's letters will help you engage with the particular points made in this presentation. It may be helpful whether working as an individual or group to use the Friendly Bible Study method evolved by Joanne and Larry Spears (Spears and Spears 1990).

3. *Quiet reflection.* This is not solely an academic exercise. Some quiet time alongside time for reading may make possible an engagement with the material which runs deeper than the intellectual alone.

4. *A mainstream interpretation. Pauline Christianity* by J. A. Ziesler (1990) is a well respected and well written presentation of Paul's theology. It refers to a variety of scholarly views but remains readable and accessible. Read alongside this argument it will become clear where the major differences are.

The knot

The science of interpretation includes the principle that in order to grasp the meaning of something we must understand the whole in terms of the detail and the detail in terms of the whole (Gadamer 1989:291). The issue of how the details of Paul's thinking relate to the whole of his theology continues to exercise scholars. It appears that Paul says contradictory things, particularly in trying to show how God could give the law only to later abrogate it and introduce the age of faith. Paul cannot say that God got it wrong but, it is argued, in trying not to say this, the coherence of Paul's theology is undermined. One explanation is that Paul is so passionate about his central conviction that God has sent Jesus to bring liberation to the world that he does not worry about making other aspects of his thinking consistent with each other (Sanders 1983:146-8). A fresh effort is made in this presentation to show how the various elements of Paul's thinking do relate coherently to each other. The approach taken in this presentation can be likened to a diagram of a knot.

Just as this diagram in order to be effective must show the way in which any one strand of the knot relates to all the others, so this presentation will primarily be concerned to show how a particular strand in Paul's thinking relates to any other.

Chapter Three

From law to faith

Timothy Peat

At the heart of Paul's message is the theme of liberation: For freedom Christ has set us free. Stand firm, therefore, and do not submit again to a yoke of slavery (Gal 5:1).

If Paul is speaking of 'liberation', what is this liberation from and to? John Ziesler is clear that Paul is speaking of liberation. In his *Pauline Christianity* he has a chapter called 'Old Life and New' and most of the subheadings within that chapter contain the idea of liberation: 'Liberated from sin'; 'Liberated from flesh'; 'Liberated from Law'; and the list continues (Ziesler 1990:viii). In this chapter we shall combine two of these: liberation from sin and liberation from law.

Soon after the above verse where Paul is speaking to the Galatians of liberation, Paul refers to the life of the Spirit:

> Live by the Spirit, I say, and *you will definitely not* gratify the desires of the flesh... [I]f you are led by the Spirit, you are not subject to the law... [T]hose who belong to Christ Jesus have crucified the flesh with its passions and desires (Gal 5:16, 18, 24, NRSV amended with the words in italics).

The point is simple but can slip away in translation. I suggest that Paul's point here is that coming to live by the Spirit involves a real change in which the 'passions and desires' no longer have any power.

It involves a real transformation in the individual. The first sentence above is usually translated:

> Live by the Spirit, I say, and do not gratify the desires of the flesh.

That is an exhortation, an encouragement. But what Paul says is:

> Live by the Spirit and *there is no way* that you will gratify the desires of the flesh (Dunn 1993:297).

He considers that a real change is possible in which fleshly passions and desires are no more. The logic is simple: 'If you are led by the Spirit, fleshly (if you like, selfish) passions and desires have died and therefore you are not under the law.' A fundamental part of the law is to provide a check upon such desires and so, if they are gone, in this respect, the need for the law has gone too. This is a vital strand in Paul's understanding. It is not that there was something wrong in religious law and all that is needed is a turning to a different way of living. It is far more radical. Paul is claiming that the life of the Spirit is one in which there is such a transformation in the individual that law is no longer required. There is an inner direction and empowerment which brings the need for an external boundary to behaviour to an end.

Very simply this is confirmed in the word Paul uses for this fundamental change. In Greek, it is the verb *dikaioō*, usually translated in English, 'to be justified'. That translation is itself misleading. It removes the connection there is in the Greek with *dikē* (right) and *dikaiosunē* (righteousness). In order to relay the sense in English the phrase 'to be righteoused' has to be coined (Sanders 1991:45-9). That gets across a sense that connects directly with Paul's claim for life in the Spirit: the one who lives by the Spirit has been 'righteoused', brought from doing wrong to doing right; such a one is no longer 'under the law'. The need for the law as a check for the desires of the flesh has simply gone.

The prophetic word

Paul consistently makes a contrast between law and faith. He speaks of being 'righteoused' by faith. It will be proposed that one key reason why Paul consistently contrasts law and faith is a simple one: law and faith both provide direction on what to do. Now that is obvious when it comes to law: if you are following the law you simply do what is prescribed. It is not so obvious when it comes to living by faith. How does faith provide clear direction on what to do? A good answer is a particular proposal for what Paul means by faith: faith understood as living under direct guidance from God; living with the confidence that God's word is active and can be discerned. We need to see if that is a legitimate interpretation of Paul.

Before coming to Paul's understanding of faith it is useful to consider some of the biblical background to this idea of direct guidance from God. Right at the beginning of the account of the first followers of Jesus in the Acts of the Apostles we find the apostles gathered in Jerusalem in fear. Something very dramatic happens which is described in poetic language and images. The Spirit is described as coming among them with a sound like rushing wind and then something like a tongue of flame rests upon each one gathered there. Out of this experience they go out on to the streets and speak words from the prophet Joel:

> "...'In the last days it will be, God declares,
> that I will pour out my Spirit upon all flesh,
> and your sons and your daughters shall prophesy,
> and your young men shall see visions,
> and your old men shall dream dreams.
> Even upon my slaves, both men and women, in those days I will pour out my Spirit; and they shall prophesy...'"
> (Acts 2:17f; cf. Joel 2:28f).

Commonly today the verb 'to prophesy' is used to mean 'to foretell the future' but the richer sense of the verb is 'to speak by divine inspiration' (Onions 1972:1688). Although the prophets of the Old

Testament were often concerned with the future, their essential task was to speak for God:

> "Son of man, go, get you to the house of Israel, and *speak with my words to them...*" (Ezek 3:4, RSV).

The prophet becoming the voice for God is understood in a literal way. This comes through very clearly in the account of the calling of Moses. Even though Moses is known primarily as the great law-giver of Israel, his was nonetheless a prophetic calling. He has an anxiety about this call from the very beginning. He says to God:

> "If I come to the Israelites and say to them, 'The God of your ancestors has sent me to you,' and they ask me, 'What is his name?' what shall I say to them?" (Ex 3:13).

In response to this God gives Moses a range of dramatic signs to perform, but still Moses is worried:

> "O my Lord, I have never been eloquent, neither in the past nor even now that you have spoken to your servant; but I am slow of speech and slow of tongue." Then the Lord said to him, "Who gives speech to mortals? Who makes them mute or deaf, seeing or blind? Is it not I, the Lord? Now go, and *I will be with your mouth and teach you what you are to speak*" (Ex 4:10-12).

Here the very literal understanding of prophecy emerges. Still Moses resists:

> But [Moses] said, "O my Lord, please send someone else." Then the anger of the Lord was kindled against Moses...(Ex 4:13f).

There now follows a section which further illuminates the literal understanding of prophecy that emerges above:

> ...and [the Lord] said, "What of your brother Aaron, the Levite? I know that he can speak fluently; even now he is coming out to

meet you, and when he sees you his heart will be glad. You shall speak to him and put the words in his mouth; and I will be with your mouth and with his mouth, and will teach you what you shall do. He indeed shall speak for you to the people; he shall serve as a mouth for you, and you shall serve as God for him" (Ex 4:14-16).

With this richer understanding of prophecy, the sense of the words of Joel is not that in the last days all shall predict the future but rather that, in those days, God will speak in all God's sons and daughters.

The prophetic word in the early Christian communities

Paul's first letter to the Corinthians contains an extensive section on spiritual gifts (1 Cor 12-14). Paul's discussion includes an appraisal of the particular gift of speaking in tongues but a modern concern to understand this unusual gift can obscure the no less extraordinary presupposition shared by Paul and his readers. The section opens with a contrast which begins to make the point. Paul describes the former life of the community when they 'were led astray to idols that could not speak' (12:2) and immediately follows this with a point about discerning when someone is 'speaking by the Spirit of God' (12:3). The main concern of the passage is about discernment but the object of that discernment is how the prophetic word of God is heard and recognised in the community. *That God is speaking in the community through its members in contrast to the idols of the past that could not speak is the unquestioned assumption of the whole passage.*

Paul considers that clear direction for action comparable to the directions given by law comes through the prophetic word of God sounding in the community. He describes how he pleads for the removal of what he calls a 'thorn in the flesh' and records the response that he receives from the Lord:

> [B]ut [the Lord] said to me, "My grace is sufficient for you, for power is made perfect in weakness" (2 Cor 12:9).

Paul goes on to use this prophetic word as an explanation of why he glorifies in weakness and hardships. Paul claims to hear this teaching directly from God and he uses it in order to advance his understanding of the God's purposes. He presents this without comment with the clear assumption that, just as he ascribes this word to the Lord, so will his readers. That the voice of the Lord is speaking in the community is a firm belief shared between Paul and his readers.

In Paul's discussion of prophecy and speaking in tongues he focuses the issue of discernment on the relative value of these two spiritual gifts to the community:

> For those who speak in a tongue do not speak to other people but to God; for nobody understands them, since they are speaking mysteries in the Spirit. On the other hand, those who prophesy speak to other people for their upbuilding and encouragement and consolation. Those who speak in a tongue build up themselves, but those who prophesy build up the church. Now I would like all of you to speak in tongues, but even more to prophesy. One who prophesies is greater than one who speaks in tongues, unless some one interprets, so that the church may be built up (1 Cor 14:2-5).

Prophecy, Paul says, is of clear and practical benefit; it builds up the church, giving encouragement and consolation:

> [I]n church I would rather speak five words with my mind, in order to instruct others also, than ten thousand words in a tongue (1 Cor 14:19).

From this last sentence it could be argued that the form of prophecy that Paul is contrasting with speaking in tongues is something akin to a considered exposition of Scripture or a discourse on morality - reasonable words (words spoken with the mind) that build up, encourage and console the community that hears them; but while, as has been said, Paul is not explicitly expounding the nature of prophecy, the passage continues to give further information about the rather more extraordinary nature of this gift:

> If, therefore, the whole church comes together and all speak in tongues, and outsiders or unbelievers enter, will they not say that you are out of your mind? But if all prophesy, an unbeliever or outsider who enters is reproved by all and called to account by all. After the secrets of the unbeliever's heart are disclosed, that person will bow down before God and worship him, declaring, "God is really among you" (1 Cor 14:23-25).

There are two Greek words here that are difficult to put into English: 'to reprove' *elegchō* and 'to call to account' *anakrinō*. One reason for that difficulty is that what Paul would seem to be describing here is not something commonly known in the modern church. One recent translation gets over the difficulty by assuming that what Paul is describing is something closer to Christian experience today:

> But if all are uttering prophecies, the visitor, when he enters, hears from everyone something that searches his conscience and brings conviction... (1 Cor 14:24, REB)

In this translation Paul is thought to be recalling a picture of 'unbelievers' entering a Christian gathering and hearing inspired words which they then apply to themselves, just as people might enter a church today and apply the words of Scripture or preaching that are heard to themselves bringing some kind of change of heart. This changes the sense in the Greek in a subtle way; while the prophetic word is spoken by all it does not therefore have a general sense which the hearer can then apply. The dramatic effect of the prophetic word implies that what is spoken through the community is specifically targeted upon the unbeliever; it is the prophetic word spoken by all but addressed to this particular unbeliever that convicts and calls to account:

> [H]e will be convinced by all that he is a sinner and he will be judged by all...(1 Cor 14:24, NIV).

It is as a consequence of this extraordinary activity of the community, by which the secrets of the heart are disclosed, that unbelievers are convinced that it is not by any human ability that the truth about themselves is revealed but that it is God who is speaking to them through the word of prophecy. It is this which leads to the declaration 'God is really (Gk. living, existing, being) among you' (1 Cor 14:25). God who knows what is in the heart of the person who enters the community speaks through the gathered assembly in a way that convinces the individual that this is God who is speaking to them.

Further evidence that when Paul speaks here of prophecy he is speaking of a gift just as extraordinary as that of speaking in tongues occurs as the passage continues. Paul gives instruction about the way things are to be done when the community is gathered:

> Let two or three prophets speak, and let the others weigh what is said. If a revelation is made to someone else sitting nearby, let the first person be silent. For you can all prophesy one by one, so that all may learn and all be encouraged (1 Cor 14:29-31).

Paul is ensuring that there is an order to the gatherings of the community so that all may benefit to the full but note once again that the reality of the prophetic word, that is, the word of God voiced within the community, here referred to as encouraging and teaching, is an unquestioned assumption of all the instructions that Paul gives.

Paul and the prophetic word

In the early part of the letter to the Galatians Paul speaks of the source of the gospel that he preaches. From the very opening of the letter he is concerned to establish that his calling did not come through any other person:

> Paul an apostle - sent neither by human commission nor from human authorities, but through Jesus Christ and God the Father, who raised him from the dead... (Gal 1:1).

Apostle means 'one who is sent'. Paul is affirming that this sending came directly from God just as the Hebrew prophets heard the word of God sending them out for a particular task. This sending has no other authority; it needs no other authority. Paul goes on to give a further insight into his calling which leads to an interesting connection:

> But when God, who had set me apart before I was born and called me through his grace, was pleased to reveal his Son to [Gk. 'in'] me, so that I might proclaim him among the Gentiles, I did not confer with any human being (Gal 1:15f).

Given the right background information, it becomes clear that Paul is making here a very specific point. For the main part of that information it is necessary to see the close parallels between the above text and the beginning of the book of the prophet Jeremiah:

> Now the word of the Lord came to me saying, "*Before I formed you in the womb* I knew you, and *before you were born I consecrated you*; I appointed you *a prophet to the nations*" (Jer 1:5) [italics added].

The parallels indicated by the sections in italics are interesting enough in themselves, indicating that Paul, knowing this text, could clearly present his calling in prophetic terms, but this is to miss the crucial point. Paul is arguing that his gospel did not come to him through any human being. His words clearly echo the passage which records the call of Jeremiah; but the essential element of that prophetic call is not the reference to being called before birth or being sent to the Gentiles but rather *the coming to the prophet of the word of God*. To make the connections as vivid as possible an extended quotation will be included. Note how in the phrases in italics the coming of the word of God is described as historical fact. The context of Paul's use of the parallel to this passage indicates that he is attributing his gospel to that same prophetic word:

have seen how he considers that he has been called directly by God. Now we turn to three texts where Paul speaks of the nature of his mission.

Galatians 3:2, 5

Paul is once again expressing astonishment at the Galatians. He starts by calling them foolish and asking who has bewitched them:

> The only thing I want to learn from you is this: Did you receive the Spirit by doing the works of the law or by believing what you heard?... Well then, does God supply you with the Spirit and work miracles among you by your doing the works of the law, or by your believing what you heard? (3:2, 5).

A detail of this brief passage needs consideration. Paul is asking a simple rhetorical question in this passage: did you receive the Spirit by doing the works of the law or by believing what you heard? There is no question that he expects there to be only one thing that comes to mind as an answer: 'by believing what we heard.' This is clearly part of a communal experience that he can assume he shares with those receiving the letter: you remember how it was when I came to you. There is clearly an experience that he can point to which all will recognise and which he can then build his argument upon.

It is important then that we get an idea of what is meant by the phrase that is translated here 'believing what you heard'. The fact is - and you would not know it by simply reading through the text of the letter in English - that what Paul means by the Greek words that he uses here is not easy to be assess (Dunn 1993:154f; Williams 1989; Hays 1983). The phrase in Greek is *akoē pisteōs.* The second bit is relatively easy. It is the genitive for the Greek word for 'faith' so can be translated the 'blank of faith' or 'faith's blank'. The first word is the noun connected with the verb 'to hear'. We do not have a noun in English which will precisely fit in this position, a noun of the same family as the verb 'to hear' which means something that is heard. So what the English translation of this two word phrase needs to relay if it is to be accurate is the idea of faith's 'heard thing'. There is no English word that does not limit what the 'heard thing' might be. So what translators have to do is to make a decision about what this 'heard thing' is and what its relationship with faith is and then, having made a decision, choose English words that get this across. It is very obvious when you run through the translations what most translators have decided.

> How was it that you received the Spirit - by practice of the Law, or by *believing in the message you heard?* (NJB)

> [D]id you receive God's Spirit by doing what the Law requires or by *hearing the gospel and believing it?* (TEV)

> [D]id you receive the Spirit by keeping the law or by *believing the gospel message?* (REB)

> Did you receive the Spirit by observing the law, or by *believing what you heard?* (NIV)

It is very clear most translators have made the decision that Paul is contrasting doing works of the Lord with hearing and believing the gospel message preached by Paul. However, what I think Paul is referring to is a contrast between the works of the law and hearing and responding to the word of prophecy, the direct word from God, that came to the community when Paul first preached. There are two other occasions when Paul uses *akoē*. To get across the alternative I will use the clumsy phrase 'heard thing'. Remember that this is not a proposal for a good English translation but an attempt to be clear about what Paul is saying:

> The only thing I want to learn from you is this: Did you receive the Spirit by works of the law or by faith's 'heard thing'?... Well then, does God supply you with the Spirit and work miracles among you by works of the law, or by faith's 'heard thing'? (3:2, 5).

Romans 10:15-17

The first text I want to look at comes in chapter 10 of the letter to the Romans. Shortly before the relevant phrase we find this:

> But what does [the righteousness that comes from faith] say? "The word is near you, on your lips and in your heart" (that is, the word of faith that we proclaim)... (10:8).

Note here the connection of faith with the word understood as a word that is intimately known; it is in your heart. This is how the section we are interested in is translated in the NRSV:

> As it is written, "How beautiful are the feet of those who bring good news!" But not all have obeyed the good news: for Isaiah says, "Lord, who has believed our message [*akoē*]?" So faith comes from what is heard [*akoē*], and what is heard [*akoē*] comes through the word of Christ (10:15-17).

These quotations come in the midst of an extended section where Paul is seeking to explain how the failure of his fellow Jews to accept the gospel does not mean that God's promises to them have been broken. If the interpretation we are suggesting is right, Paul is using a quotation from the prophet Isaiah to argue that, just as the failure to accept the prophetic words of Isaiah in his time did not mean that God's word was false, so the failure of the Jews to recognise the prophetic word spoken through Paul and his fellow apostles is, again, not a sign that God's word is false or has failed. This is an alternative version:

> As it is written, "How beautiful are the feet of those who bring good news!" But not all have heard and responded to the good news: for Isaiah says, "Lord, who has believed our 'heard thing' (*akoē*)?" So faith comes from the 'heard thing' (*akoē*), and the 'heard thing' (*akoē*) comes through the word of Christ.

1 Thessalonians 2:13

The second passage provides the strongest confirmation that we are on the right track with this interpretation. For this section of the first letter to the Thessalonians the most literal English translation of the Greek is that made in the *Revised Version*:

> And for this cause we also thank God without ceasing, that, when ye received from us the word of the message (*akoē*), even the word of God, ye accepted it not as the word of men, but, as it is in truth, the word of God, which also worketh in you that believe. (1 Thess 2:13, RV [translators' italics]).

Problems of translation

> [T]he meaning of a word depends not on what it is in itself, but on its relation to other words and to other sentences which form its context (Thiselton 1979:78f).

This reflects the vital concern to take seriously the context in which a word is used. But there is a balance to be struck. While the meaning of a word is shaped by the context in which it is used, there is something consistent that is retained in a word as it moves from context to context:

> There is no getting away from the fact that single words do refer to certain referents, and not to others, and that this characteristic is the indispensable basis of all communication. It is on this basis that the speaker selects his [*sic*] words, and the hearer understands them...(Stern 1931:85).

Turning to a dictionary provides a range of meanings for a word based on characteristic contexts where the word is used. In studying the writings of Paul, some sharpness of definition becomes possible by seeing how he uses particular words. The context in which a word is used by Paul will mean that it can only carry a certain limited range of meaning. If that same word can be used in other settings with that limited or even further reduced range of meaning this will strongly suggest that the word carries a sharp and specific meaning for Paul:

> The mutual limitations exercised by the word meanings in a phrase may be sufficient to make the total meaning perfectly definite, and to reduce the number of possible phrase referents to one...(Stern 1931:141).

'Heard thing' (*akoē*) is rendered above as 'the message'. A second point brings a further sharpening of the translation. The translators of the *Revised Version* were particularly concerned with remaining close to the Greek and whenever they added words not in the Greek in order to make the sense in English clearer they put them in italics. In the phrase, 'the message, even the word of God', 'even the word' is in italics and is not in the Greek; 'it' and 'as' in the following phrase can be omitted on the same basis. With these changes the passage now reads:

> [W]hen ye received from us the word of God's 'heard thing', ye accepted not the word of men, but, as it is in truth, the word of God, which also worketh in you that believe (1 Thess 2:13, adapted RV).

If 'God's "heard thing"', like 'faith's "heard thing"' in the Galatians passage, is used in this passage, it can be seen that the interpretation of this phrase as 'the inner voice' or 'word of prophecy' makes good sense in this context. It can be seen that, of the three passages, this verse most dramatically favours this interpretation. It evokes an image of Paul speaking the word of God, understood as words from God, spoken as a prophet speaks, accepted as such by the community ('ye accepted not the word of men, but...the word of God'), which then, as a consequence, becomes a medium of the same prophetic word ('which also worketh in you that believe').

Conclusion

In the three passages examined in the last section of the chapter, it is possible to maintain a consistent translation of the single Greek word *akoe* if Paul is understood to be speaking of something heard within the believer. I am proposing that this is indeed what Paul means and that what is heard in association with the coming of the Spirit is the prophetic word from God guiding the actions of those who receive it. It is with this word that Paul claims to speak. In what Paul writes to the Thessalonians he indicates that by their recognition of the prophetic word spoken by him they themselves become recipients of the same prophetic word. This points to the possibility that in speaking of 'righteousness by faith', that is, the way of doing what is right by faith, Paul is referring to a life guided by this voice from God which sounds within. If this is correct then Paul's question to the Galatians examined earlier can be understood with this sense in the following paraphrase:

> Was it through works of the law or when you heard the word of God spoken through me that you received the prophetic Spirit that empowers and guides, the same Spirit by which I spoke?

The Spirit and prophetic word can be understood as being directly from God. Paul can sharply contrast righteousness by faith with righteousness by the law because they are both ways of knowing what to do. One difference is in the directness or immediacy of guidance by the prophetic word from God. The other is that the liberation Paul speaks of includes a liberation from sin; the one who walks by the Spirit will definitely not sin. In Paul's understanding, for those who have been set free from sin and have the way of doing what is right through faith, the mediation of law is no longer required.

Chapter Four

Face to faith: tied up in knots

Timothy Peat

Paul and Palestinian Judaism

When in 1982 I went as an undergraduate to study theology I was very interested in the issues of theology: the nature of God; the big questions of human existence; the questions of how and why we act as we do. But I had no expectation that I would get especially interested in the Bible or in the thought of Paul in particular. I was a student at Durham University and had the privilege of studying in a system which, along with lectures and seminars, provided a personal tutor to meet with each week whose task was to determine what reading and essays would enable the student to get most from the course. In my second term there began a course on Paul's letter to the Romans and so I was directed to tackle a series of essays on Paul.

I quickly became aware of a book that had been published five years earlier, a book by an American scholar, E. P. Sanders, Paul and Palestinian Judaism *(Sanders 1977). It was clear that this book had been more than influential. It had demolished one of the central foundations upon which the interpretation of Paul had been based. I need to get across what that foundation was and why it was important.*

You do not need to read far in Paul to find that he says some negative things about the Jewish law, in particular, contrasting it detrimentally with faith. Partly because of these negative statements, partly because of the gospel accounts of the struggles of Jesus over the law, there was established in Christian scholarship a particular view of the Jewish religion at the time of Jesus: a view of Judaism as a religion of interminable struggle with petty regulations, of a constant failure to meet the demands of a judging God; and, in particular, a religion in which there was the need to earn the grace of God through works. Paul was seen as the prime exemplar of someone locked in this guilty struggle, never able to get it right, wanting to so badly that he was prepared to persecute the emerging dissident followers of Jesus and finally, with all this emotional friction, having some kind of crisis which led to his conversion to the Christian way and to a new life of grace, faith, peace and freedom.

It is this foundation that Sanders demolishes, in two ways. First, and this is the major part of his book, he presents a picture of Judaism at the time of Jesus and Paul. This is an extraordinary piece of scholarship. What he establishes is that nowhere is there to be found in the Jewish writings the picture of Judaism that I have just presented. Everywhere - in the many writings that Sanders surveys - the law is understood as a gift. Everywhere there are echoes of these words from Psalm 119:

> *Oh how I love your law!*
> *It is my meditation all day long.*
> *Your word is a lamp to my feet*
> *and a light to my path.*
> *Your decrees are my heritage forever;*
> *they are the joy of my heart.*

The law is part of the covenant between God and Israel. Obedience to the law is important, it maintains that covenant relationship between God and each individual, but it does not earn God's grace. What is more it is quite possible to fall short of the law and not fall from grace with God. Within the law there is a whole framework for reconciliation with God and neighbour.

So that is the first part of Sanders' achievement: a presentation of the Jewish tradition at the time of Paul and Jesus which completely undermines the established view. What it also does is raise an issue that could not be clearly seen prior to this point. If Judaism at the time of Jesus and Paul was not this caricature that I have briefly sketched, then why are there such strong statements against the law in the writings of Paul (and in other parts of the Christian Scriptures)? This is a simple but important point. Paul still makes a huge distinction between faith and the law. If there was something fundamentally wrong with the law, if it was causing him personally to be in a state of acute religious anxiety, if it was giving him no peace, then this antipathy, this massive distinction can be easily explained. But if not, why does he make the distinction?

Sanders discovers an extremely interesting thing about Paul's way of thinking and it is summed up in a phrase that you will probably come across if you do any reading on Paul. What Sanders discovers is that Paul's thought, his understanding, moves 'from solution to plight'. Paul has a dramatic experience, a transforming experience, in which Jesus Christ and in particular the death and resurrection of Christ are central. It is an experience of reconciliation and liberation. Paul comes to a new life. This is reflected in the language he uses: death to rebirth; liberation from slavery; a new creation. It is this experience that is the starting point of Paul's understanding, his theology. He has a dramatic and positive experience. He experiences what he feels is the solution to the whole of the world's suffering and sin. He experiences the solution first. It is only from that perspective that he then describes 'the plight', 'the problem' of which 'the law' is a significant part. Some words from Paul might help here. He says:

> *Indeed, what once had glory has lost its glory because of the greater glory... (2 Cor 3:10).*

The glory of the law has been overwhelmed by the glory of what has come. The law really was glorious but in the light of what has come that glory is no more seen. In this same passage, Paul describes the law as 'the ministry of death' (2 Cor 3:7). He would never have described the law in this way before this new experience. It was not that he had experienced the law as a ministry of death. But it is in the light of what he has now encountered that he describes it so. There was something wrong or inadequate about the law, only in relation to what he has now come to.

And this is where understanding Paul really came alive to me because at the end of studying this work by Sanders, I was left with a question, a question that I had already asked myself but one which was reinforced by this work on Paul. If Paul was going along happily in his Jewish faith, then went through a transformation which could make him look back on that Jewish faith and describe the law in the negative way that he does, what was it that made the difference; what had happened to him? It is a question that Sanders himself asks: what was the nature of the transformation that Paul had gone through; what new perception did it bring him? Sanders is clear: it was more than just a revised understanding of himself and the nature of God, it was not just magic. Something really happened, but what? Towards the end of his book, Sanders says, very humbly:

> *I do not have a new category of perception to propose here. This does not mean, however, that Paul did not have one (Sanders 1977:522f).*

'A new category of perception' is an idea that interests me. It intrigued me then; it still intrigues me now. And it fuelled my interest in Paul.

New Testament Greek

The most useful thing that I did as an undergraduate - struggle though it was - was to learn some New Testament Greek. What I learned then and what I continue to use opened up possibilities of understanding that would otherwise have been closed to me. There is one particular problem of translation that made it very clear how important the work of translation is. The aim in looking at the following text is to see this issue of translation rather than to examine the meaning of the text, but it may help to know that Paul is here arguing how those who live by faith are the true children of Abraham, because he lived by faith. He was faithful before the law existed.

Just as Abraham "believed God, and it was reckoned to him as righteousness",

so, you see, those who believe are the descendants of Abraham.

And the scripture, foreseeing that God would justify

the Gentiles by faith, declared the gospel beforehand to Abraham ...

(Gal 3:6-8, New Revised Standard Version)

Figure 1

Without knowing the Greek there is no way of knowing from this translation that 'believe' and 'faith' are translating the same Greek root - believe for the verb, pisteuō, *faith for the noun,* pistis *(Sanders 1991:45-49). There is no difference. To translate the noun and the verb consistently into English is tricky. The noun 'belief' would mean something different, something closer to the idea of opinion or thought: 'that God would justify the Gentiles by belief' means something different from 'that God would justify the Gentiles by faith'. The same issue affects the translation of the second word above but involves a weightier issue. 'Righteousness' is the obvious translation of the noun,* dikaiosunē. *We do not have in English the verb 'to righteous' as a way of translating the verb,* dikaioō, *and instead we have in most translations 'to justify'. For the reader in English there is no way of knowing that the two words are from the same root: 'it was reckoned to Abraham as righteousness' is directly connected with 'scripture, foreseeing that God would righteous the Gentiles by faith'.*

Now this is a really substantial matter and takes us back to the last point of Sanders' that I made above. What Paul is using here is a word to describe something closely connected to that dramatic change, that new perception that we spoke of above. And in English at this point, our translations obscure what Paul is saying. What this did for me as I made this exploration as an undergraduate was to open up the value of translation work. Without getting some help in getting at the original language, the reader in English is very much at the mercy of the particular understanding of the translator.

In 1990, I was studying at Oxford. I was by this time in contact with Friends. My wife and I were wardens at the Quaker Meeting House in Aylesbury and I was becoming familiar in a very practical way with the particular practices of Friends. I had a term of study where to a large extent I was left to my own devices. And I picked up on the work that I had done as an undergraduate. The most interesting thing going on was a seminar on Paul's letter to the Galatians and prompted by this I began to translate the letters of Paul, with a commitment to translate all verbs and nouns from the same Greek root consistently through all the letters. A very interesting thing occurred. What I found when I translated words consistently was that Paul's thinking seemed to come into sharp focus, particularly his thinking around this idea of a 'new perception'. There were a number of elements to the emerging picture. In summary, these are the main points that I think he is claiming for this new perception that he had come to: Jesus is alive and has appeared to the apostles; Jesus continues to live and speak in us as God acted and spoke in him; living by faith is living by this direct guidance from God; the Spirit of Christ which is now in us puts an end to sin, there is no longer any struggle to do right, but right action arises from a natural obedience to the voice of faith sounding within; because, in us, sin is at an end, there is freedom and no need for the law, including the need for special rituals, times and seasons; what has come to us now is a promise of what is to come to all.

There are two major themes running through this: one is the importance of direct guidance from God, the idea that the community can be guided by faith, in the same way that Jesus was guided; the second is the idea that this change Paul is speaking of is a real liberation from sin. I do not think it is overstating the situation to say that in mainstream biblical scholarship neither of these is seriously considered as a key element in the lives of the early Christians. That the early Christian communities considered that the word of God was sounding among them is acknowledged but not given a central place (eg. Dunn 1991:92). More controversial still is the idea that there was a claim among at least some of the early Christians to be free from sin. This receives no backing. And as a consequence of pursuing this line I found myself seriously at odds with mainstream scholarship, right out on a limb.

Apocalypse of the Word

Some years on, while visiting Friends House in London, I came across a book about the message of George Fox entitled Apocalypse of the Word *(Gwyn 1986). As a result of the material that Doug presents in this work, I suddenly found myself not alone out on this limb, but joined to a whole community of people who were saying very similar things as I had found in my approach to Paul. What Doug makes very clear is that the early Friends made both of those central claims that I had found in Paul: to be directly guided by God; to be liberated from sin.*

Since taking up the position of Biblical Studies Tutor at Woodbrooke I have been exploring these links between the first Christians and the first Friends. There are, of course, many Friends in the past and present who have made connections between these two groups (e.g. Cadbury 1957). I think the one difference in my approach is that my starting point has been a fresh reading of Scripture rather than an interest in Friends. It was only after some years of studying Paul that the Apocalypse of the Word *came to hand.*

What this connection has done is provide two openings. One is professional. Most students who come to Woodbrooke do not come for biblical studies. Looking at the Bible through this particular lens of the experience of early Friends has, I think, been a way to enable the Bible to be taken seriously by people who are hesitant about approaching it or who see it as having nothing to say to them.

The second opening has been personal. Placing the experience of the early Friends alongside that of the early Christians simply emphasises the interest that came out of the earlier study of E. P. Sanders: the recognition that something dramatic happened among these groups, something that brought real change. My belief is that real change can still happen. And the experience of the early Friends and early Christians is dramatic confirmation of its reality.

This is not a line of research that is 'academic' in the sense of detached impersonal enquiry. To know what it was that inspired the early Christians and the early Friends seems vital to me. And it has a direct bearing on my own faith position. For I find myself now uncomfortably straddling two communities. I keep a foot in the traditional church; I have a foot in the Quaker community. I certainly do not feel inclined to place both feet back in the traditional church. I have stepped out of it and there is no going back. But I hesitate to place both feet in the Quaker community. I have spoken of how coming to an appreciation of the early Friends was a real support for coming to an understanding the early Christians. That is only one side of the equation. If light is thrown from the early Friends upon the early Christians, then it is certainly true the other way round - light is thrown from the early Christians upon the early Friends. Without an understanding of the Christian tradition, there is a whole depth of understanding missing from Quakerism.

There is something analogous here to the way Christianity grew out of Judaism. To take Paul's writings as an example: on the one hand, they are emphasising a serious break with what has gone before, a radical change which he can describe as a new creation; on the other, they are steeped in Jewish ways of thinking, in Jewish theology. It is a combination reflected in the very layout of the Bible. In the Christian Bible there is a new testament, a new covenant, a radical break with the old, but the old is also there bound together with the new, forming a unity. As I grow in experience of the Quaker way, I find my appreciation of the living Christian foundation of Quakerism becoming more not less important... and so I keep one foot in the traditional church, not wanting to lose the foundation which has brought me to a Quaker understanding and which I find is needed to inform it.

Chapter Five

Childhood under law

Timothy Peat

As was noted in Chapter 2, the image of history coming to an end in a major spiritual upheaval is not an easily accessible one. It is hard for us to comprehend what that might mean, and it is not the image that Paul uses. He speaks of a time when Jesus will return, when Christ will be all in all, when the kingdom of God will be inherited. There is one image that Paul uses that I think is extremely helpful in getting some idea of his vision for the future. It is that of a change for all humankind analogous to the change every individual goes through from childhood to adulthood. One very important strength of this image is that it is universally accessible; it is something everyone has experience of. It is an image that combines a number of elements in a subtle way. The image includes the idea of a real break with the past, a real ending to what has gone before, but also a continuation of life, connected with the past, but now transformed. It is an image which illuminates Paul's vision of a real change but one that essentially does not come by learning or achievement. As we shall see, these are helpful elements for understanding what Paul is saying.

The law is for childhood

When we come to investigate what Paul means by this image of adulthood, what I want to suggest is that this side of the image is associated with liberation. The adult who has come successfully through childhood has internalised the checking and guiding voice

Second Coming scripture outside Paul

As was suggested in Chapter 2 (p.10), the words of Jesus in Luke 17:21 are more accurately interpreted as 'the kingdom of God will be suddenly in your midst' rather than 'the kingdom of God is within you' (Jeremias 1971:101). This interpretation is in line with the sense of the kingdom of God in the teaching of Jesus as something essentially in the future - not far off, to be sure, but a future event.

The synoptic gospels - Matthew, Mark and Luke - all contain their own versions of a discourse of Jesus which they all place shortly before the end of his life (Mt 24-25; Mk 13; Lk 21). In this Jesus speaks of "'the Son of Man coming in clouds' with great power and glory" (Mk 13:26) but says that this event will be preceded by a time of violent upheaval with wars, famine and disease. "When you see these things taking place," says Jesus in Luke's gospel, "you know that the kingdom of God is near" (Lk 21:31). So the Second Coming is tied together with the coming of the kingdom or rule of God.

The book of Revelation contains the most vivid imagery to relay the meaning of the Second Coming. Jesus is envisaged as returning, knocking at the door. For those who invite him in he will come in and eat with them (Rev 3:20). As with the picture in the synoptic gospels there is a time of huge upheaval and suffering before the kingdom comes (Rev 8-20). Towards the end of the book, we are presented with the image of humankind in a state of intimacy with God. Combined with the return of Jesus there is placed the image of a new city, the new Jerusalem descending out of heaven like a bride adorned for her husband (Rev 21:1 - 4; 21:22 - 22:1 - 7). Death is no more; darkness is no more. The city is filled with the light of God. There is no temple in the city because God and 'the Lamb' are its temple. This is an image of a unity between God and humankind, of heaven on earth.

of the parent. The external guidance of the parent is no longer needed because it has become established within the individual. There is a way of understanding here how a childhood for humankind is tied together in Paul's mind with the external law. Just as the child needs the external word of the parent, so humankind in its childhood needs the external guidance of the law. Once the child comes to maturity, the voice of the parent becomes part of the child. In a similar way, in the adulthood of humankind it is that inner voice from God, that inner word of faith that guides each individual (see Chapter 3). There is a real change so that just as the adult can now act with freedom, so can humankind in its adulthood. But a further point is this: just as the external guidance of the parent is necessary for childhood so, in Paul's thinking, the law has had a similar purpose in bringing the child safely through to adulthood. Unfortunately this whole image of the movement from childhood to adulthood can be lost in translation and we can now look at how this happens.

The law as 'child-leader'

In this section the three italicised words in the following brief passage will be examined:

> Now before faith came, we were *confined* [*phroureō*] under the law, *kept under restraint* [*sug̃kleiō*] until faith should be revealed. So that the law was our *custodian* [*paidagōgos*] until Christ came, that we might be justified by faith. But now that faith has come, we are no longer under a *custodian* [*paidagōgos*]; for in Christ Jesus you are all sons of God through faith (Gal 3:23-25, RSV).

The word translated 'custodian' (*paidagōgos*) is a Greek word with a very particular meaning. The problem in translating it lies in the fact that there is no English equivalent for what it is conveying. An authoritative dictionary of New Testament Greek (Bauer *et al* 1979) gives this definition: 'literally, boy-leader, the man, usually a slave whose duty it was to conduct the boy or youth to and from school and to superintend his conduct; he was not a "teacher".' This indicates that the word is describing a very particular task but one which has no precise equivalent in the modern English-speaking world. Following the Bauer definition, it is clear that 'schoolmaster' (AV), and 'a kind of tutor' (NEB) are misleading translations; the role that Paul is ascribing to the law is not educational although it is directed towards a child. 'Custodian' is a good translation if it is taken to mean 'one who keeps safe, protects, a guardian' but this

English word also carries the meaning of 'an officer of the justice who keeps in confinement or imprisonment' and this is a long way from the sense in the Greek.

Other translations define the figure evoked here as a custodian in the sense of an imprisoning jailor. This comes about because a prior assessment of how Paul understands the law is made by translators and shapes the image. The NIV is a good example:

> Before this faith came we were *held prisoners* by the law, *locked up* until the faith should be revealed. So the law was *put in charge* to lead us to Christ that we might be justified by faith. Now that faith has come, we are no longer *under the supervision* of the law (Gal 3:23-25, NIV).

In this translation, the problem of defining *paidagōgos* which might be rendered 'childminder', is solved by turning a noun into two different verbs: 'to be put in charge', and 'to supervise'. It is true that these are appropriate words for aspects of the role Paul is referring to but the particular crispness of the image, difficult as it is to render into English, has disappeared altogether. To make the point another way: many roles include 'being in charge' and 'supervision', including that of a jailor, but it is the particular role of the slave conducting the child to school, a role unknown today, which Paul is deliberately choosing as an image of the law.

What about the Greek word (*sugkleiō*) which is translated 'to lock up' in the NIV and 'to keep under restraint' in the RSV? The one other use of this exact word in the New Testament is in a gospel description of fishing: 'they *enclosed* a great shoal of fish' (Lk 5:6). However, it is closely related to the word for 'to shut' (*kleiō*), normally used with 'door' and in one passage a 'prison door', but also with 'heaven' and 'heart'. From these uses, a consistent idea can be seen operating behind the word, that of 'closing' and also of 'restraint', with an additional component of 'all around'. These observations prove nothing except to strongly suggest that the association of the word with 'imprisonment', although possible, is not a necessary one.

The word can be used in a variety of contexts to indicate 'restraint' or 'enclosing'. This is not a clinching argument for a particular translation but gives an awareness of the issues involved in coming to an accurate translation, sensitive to the nuances in Paul's thought. It is important to remember at this stage that behind these subtle matters of definition, there is a substantive issue: it matters a great deal in appreciating Paul's understanding of the law if his conception of the law is more accurately represented by a jailor or a child-leader.

The third word can be dealt with quickly before moving on. The issue here is more straightforward. The verb used [*phroureō*] is related to the noun, 'a guard' (*phrouros*), consequently there is no problem in seeing how the image of imprisonment can be found here. However there are two sides to the English word, 'to guard', which are also in the Greek. 'To guard' is not only used of keeping prisoners restrained but is also used meaning 'to protect'. So, as with the previous word, while there is clearly the potential for this word also to be used of the restraint associated with imprisonment, this is not its necessary meaning.

The argument so far has been leading to the following conclusion: the meaning of *paidagōgos* indicates that, to clarify the function of the law, Paul is using the image of the protective restraint of a wandering child rather than, as is usual in modern translations, the custodial restraint of an offending adult. The two other words in the passage can comfortably carry the meaning of protective restraint from danger just as easily as that of imprisonment. *Sugkleiō* can carry the sense of 'to restrain' just as well as 'to lock up'; *phroureō* can carry the sense of 'to protect' just as easily as 'to guard'. The interpretation hinges on the meaning of *paidagōgos:*

> Now before faith came, we were *restrained* under the law, *protected* until faith should be revealed. So that the law was our *child-leader* until Christ came, that we might be justified by faith. But now that faith has come, we are no longer under a *child-leader*, for in Christ Jesus you are all sons of God, through faith. (Gal 3:23-26, adapted RSV).

Clear confirmation for this interpretation comes in following Paul's argument a little further. He continues to contrast being a child or infant with coming of age or full sonship:

> I mean that the heir, as long as he is a child, is no better than a slave, though he is owner of all the estate; but he is under guardians and trustees until the date set by the father. So with us; when we were children, we were slaves...But when the time had fully come, God sent forth his Son, born of woman, born under the law, so that we might receive adoption as sons (Gal 4:1-5).

Right through this passage from the letter to the Galatians, Paul is speaking of the law in connection with the image of childhood. This provides further support for the argument that *paidagōgos* is rightly understood as illuminating the purpose of the law because it refers to a particular role in relation to a child - a role concerned with restraint but not imprisonment.

In concluding this section, it is worth developing Paul's image of the wandering infant while returning to the first response which Paul makes to his own question, 'Why then the law?' What he says is this, 'It was added because of transgressions...' (Gal 3:19). Once a baby becomes a toddler, parents have to be vigilant in ensuring that the child, who does not understand danger, does not wander where it might come to harm. The law was added because of 'wandering', which is what the word 'transgression' means. The child being taken upon the road to school is inclined to wander into danger and one purpose of the 'childminder' is to restrain the child within the safe boundaries of the pavement. So, the aim has been to demonstrate that, in Paul's conception, the law was given to infants to prevent their wandering, their transgression. *Paul, as indicated by his positive affirmation of the law as a gift to Israel, is not working with an image of the law as a imprisoning jailor, but rather as a childminder for the wandering infant.*

Why study the Bible at all?

> 'And their Gospel is dust, Matthew, Mark, Luke and John, which is the Letter, and all this is in the carnal mind, feeding of which is the enemy against God, which is without God, in the generation of Cain and the wicked...' (Fox 1654:14).

There is no shortage of similar quotations that could be picked out of the pamphlets of Friends from the early days of the movement. In this extended diatribe, Fox links together a sequence of words to describe those people and things that are 'without God', in other words 'outside of God'. Such things are 'in the generation of Cain', 'dust', 'carnal', 'external', 'death', 'under the dominion of Satan'. Fox places 'their gospel... Matthew, Mark, Luke and John' in that category. It is 'the Letter' and, as such, it can only feed the 'carnal mind'. Yet in this pamphlet, sentence after sentence is rich in biblical allusion if not direct quotation. The margins of the pamphlet note biblical references. Making sense of this from the words of Fox is not difficult. He is targeting a dependence on the Bible which is detached from the life that the Bible points to and at the same time claiming that it is possible to have the direct contact with God that brought forth the Scriptures:

> [F]or all the prophets were taught of God immediately alone, and God was the living fountain of mercy, and who turned from God, forsook the living mercies, and Christ said, ye shall be all taught of the Father, and the Apostles were taught of God, taught of Jesus Christ, and so they all witnessed one Fountain, one Godhead, from whom all living springs come, and this do we witness now with the Apostles, and all the servants of the Lord, and sons and daughters of God (Fox 1654:39).

This is at the very least a powerful argument for a distinctive approach to the Bible among Friends. The experience of the early Friends gave them a certainty that they were being 'taught of God immediately alone'. If this is possible, why study the Bible? *Advices and Queries* points to one reason:

> Take time to learn about other people's experience of the Light. Remember the importance of the Bible, the writings of Friends and all writings which reveal the ways of God (*Quaker Faith and Practice* 1.02, n.5).

The Bible speaks of 'other people's experience of the Light' and is one of those writings which 'reveal the ways of God'. But surely Fox would reply with words such as these: 'Know the Light for yourself! Discover the Light that leads to God and follow it!'

The early Friends understood and relayed their experience in biblical terms. They felt themselves living at a moment when God was initiating a particular movement forward in the human story - the human story that the Bible tells. Without knowing something of that biblical story it is impossible properly to understand what those early Friends were saying and then it becomes difficult to see how Friends relate to that same story today. Does that matter? There is a story in the Acts of the Apostles of Paul coming to Ephesus and meeting some disciples there. He asks them, 'Did you receive the Holy Spirit when you became believers?' They reply, 'No, we have not even heard that there is a Holy Spirit' (Acts 19:1f). It is only once they have heard of this possibility that they can come to the experience of the Holy Spirit. Without some knowledge of the Bible there is a similar situation for many Friends: 'When you became Friends did you discover what it is to be taught by God, taught by Jesus Christ as were the apostles?' Without study of the Bible the reasonable reply might be: 'No, we have not even heard about the apostles, about Jesus Christ, about God.' Without knowledge of the possibility, the experience cannot be looked for.

The knowledge of good and evil

If the above presentation is not accepted and we assume that Paul is saying that God gave the law to act as a kind of jailor, locking up people until the arrival of faith, what kind of God is this? If this is the view taken, and it is very common as we see from the translations, then an interpreter has to start explaining in this sort of way. Paul was so overwhelmed by his positive new experience of faith and so caught up in the argument against going back to the law that he was drawn to say things about the law that did not add up (Sanders 1991:84-100). He wants to affirm that the law was God-given but also to affirm that faith is so much better. It is held that it is this awkward combination that has led him to say very negative things about the law, things which then raise questions about the sense of his view of God. Why should God give the law - a kind of jailor - only to decide later to drop the law and introduce the way of faith?

In the translation work above, I hope it has been possible to see that Paul may well have had an idea of the law as something given for a kind of childhood of humankind, something given for a temporary purpose. There are still problems with this interpretation but it does not present God as either a capricious despot, deciding what will be done with humankind at a whim, or an incompetent, giving the law only to decide later that faith is better. So what can be made of this image of childhood? For this interpretation the frame needs to be the one we began this chapter with: the biblical frame beginning with Genesis and ending with Revelation. This is a picture of humankind first created with an intimacy with God and then that intimacy gloriously restored in the future events of Revelation.

Now we have an important question to deal with from within this frame: why was the intimacy with God lost, given that humankind was created in the image of the perfect God? Is this in itself not a challenge to God's all-powerful perfection? Why the Fall? To put this another way, why did sin come into the world? And connected with this is the question that Paul asks: why the law? For the law and sin are bound together. Law is necessary because sin exists.

Let me point to a section of the Genesis story of creation. At the point at which the serpent tempts the woman to eat of the forbidden tree, the serpent says:

> "...God knows that when you eat of this tree your eyes will be opened, and you will be like God, knowing good and evil..." (Gen 3:5).

Right in the middle of Paul's letter to the Romans is a very famous passage:

> I can will what is right but I cannot do it. For I do not do the good I want, but the evil I do not want is what I do. Now if I do what I do not want it is no longer I that do it, but sin that dwells within me (Rom 7:18-20).

I have a simple proposal to make. In a brief span, all the supporting arguments cannot be given but it does offer an explanation of both the positive and negative things that Paul says about the law. The simple proposal is that in this passage what Paul is describing is the knowledge of good and evil. The universal sense of struggling to do right, struggling against wrongdoing. It is known to all people to a greater or lesser extent. We all have this knowledge of good and evil in ourselves. And Paul, in the earlier part of this passage, is referring back to the Genesis story, using the image of the development from childhood to adulthood, to understand the meaning of this struggle. How and why did this struggle with wrongdoing come about? I will present what I think is his understanding very briefly. God creates humankind in God's own image with dominion over all that is created. The climax of the Genesis account of creation is the creation of woman. At this point the man says, 'Here at last is flesh of my flesh, bone of my bone.' It is a joyful affirmation of intimacy and companionship. What is odd at this point is that, having given humankind dominion over all that is created, God places a prohibition on this creature: 'you can eat of all the trees in the garden, except that one tree.' There is an inconsistency here.

It is worth pausing to draw out some connections with the image of childhood. Every healthy child has an unlimited desire to enquire and explore. Parents encourage this exploration, giving whatever is needed to support it except in one respect: where something might endanger the child, the parent prohibits. From the child's point of view there is a fundamental inconsistency. The child's motivation for enquiry is not limited to those things that are safe and the child cannot help but rebel against the parent, however subtle or non-confrontational the parents are. At that point there is a division between child and parent. The child is confirmed in its separateness from the parent. Putting this in modern terms, the ego comes to life. This parallels the picture in Genesis. Humankind, given absolute dominion over all that is created, is then subject to a prohibition. To be true to its God-given dominion, humankind finds itself asserting its own will against God. And in this assertion of a separate human will there comes a separation from God. Through this assertion, humankind, in the separate striving of each individual, comes to an intimate knowledge of good and evil. So the law – the prohibition – both brings the separate ego – the sin – into existence, and provides a check for it. It prevents wanderings, transgressions.

From within this frame of separate fleshly existence under the check of the law, there is no way out. There is no way that the ego can free itself. Every act is mixed with selfishness. And Paul includes a cry for help at the end of the Romans 7 passage:

> Wretched man that I am! Who will rescue me from this body of death? (Rom 7:25).

Through the law comes the separate ego - the sin - and direct knowledge of good and evil through the struggle that goes on in each individual, but, from within this frame, there is no possibility of liberation from sin. There is no way that a child can be educated into adulthood. A physical transition into maturity is needed, something that the child is unable to effect for itself.

Chapter Six

Adulthood: incarnation and the kingdom of God

Timothy Peat

> God of power and mercy,
> open our hearts in welcome.
> Remove the things that hinder us from receiving Christ with joy,
> so that we may share his wisdom
> and become one with him
> when he comes in glory
> (*The Roman Missal* 1975:10).

This is the prayer that is said in the Roman Catholic Church on the second Sunday of the season of Advent. Advent is the time when the church is awaiting and preparing for the celebration of Christmas. But its prayers are also focused on another sense of waiting - waiting for the time when Jesus 'comes in glory'. This is not a reference to the First Coming of Jesus, born in Bethlehem. These prayers are referring to the Second Coming of Jesus, the expectation that Jesus will return to bring to fulfilment the work begun in his First Coming - to bring 'the kingdom or dominion of God' in its fullness.

Paul speaks of Jesus as 'the image of God', 'the son of God', 'the Christ'. He is clear that something was effected through Jesus which is of significance for all. What is also clear is that what was done is still to be fully realised. The dominion of God is still in the future; it is an inheritance that is still to be received.

The faith of Jesus

The view that Paul usually speaks of 'the faith of Jesus' as opposed to 'faith in Jesus' has been gaining support over the past ten years or so (Hays, 1983; Hooker, 1990). Compare:

> ...to prove at the present time that [God] himself is righteous and that he justifies [makes right] the one who has faith in Jesus (Rom 3:26).

with

> ...to prove at the present time that (God) himself is righteous and that he justifies *the one who has the faith of Jesus* (Rom 3:26, NRSV replacing main text with footnote [in italics]).

This understanding of faith adds further support to the idea that, in Paul's understanding, those who come to faith are coming into the same kind of transparency to God that was in Jesus. As God worked through the faith of Jesus, guiding his every word and action, now God can work through those who have come to that same faith, who are now themselves directly guided by God. And yet Paul does speak of faith having some kind of beginning with Jesus. We must consider further this idea of 'the faith of Jesus'.

'Faith of' or 'faith in'

An accurate understanding of the phrase translated above 'the faith of Jesus' *(ek pisteōs Iēsou)* is obviously important for closely related phrases occur in several passages that are important for understanding Paul:

> ...the life I now live in the flesh I live *by faith in the Son of God...* (Gal 2:20).
> ...the life which I now live in the flesh I live *by the faith of the Son of God...* (Gal 2:20, AV).
> ...that I may gain Christ and be found in him, not having a righteousness of my own that comes from the law, but one

> that comes *through faith in Christ*, the righteousness from God based on faith (Phil 3:8f).
> ...not having my own righteousness, which is of law, but that which is *through the faith of Christ*... (Phil 3:8f, AV).

> But now, apart from law, the righteousness of God has been disclosed,... the righteousness of God *through faith in Jesus Christ* for all who believe. (Rom 3:21f).
> But now the righteousness of God without the law is manifested,... even the righteousness of God which is *by faith of Jesus Christ* unto all and upon all of them that believe (Rom 3:21f, AV).

Most modern translations replace the phrase rendered 'by the faith of Jesus Christ' in the AV translations above with the phrase 'through' or 'by faith *in* Jesus Christ' (RSV, NIV, NJB, REB, TEV). Interpreting the phrase as 'faith *in* Jesus Christ' places a division between those who have faith on the one side and Jesus Christ on the other. When this is combined with Paul's description of Jesus as the Son of God and as the one 'who knew no sin' (2 Cor 5:21) then this supports the view that Paul conceives of Jesus as being firmly on the side of God with those who come to faith in him as firmly on the other side. The translation 'faith of Jesus Christ' leads to a different interpretation; it means that if Jesus Christ lived by faith then others who come to faith can be understood as having a fundamental connection with him in their way of living. It is this issue that can be seen to have distorted the plain sense in the Greek which, if there was no other issue involved, would undoubtedly be translated 'faith *of* Jesus Christ' rather than 'faith *in* Jesus Christ'. Clearly if Jesus Christ is the one 'who knew no sin' then he is separated from all the rest who 'have sinned and fall short of the glory of God' (Rom 3:23); if living by faith is solely associated with continuing sin then it is not something that describes the way Christ lived. However it has been suggested that central to understanding what Paul means by faith is the idea of seeking to live by direct guidance from God (see chapter 3, pp.19 and 32).

The beginning of faith

It is important to note alongside this proposal that, recognising a deep connection between the faith of Jesus and that of those who come after him, Paul still ascribes a particular significance to the faith of Jesus; there is an important sense in which faith has a beginning in him. This was clear in the text we examined in chapter 5 (pp.44ff):

> Now before faith came, we were *restrained* under the law, *protected* until faith should be revealed. So that the law was our *child-leader* until Christ came, that we might be justified by faith. But now that faith has come, we are no longer under a *child-leader;* for in Christ Jesus you are all sons of God, through faith (Gal 3:23-26, adapted RSV).

This passage was examined as part of the argument in the chapter on the law indicating that the law has a temporary function. Here the concern is with the idea that faith has a beginning: 'before faith came'; 'the faith which should afterwards by revealed'; 'after that faith is come'. Clearly Paul has a specific event in mind when he speaks in this way. He could be interpreted as speaking here of the coming of faith in the individuals who come after Christ - that once a person has come to faith he or she has no more need of the law to act as a child-leader; however the context of the whole passage is the discussion of the purpose of the law in human history as a whole, not just on the individual scale. As has been argued, what Paul has in view is not the transformation of isolated individuals but a transformation for the whole of humankind.

Greater clarity can be found about what Paul means by 'faith' by considering in more detail what he means by the 'faith of Jesus Christ'. We have seen that Paul speaks of the faith of Christ as some kind of starting point. It might be thought that Paul is referring to the actions of Jesus throughout his life as an example of living by faith which others can now follow. The lack of references in the letters of Paul to events in the life of Jesus gives one important indication that this is not his meaning. There is however one action of Jesus to which Paul does regularly refer, his death on the cross:

> And being found in human form he humbled himself and became obedient unto death, even death on a cross (Phil 2:8).

Confirmation that when Paul is referring to the faith of Jesus he has in mind the death of Jesus comes in a curious way.

The faith of Abraham

In order to present the primacy of faith, Paul sets out to demonstrate in the letters to the Galatians and the Romans that the response of Abraham to God was the response of faith and that, therefore, the first of the people of Israel lived by faith and not by law. For Paul to speak of the faith of Abraham would seem to undermine the idea that the faith of Christ was some kind of beginning of faith for others. This would indeed be so if Christ's whole life were being presented as the example of faith. It would then make no sense for Paul to present for his argument the faith of Abraham, who could hardly have been following the example of Jesus. However what is being proposed here is that it is faith with two particular qualities which Paul is indicating when he speaks of the faith of Abraham and, by implication, the faith of Christ: confidence in the face of death and the immediacy of guidance from God. It can be seen in the following passage how when, in describing Abraham's faith, Paul repeatedly shows how Abraham did not lose faith when faced with the power of death:

> [Abraham] is our father in the sight of God, in whom he believed - *the God who gives life to the dead and calls things that are not as though they were.* Against all hope, Abraham in hope believed and so became the father of many nations, just as it had been said to him, "So shall your offspring be." Without weakening in his faith, *he faced the fact that his body was as good as dead - since he was about a hundred years old - and that Sarah's womb was also dead.* Yet he did not waver through unbelief regarding the promise of God, but was strengthened in his faith and gave glory to God, being fully persuaded that God had power to do what he had promised (Rom 4:17-21, NIV).

Abraham is also for Paul the exemplary man of faith because he believes and obeys the unmediated word of God. His first appearance in Scripture is an account of the word of God sending him away from his own country:

> Now the Lord said to Abram, "Go from your country and your kindred and your father's house to the land that I will show you. And I will make you a great nation..." (Gen 12:1f).

Paul quotes the book of Genesis when it recounts how Abraham is promised that his descendants will be as many as the stars. The faith of Abraham is that the word spoken to him by God will be fulfilled. This is the point made about Abraham in Genesis, after he has been tested to the extent of having to offer his son Isaac:

> "...by your descendants shall all the nations of the earth bless themselves, *because you have obeyed my voice"* (Gen 22:18).

Abraham stays confident in and obedient to God's inner voice, even though his body was as good as dead and the womb of Sarah was dead. Even when he is asked to kill Isaac, the apparent fulfilment of God's promise that he would have descendants by Sarah, his obedience to the word of God does not falter. In the first place, it is Paul's presentation of Abraham's confident obedience in the unmediated word of God even in the face of death which connects his faith with the faith of Jesus.

The death of Christ as one accursed

It is necessary to consider a difficult passage in which Paul places together apparently contradictory texts from the Hebrew Scriptures. He finds a harmonious interpretation for them through his understanding of the death of Jesus. The four texts from the Hebrew Bible are presented symmetrically and by italicising the key words it can be seen that the two outer ones belong together as do the two inner ones:

> *"Cursed be every one* who does not abide by all things written in the book of the law, and do them" (Gal 3:10, RSV, quoting Deut 27:26).

Is the model necessarily Christian?

If those scholars who are suggesting that 'faith of Jesus' is the appropriate translation of *pistis Iēsou* as opposed to 'faith in Jesus' are right this has the potential for bringing a shift in understanding Paul. What becomes possible is faith understood not as reliance upon something outside the believer, whether of the person of Jesus or the message of Jesus but an understanding of faith as a potentially universal way of being: to live not by faith in Jesus but by the faith of Jesus - living by the same kind of faith that Jesus had.

That said, Paul speaks of a beginning of faith and it is clear that he believes a new way of life for all people was effected through the death of Jesus. In the model this past historical event is tied together with an understanding of the Second Coming as a future historical event. As the model becomes helpful to someone in understanding Quaker history it does also face that person with questions which the mainstream Christian tradition has grappled with and continues to grapple with: who was Jesus? How could Paul consider that the death of this one man could have an effect for all humankind?

> "He who through faith is righteous *shall live*" (Gal 3:11, RSV, quoting Hab 2:4).
> "He who does them *shall live* by them" (Gal 3:12, RSV, quoting Lev 18:5).
> *"Cursed be every one* who hangs on a tree" (Gal 3:13, RSV, quoting Deut 21:23).

Probably because, as evidenced by the systematic way that he presents these texts, Paul is using a formal but now obscure method of demonstration, it is very difficult to follow him through his precise explanation of these texts. What also makes him difficult to follow is that, while he seems to be using an argument to demonstrate a case, it would be more appropriate to describe what he is doing as showing how his conclusion is compatible with the Hebrew Scriptures. In the context of the letter to the Galatians this is important. Paul is arguing for both the continuity and discontinuity of his gospel in relation to Jewish law and Scripture: continuity because he is claiming obedience to the God of Abraham; discontinuity because he is advocating an abrogation of the Jewish law as the way of discerning what is right to do. Once this is understood it is possible to gain a clear picture of the thought Paul is seeking to express in juxtaposing these texts. In all these texts Paul is seeking to make clear something about Jesus Christ. The element which is, in effect, part of Paul's conclusion but without which his demonstration makes no sense, is that the God of Abraham, the God who gave the law, brought Jesus back to life from the dead; what Paul is demonstrating is the consequence of this for the law and the meaning it gives to the death of Christ.

The outer two texts need to be taken first and are the more important. The first text is a shorter version of a classic text in Deuteronomy. The following are presented there as the words of Moses:

> "See, I have set before you this day life and good, death and evil. If you obey the commandments of the Lord your God which I command you this day... then you shall live and multiply, and the Lord your God will bless you... I call heaven and earth to witness against you this day, that I have set before you life and death, blessing and curse..." (Deut 30:15f, 19, RSV).

The sense of the shorter text is the same. The second curse text is very significant for understanding Paul. It is worth looking at the full sentence in Deuteronomy from which it is taken:

> "And if a man has committed a crime punishable by death and he is put to death, and you hang him on a tree, his body shall not remain all night upon the tree, but you shall bury him the same day, for a hanged man is accursed by God, you shall not defile your land which the Lord your God gives you for an inheritance..." (Deut 21:22f).

Paul is making explicit here a theme that recurs elsewhere. Jesus died as one who, through the law, was accursed by God. Although in him there was no assertion against God, because he was accursed by the law he died as one who was apparently completely over against God:

> For our sake he made him to be sin who knew no sin... (2 Cor 5:21).

In the last section consideration was given to how Paul can present the faith of Abraham as the faith of Jesus. It was argued that it was Abraham's faithfulness in the face of death that connected the two. One further vital connection can be made. Abraham is absolutely faithful to God's immediate word *even when it apparently leads to conflict with God's purposes.* This additional element is clear in his story. Abraham was absolutely faithful to the immediate word of God *even when that word appeared to contradict itself.* Consider the promise to Abraham of Isaac:

> God said to Abraham, "As for Sarah your wife, you shall not call her name Sarai, but Sarah shall be her name. I will bless her, and moreover I will give you a son by her. I will bless her, and she shall give rise to nations; kings of peoples shall come from her." Then Abraham fell on his face and laughed, and said to himself, "Can a child be born to a man who is a hundred years old? Can Sarah, who is ninety years old, bear a child?" ...God said, "No, but your wife Sarah shall bear you a son, and you shall name him Isaac. I will establish my covenant with him as an everlasting covenant for his offspring after him..." (Gen 17:15-17, 19).

Once Isaac has grown the word of God comes again to Abraham:

> After these things God tested Abraham. He said to him, "Abraham!" And he said, "Here I am." He said, "Take your son, your only son Isaac, whom you love, and go to the land of Moriah, and offer him there as a burnt offering on one of the mountains that I shall show you. "...When they came to the place that God had shown him, Abraham built an altar there and laid the wood in order. He bound his son Isaac, and laid him on the altar, on top of the wood. Then Abraham reached out his hand and took

> the knife to kill his son. But the angel of the Lord called to him from heaven, and said, "Abraham, Abraham!" And he said, "Here I am." He said, "Do not lay your hand on the boy or do anything to him; for now I know that you fear God, since you have not withheld your son, your only son, from me" (Gen 22:1f, 9-12).

Abraham's faith in God's inner voice remains, even when God's own promises appear to be contradicted.

What of Jesus? Paul is not concerned to relay the facts of his life and death. What he does is to speak specifically of the faith of Jesus in connection with his death. And just as with the faith of Abraham, it is not simply a faith that goes beyond death with which Paul is concerned, but a faith that perseveres even when God's promises appear to be contradicted. Far from fulfilling the will of God revealed to the people of Israel in the law, the obedience of Jesus to God leads him to the apparent contradiction of it.

> Let the same mind be in you that was in Christ Jesus, who...humbled himself and became obedient to the point of death - *even death on a cross* (Phil 2:5, 8).

Note first that 'cross' is translating a Greek word meaning 'a spiked wooden stick'. The significance of the phrase, 'even death on a wooden stake' becomes precisely the same as was found above. It is not simply going to death in obedience to God that demonstrates the faith of Jesus, it is, very particularly, death on a tree - *death as one accursed by God.*

In this, Paul is saying how Jesus becomes identified with the fundamental state of sin, the fundamental assertion of humankind against God, how 'God made him to be sin who knew no sin'. But, of course, for Paul, that is not the end. God raises Jesus from the dead. In Paul's understanding it is not Jesus that dies, but 'the sin'. Those who encounter the risen Jesus are, in and through that encounter, liberated from sin. As Paul claims, they no longer identify their existence with the physical body; the illusion of death is ended.

> I have been crucified with Christ; and it is no longer I who live, but it is Christ who lives in me (Gal 2:19f).

Two incarnations

The last quotation above gets across the extraordinary nature of what Paul is suggesting, his understanding that what is now possible is to live the same kind of life that Christ lived, to live in the same intimacy with God as he had. To make this point boldly this section is headed 'two incarnations'. In traditional Christian understanding, God was 'incarnated' in Jesus, God was 'enfleshed' in Jesus. The suggestion of this chapter is that Paul did not pull back from the idea that the very purpose of this first incarnation was that, as a consequence of the faithfulness of Jesus in being totally obedient to the directly given word of God (even when that word in human understanding seemed inconsistent), that same faithfulness was now to come for all, so that now there might be a second incarnation: the whole of humankind as the incarnation of God.

Jesus as the image of God ➠ ➠ ➠Humankind as the image of God exercising the dominion of God in creation

Just as Adam was made in the image of God so Paul describes Jesus:

> ...the glory of Christ, who is the image of God... (2 Cor 4:4).

But Paul also speaks of the image of God when referring to a transformation that is underway in humankind:

> And all of us, with unveiled faces, seeing the glory of the Lord as though reflected in a mirror, are being transformed into the same image... (2 Cor 3:18).

The idea of Jesus and of humankind as 'the image of God' clearly evokes the creation of humankind in Genesis. In Jesus it is possible to see the image of God and the implication of Paul's words is that the same image is being restored in humankind.

The phrase 'the kingdom of God' does not immediately evoke the Genesis account of creation but a brief note can reveal the connection. The phrase usually translated 'the kingdom of God' can best be understood as referring to an activity rather than a fixed state. It is the activity of 'ruling' or 'exercising dominion' to which the phrase refers. When Paul speaks of inheriting the kingdom of God, he is referring to the inheritance of a way of acting rather than an object. This does take us into the Genesis account of creation:

> "Let us make humankind in our image, according to our likeness; and let them have dominion ..." (Gen 1:26).

It is God who has dominion over all that is created. When humankind inherits the kingdom, that is, *inherits the dominion*, it is the activity of rulership that is inherited. In Paul's view inheriting God's kingdom is inheriting God's dominion. Humankind, the image of God, will then be exercising God's loving care over all that is created.

Jesus as the Son of God ➠ ➠ ➠ 'sons' in the Son

'Son of God' is a phrase loaded with the weight of subsequent Christian doctrinal development. What it certainly does indicate in Paul's thinking is that Jesus had a unique closeness to God and a unique role in God's activity:

> God was in Christ reconciling the world to himself...(2 Cor 5:19, RSV).

Inclusive language translations of the Bible can obscure the force of what Paul is saying when he speaks of believers becoming '"sons" in the Son'. Those who come to faith do not become children of God in a general way, they are clothed in Christ. They receive the 'Sonship' - that intimacy of relationship with God - that Jesus had.

> [F]or in Christ Jesus you are all sons of God, through faith. For as many of you as were baptized into Christ have put on Christ (Gal 3:26f, RSV).

Jesus as 'the Christ' ➠ ➠ ➠ Humankind 'in Christ'

Those who have 'put on Christ' are now 'in Christ'. The liberation effected by this Christ - this deliverer or saviour of Israel - has not been what was expected. It is a liberation from division, a reconciliation with God and with each other:

> There is neither Jew nor Greek, there is neither slave nor free, there is neither male nor female; for you are all one in Christ Jesus (Gal 3:28).

Jesus as one without sin ➠ ➠ ➠ Humankind liberated from sin

In Paul's understanding, Jesus is the one in whom there is no opposition to God, completely united with the will of God:

> For our sake [God] made him to be sin who knew no sin...(2 Cor 5:21)

The points made above about how those who live by faith come to be '"sons" in the Son' and are 'in Christ' are confirmed by the idea already proposed (see chapter 3) that those who follow the way of faith as understood by Paul are genuinely liberated from sin:

> Live by the Spirit and you definitely will not gratify the desires of the flesh (Gal 5:16, author's translation).

Living by the Spirit brings a real change which necessarily results in a liberation from sin.

Summary
The diagram overleaf summarises the above presentation. The First Coming is God incarnate in the life of Jesus; the Second Coming is God incarnate in all humankind. All humankind comes into the relationship with God that Jesus had.

First Coming First Incarnation The Life of Jesus		**Second Coming Second Incarnation The Life of All Humankind**
image of God		humankind - the image of God exercising the dominion of God
the Son of God 'God was in Christ'		'sons' in the Son
	➠ ➠ ➠	
the Christ		in Christ
one without sin		humankind liberated from sin
living by faith		living by faith

Figure 2: Two incarnations

Conclusion

Paul's claim is that a dramatic change for all humankind has been effected by the life, death and resurrection of Jesus. It is a coherent picture. In the time when Paul is writing he considers that the risen Christ has encountered only a few people; his vision is that when the Second Coming happens the risen Christ will encounter all people and that there will be a transformation for all humankind. This can be understood as a second incarnation of God in that there is an end of all that keeps humankind separate from God. Just as Jesus lived by faith performing only God's actions, speaking only God's words, so humankind will do God's will, speak God's words, live by only faith but in freedom, knowing good and evil.

But, most obviously, despite the extraordinary impact of the spread of the Christian gospel in the world, the claims were not being realised in the time of Paul, nor are they now. A key to understanding this limitation lies in Paul's image of a transition for humankind from childhood to adulthood. In human experience this change does not happen all at once. There is an interim time: adolescence. Paul's understanding of the time of transition is the subject of the next chapter.

Chapter Seven

Adolescence and the church

Timothy Peat

The coherence of Paul's vision

If we are going to take what Paul says seriously we are faced with a problem. I have suggested that Paul is talking about real historical events which, in his understanding, have real historical effects. The death of Jesus was an event which, Paul claims, has universal significance. He claims the same for the resurrection of Jesus. They are presented in Paul's theology as events which will have a transforming effect upon the whole of humankind. The basic problem for this view is, where is the evidence?

It is worth first taking seriously an extraordinary historical fact. In the introductory chapter to this section, a point was made about the particularity of these letters of Paul. Paul was not writing for posterity. He was in the middle of a fierce argument within the Christian tradition – an argument that there was no guarantee he would win. The question was: do those who come to faith need to become Jews? He did win that argument. Christianity became the faith of thousands of millions of people down the ages. Those ephemeral documents have been heard and read and studied in a way that was utterly inconceivable from the perspective of their writing. Paul was claiming in the death and resurrection of Jesus an event of universal significance; he was claiming that he had been called to be the apostle of the Gentiles; two thousand years after this claim we, like millions of our contemporaries, like millions of those before us, are giving attention to his writings and considering his witness to the resurrection of Jesus. There is something to ponder here.

There is another view of the fulfilment of Paul's expectation of the kingdom and that is made by those who claim that the kingdom is realised in the life of the church. This may be felt at times within renewal movements, but it is also there in the mainstream churches. At various times the sense has been expressed that the church is the kingdom of God here on earth in the process of spreading that kingdom to all. The Orthodox church, for example, has a very strong sense of the divine and human meeting in the worship of the church, the kingdom being present as the church celebrates the divine liturgy. The church has spread from its small beginnings, the beginnings that provide the context for Paul's letters, to be the organisation that we know today. Whatever your reservations about the church, the situation now, in terms of scale, is again a picture unimaginable from the small beginnings that Paul was involved in.

And yet, even these extraordinary facts do not remotely fulfil the expectations that Paul's vision raises. The picture of the kingdom that was presented in the last chapter is one where humankind as a whole is transformed, where creator and creation are brought together in humanity, a reconciliation of Spirit and flesh, where there is an end to wrongdoing. Coming to the end of this most violent century, where is the evidence for this?

This would seem to be the point in our exploration of Paul when we have to leave behind Paul's understanding on its own terms and start to reinterpret Paul. Does our question now not have to be: 'well, we know that Paul was wrong about the coming of the kingdom in the dramatic and universal way that he anticipated, but can we still draw useful teaching from his vision? We have said that he thought a dramatic event was to come in the future. We know now that he was wrong but we can reinterpret this.' If we start to reinterpret we might draw on the themes of chapter 3, the movement from the external guide of the law to the inner guidance of faith. Here is a theme that is rich for individual growth. It can be usefully explored without the main theme of chapters 5 and 6 of a transformation for all impingeing. We might want to argue that Paul's image of a radical transforming event is one that can be usefully placed alongside the more popular modern view of spirituality as a steady process of development. It can work as a corrective to the sense of the spiritual as something that is only connected with human effort and achievement. Lots of reinterpretations are possible.

This chapter aims to indicate why an effort to reinterpret Paul at this stage is premature. It will be shown that his theology is large enough to cope with the situation we have described. The fact that the kingdom has not come yet in the way that he envisaged does not destroy his theology. The reason is that his theology contains the idea of the kingdom or the Spirit coming 'in part' as a prelude to it coming 'in fullness'. It includes very serious qualifications about the present reality of the kingdom. What Paul says about the present reality of what has been effected by the death and resurrection of Jesus is that it is only a partial realisation of what is to come.

We have seen that Paul has a view of a dramatic future transformation for all. The aim here is to make clear how Paul understands this future transformation to be only partially realised in the present. In terms of the image of a transition from childhood to adulthood, the time in which he is writing and the time in which we are reading is a kind of 'adolescence' - a time when there is only a partial realisation of the change that is to come in the future.

A 'partial' transformation

It is time to work on a text again, the most well known passage of Paul: the hymn to love in 1 Corinthians 13. Our concern is with the translation of the last section:

> Love never ends. But as for prophecies, they will come to an end; as for tongues, they will cease; as for knowledge, it will come to an end. For we know only in part, and we prophesy only in part; but when the complete comes, the partial will come to an end.

> When I was a child, I spoke like a child, I thought like a child, I reasoned like a child; when I became an adult, I put an end to childish ways. For now we see in a mirror, dimly, but then we will see face to face. Now I know only in part; then I will know fully, even as I have been fully known. And now faith, hope, and love abide, these three; and the greatest of these is love (1 Cor 13:8-13).

Paul is speaking here of a change that is still to come and to illustrate that change he is using the image of the movement from childhood to adulthood. There is a very straightforward sentence that we can begin with:

> When I was a child, I spoke like a child, I thought like a child, I reasoned like a child; when I became an adult, I put an end to childish ways (1 Cor 13:11).

'Childish ways' is a slightly loaded phrase in English. It can be read as a negative judgment, a sense that is not there in the Greek. All that is said there is that 'I put away the things of a child'. This is a clear image and very helpful in illuminating Paul's theology. Childhood involves a way of speaking, a way of thinking, a way of reasoning. The child cannot speak, think, reason like an adult. But when a person becomes an adult, the things of childhood are put behind. Not rejected with any negativity but naturally left behind. There is a fundamental change which cannot be effected by the efforts of the child but happens at the right time. A coming to maturity in which there is this change of speaking, thinking and reasoning. It is a simple and universal image.

Paul is using it here to illuminate something else. Speaking as one who has come to faith, a member of the body of Christ, he says this:

> For we know only in part, and we prophesy only in part... (1 Cor 13:9).

This needs to be registered. Paul is saying something about the partial knowledge and prophecy of those in Christ, those who are living by faith. The knowledge and prophecy are not complete or full; they are partial. Then he speaks of 'the partial' coming to an end and at this point in the NRSV that we are using here, there is an issue of translation to consider:

> ...but when the *blank [teleion]* comes, the partial will come to an end (1 Cor 13:10).

What is the *blank*? The Greek word, *teleion*, can be translated in a number of different ways, all with the sense of completeness: the end or the fullness or perfection of something but also maturity or adulthood. What happens in the NRSV translation is the contrast with 'in part' determines the English word used:

> when the *complete* comes, the partial will come to an end.

If you think about it this is not very helpful. It is tautologous. If the complete comes then, of course, the partial comes to an end. But what is Paul speaking of here? What follows this sentence is the image of putting away childhood things once adulthood is reached. That image is there to illuminate and develop what has just been said. To paraphrase:

> For we know only in part, and we prophesy only in part, but when this change occurs, this change which can be compared to the change from childhood to adulthood, then the partial will be at an end.

It is certainly a change which involves completeness or the end of something but is more accurately understood as something like a 'coming of age'. As each individual goes through childhood, comes of age, becomes an adult and puts away the things of childhood so, he says, we (and he is speaking here of all those of faith), in this childhood time that we are in, know and prophesy in part, but when the transition to the fullness of life, the completeness, the perfection of life comes, *when the coming of age happens*, then the partial will be at an end. And then he goes on to use another image for the change from the partial to the full.

> For we know only in part, and we prophesy only in part; but when the coming of age happens, the partial will be at an end....For now we see in a mirror, dimly, but then we will see face to face (1 Cor 13:9, 10, 12, adapted NRSV).

And Paul goes on 'now I know only in part...'. To recall the image, now I have knowledge like that of a child in relation to an adult, but then, when this change occurs, this change like a collective coming of age, I will know fully, even as I have been known.

There are two points to draw from this:

1. The further use by Paul of this image of childhood and adulthood, and a future change like a coming of age.

2. The knowledge and prophecy of the present Christian community, as understood by Paul, is partial. It is not that those who have faith have already reached the goal and are working to make others like them. Those of faith are also waiting, looking forward to a future change.

The final image in this section of text is an understanding of the expected 'adulthood' as being a state of transparency, openness to God:

> I will know fully, even as I have been known (1 Cor 13:12).

Here is confirmation of the picture of Paul that has been presented in which adult life involves a real change consisting of an end to sin or the ego, an end to anything in the individual that is not of God. God's knowledge now fills the individual.

We can now look at two more ways in which Paul places a serious qualification on what has been presently effected by the death and resurrection of Jesus.

The first instalment of the Spirit

On several occasions when Paul speaks of the gift of the Spirit he qualifies the way he speaks of it in a consistent way. He speaks of the 'first-fruits of the Spirit' (Rom 8:23) or the 'promise of the Spirit' (Gal 3:14). A further expression he uses is what the older English translations render 'the earnest of the Spirit' (2 Cor 1:22; 5:5), in Greek, the *arrhabōn* of the Spirit.

Let us look at a modern English translation of one of these passages:

> But it is God who establishes us with you in Christ and has anointed us, by putting his seal on us and giving us *his Spirit* in our hearts *as a first instalment* (2 Cor 1:21f).

The old *Authorized Version* renders the last phrase: 'given the earnest of the Spirit in our hearts'.

The first point to draw from the *New Revised Standard Version* translation is a worthwhile one. 'First instalment' is a very good translation of *arrhabōn*. The word is used for a kind of down-payment, part of the full payment to come, given as a promise that full payment will be made.

The second point to make here is the key issue. In the new translation, and this is the usual way that it is translated, the Spirit is seen as given to those in Christ as the first instalment of what is to come. That is, those in Christ receive the whole of the Spirit as a down-payment, a promise that this Spirit will come to all in the future. With this interpretation a clear dividing line is drawn between those in Christ and those on the outside. Those inside have the Spirit, those on the outside do not. A perfectly reasonable alternative translation would lead to the sense that those in Christ have received ' the first instalment of the Spirit', a promise that it will come in its fullness in the future, for both those in Christ and those on the outside:

> But it is God who establishes us with you in Christ and has anointed us, by putting his seal on us and giving us *the first instalment of the Spirit* in our hearts (2 Cor 1:21f: adapted NRSV).

What determines which translation is used is the sense the translator has of what Paul is saying. I have been suggesting that Paul has a radical idea of life in the Spirit as a life liberated from sin. Yet in the early Christian communities to which Paul is writing there is plenty of evidence of continued struggle with wrongdoing. This leads to the question, can this radical picture of life in the Spirit as life liberated from sin be maintained? Yes, if what Paul is saying is that it is only part of the future gift that has been given, a part which points to that future when the promise contained in the present gift is received in its fullness and there is no longer any sin, no longer any separation from God.

We must now consider a further qualification Paul makes about the life of the Spirit in the early Christian communities.

Apostleship

It is not hard to indicate that Paul considers there to be a significant division between himself, as one of the apostles, and the members of the communities to which he writes:

> And so, brothers and sisters, I could not speak to you as spiritual people, but rather as people of the flesh, as infants in Christ. I fed you with milk, not solid food, for you were not ready for solid food. Even now you are still not ready, for you are still of the flesh (1 Cor 3:1f).

Paul does not consider himself to be an 'infant in Christ'. He is the one feeding the community, making the decisions about what it is or is not ready for. The shape of the relationship between Paul and the communities to which he writes is so much a part of the letters that it is remarkably easy to forget that the very fact that Paul writes in the way that he does demonstrates a clear authority over the communities. Another example:

> I am not writing this to make you ashamed, but to admonish you as my beloved children. For though you might have ten thousand guardians in Christ, you do not have many fathers. Indeed, in Christ Jesus I became your father through the gospel. I appeal to you, then, be imitators of me (1 Cor 4:14-16).

So what does Paul say of himself? If he is not a 'babe in Christ', what is he? In the first letter to the Corinthians, Paul is concerned to establish that his authority is not based on any worldly achievement at the same time as he affirms that there is a new way of seeing things - a new 'wisdom' - not available to those who are 'babes in Christ' but only to those who are 'mature' or 'adult':

> Yet among the mature [the adult] we do impart wisdom, though it is not a wisdom of this age or of the rulers of this age, who are doomed to perish. But we speak God's wisdom, secret and hidden, which God decreed before the ages for our glory (1 Cor 2:6f).

Paul speaks in a very similar way of apostles:

> [M]en ought to regard us as the servants of Christ and as those entrusted with the secret things of God (1 Cor 4:1, NIV).

I am suggesting that what Paul means by this new wisdom is an end to the identification with the flesh: in more modern terms, an end to the ego. In the letters to the Corinthians, Paul is having to defend his apostleship against those whom he calls 'pseudo-apostles'. This is what he says marks them out as pseudo-apostles:

> Not that we venture to class or compare ourselves with some of those who commend themselves. But when they measure themselves by one another, and compare themselves with one another, they are without understanding (2 Cor 10:12, RSV).

In contrast the true apostle can boast only of weakness:

> For I think that God has exhibited us apostles as last of all, as though sentenced to death, because we have become a spectacle to the world, to angels and to mortals. We are fools for the sake of Christ, but you are wise in Christ. We are weak, but you are strong. You are held in honour, but we in disrepute. To the present hour we are hungry and thirsty, we are poorly clothed and beaten and homeless, and we grow weary from the work of our hands....[W]e have become like the rubbish of the world, the dregs of all things, to this very day (1 Cor 4:9-13).

So apostles have and impart the wisdom of 'the mature', 'the adult' - 'the secret things of God' - yet Paul connects this exalted calling with weakness and, particularly, folly. He goes on to say that the wisdom of the world, human wisdom, is foolishness to God but with a very particular sense: *human wisdom is an actual obstacle to perceiving the things of God.*

> Do not deceive yourselves. If you think you are wise in this age, you should become fools, so that you may become wise. For the wisdom of this world is foolishness with God (1 Cor 3:18f).

What Paul does is to boast in the weakness of the apostles. Why? There is a simple reason that he gives: because this weakness is so clearly evident it can be known without doubt that it is God's power at work and not that of any individual apostle:

> But we have this treasure in clay jars, so that it may be made clear that this extraordinary power belongs to God and does not come from us (2 Cor 4:7).

In the first letter to the Corinthians, Paul expresses this same sense but with more detail:

> When I came to you, brothers and sisters, I did not come proclaiming the mystery of God to you in lofty words or wisdom. For I decided to know nothing among you except Jesus Christ, and him crucified. And I came to you in weakness and in fear

> and in much trembling. My speech and my proclamation were not with plausible words of wisdom, but with a demonstration of the Spirit and of power, so that your faith might rest not on human wisdom but on the power of God (1 Cor 2:1-5).

I see no reason not to consider this a genuine picture. Paul presents himself as a poor preacher and teacher. What happens in those to whom he speaks is out of all proportion to the abilities of this earthen vessel through which the teaching comes.

What Paul is claiming is not simply that, as might be said today, he and his fellow apostles are inspired by God, but rather that the work that they do is truly God's activity. In the human order of things it is wisdom and strength that are effective; what Paul is proclaiming is an inversion of this order. It is precisely because he proclaims his foolishness and knows his weakness that God's power can work in him. Something happens when Paul preaches; he can remind those to whom he preached of the objective reality of what happened to them but he also affirms that whatever happens arises even though he is subjectively aware of his weakness and folly; it is this combination of real power and real weakness that affirm that the power that is at work comes from beyond the individual preacher. Paul is saying that his preaching and work are not any individual activity, that is, it is not 'according to the flesh', it does not arise out of any individual wisdom, but it is from God.

It is possible to miss how powerfully what has been stated is integrated in Paul's thinking and what an extraordinary claim he is making. If to live according to the flesh is to be identified with what is created - that which is seen and mortal - then Paul is claiming without any doubt that the apostles are living by the Spirit. They are already 'on the side of God' in a way that others in Christ will only be in the future. In them, the inversion of the place of humanity in the created order which occurred in the fall is being reversed. The flesh - 'that which is created' - is no longer worshipped and served; it is no longer the source of motivation. This is precisely what Paul says of himself:

> I have been crucified with Christ; and it is no longer I who live, but it is Christ who lives in me. And the life I now live in the flesh I live by faith in the Son of God, who loved me and gave himself for me (Gal 2:20).

With the ego crucified, it is only God who acts and speaks in the individual. Just as, Paul says, there was no sin in Jesus - he was transparent to God - so the same can now be said of the true apostles.

Witnesses to the resurrection

So, as we have seen, Paul describes the apostles as a particularly significant group. They have an authority but this authority is based upon what is communicated through them. In themselves, Paul says, they are fools, but what they communicate comes directly from God; they are sent as the prophets before them were sent. Paul is explicit: Christ is speaking in me (2 Cor 13:3). I have suggested above what I think Paul is claiming for the apostles; that they have come to a state of liberation from sin, of freedom from the ego.

There is one specific event which, in Paul's understanding, marks out the apostles as a distinctive group: he claims that they are witnesses to the risen Jesus. When he is defending his apostleship this is what he says:

> Am I not an apostle? Have I not seen Jesus our Lord? (1 Cor 9:1f).

In Paul's mind, the future transformation that we have been talking about is bound together with the return of Jesus. This is how he describes this future coming:

> For the Lord himself, with a cry of command, with the archangel's call and with the sound of God's trumpet, will descend from heaven... (1 Thess 4:16).

Paul uses exactly the same image of the sounding of the trumpet in another passage where his focus is the nature of the change in humankind that is to come:

> Listen, I will tell you a mystery! We will not all die, but we will all be changed, in a moment, in the twinkling of an eye, at the last trumpet. For the trumpet will sound, and the dead will be raised imperishable, and we will be changed (1 Cor 15:51f).

The passage continues by presenting an image of what is mortal, perishable and corruptible being covered over by what is immortal, imperishable and incorruptible:

> When this perishable body puts on imperishability, and this mortal body puts on immortality, then the saying that is written will be fulfilled: 'Death has been swallowed up in victory' (1 Cor 15:54).

This is the picture of a transformed earthly state, not an ending of earthly existence, but a swallowing up of the mortal fleshly life in the immortal, imperishable life of the Spirit. So there is this important combination in Paul's thought: the future transformation is bound up with the Second Coming when the risen Jesus will come in glory in a way which can be witnessed by all.

And here we come to the last and perhaps most important qualification that Paul makes for the present change in those who have come to faith. In Paul's picture of the present situation of the early Christians he says that there is prophecy 'in part'. Earlier in the chapter it was suggested that this partial prophecy and knowledge fits with an understanding of those in Christ having received the first instalment of the Spirit, a down payment of the promised future fullness of the Spirit. Now we have a final vital qualification. Among the Christian community there is this core group, the apostles. Paul claims that, in them, the life that is to come is already being lived. There is a reason that Paul presents that can give grounds for this claim. The apostles are those who have already encountered the risen Jesus in a way fundamentally different from the rest of the early Christian community. This is what Paul says. Note his concern for accuracy in what follows. He is wanting it to be clear that he is describing a factual sequence of events:

> For I handed on to you as of first importance what I in turn had received: that Christ died for our sins in accordance with the scriptures, and that he was buried, and that he was raised on the third day in accordance with the scriptures, and that he appeared to Cephas [Peter], then to the twelve. Then he appeared to more than five hundred brothers and sisters at one time, most of whom are still alive, though some have died. Then he appeared to James, then to all the apostles. Last of all, as to one untimely born, he appeared also to me (1 Cor 15:3-8).

In Paul's picture, there is a sequence of resurrection appearances which are tied together with a real transformation of those who go through them. The apostles themselves are a kind of first-fruits or first instalment. They speak out of the experience of liberation from self that is the effect of their encounter with the risen Jesus. So, in their encounter with the risen Jesus, the risen life becomes theirs. Christ speaks in them and because they are no longer identified with the mortal body, their fleshly existence, they are quite prepared to suffer and die in witness to the gospel they teach.

In a famous passage in 2 Corinthians, Paul is actually speaking of the apostles, not all Christians, when he says:

> All this is from God, who reconciled us to himself through Christ, and has given us the ministry of reconciliation; that is, in Christ God was reconciling the world to himself, not counting their trespasses against them, and placing in us the word of reconciliation. So we are ambassadors on behalf of Christ, since God is making his appeal through us; we entreat you on behalf of Christ, be reconciled to God (2 Cor 5:18-20, adapted NRSV).

Conclusion

In order to see the coherence in what Paul says, the material that has been presented is here organised in the following fold-out diagram.

The columns of the diagram indicate two historical events separating three phases of history. The first of the historical events is divided into three parts: the life, death and resurrection of Jesus. The second of the historical events is the Second Coming. Before Jesus there is the 'childhood' of humanity; after Jesus is the 'adolescence' of humanity; after the Second Coming, which is also described as a 'coming of age', is the 'adulthood' of humanity.

Each row of the diagram follows a particular aspect of Paul's theology through this historical sequence.

1. Childhood is life before Jesus and life before faith; adulthood can also be described as the 'kingdom of God'.

2. This childhood of humanity is what is pictured in the Genesis story as the state of humankind after banishment from the Garden of Eden; it is humanity in its fallen state with the image of God in which it was created somehow obscured. Jesus is presented by Paul as the image of God and, as a consequence of his life, death and resurrection, Paul expects that in the future all of humanity will be the image of God exercising God's creative power in all that is created.

3. In this childhood, humanity is separated from God. In Jesus, God alone is at work so that he is called the 'Son of God' and Paul says of him that 'God was in Christ'. As a consequence of his resurrection, a first instalment of the Spirit of God is given to humankind, the same Spirit that was in Jesus. At the coming of age when the time of inheritance is reached, Paul's expectation is that the full gift of the Spirit will be poured out on humankind. Living totally in the Spirit with no separation from God will be the adult state of humanity.

4. Paul is not using the image of childhood to evoke innocence; in this scheme it is the light the image throws on the movement of humankind from a kind of childhood to a kind of adulthood. In the childhood phase humanity is under the power of sin. There is a struggle between the Spirit of God and individual fleshly desire - a

	Childhood			
1	life before Jesus life before faith	life of Jesus	death of Jesus	resurrection of Jesus
2	in the Fall	image of God		
3	separation from God	the Son of God 'God was in Christ'	the first instalment of the Spirit	
4	slaves to sin flesh ► ◄ Spirit	'one without sin'	death as one apparently cursed by God 'made to be sin'	for the few witnesses: end of identification with flesh; end of illusion of death; liberation from sin
5	expectant waiting	Jesus the Christ	Christ died in place of us: Christ died in place of our sins	Christ appears to a few witnesses
6	living under law	living by faith	faith of Jesus faith of Abraham	
7		incarnation I		historical event: the risen Christ encounters a few: their witness preserved in the Christian Scriptures and the Church

'Adolescence'	Coming of age	Adulthood	
	resurrection encounter	kingdom of God	1
time		humankind the image of God exercising the dominion of God	2
	time of inheritance	living in the Spirit	3
of the	for all humankind: end of identification with flesh; end of illusion of death; liberation from sin	humankind liberated from sin (Spirit (flesh))	4
Church	Christ appears to all	in Christ	5
		living by faith; directly guided by God	6
	the risen Christ encounters all	incarnation II	7

struggle which is a reality for all of humankind. Jesus comes as 'one without sin', one who is outside of this struggle. Yet he dies 'cursed by God', as one who is identified with sin ('made to be sin'). When, after his death he encounters others, they experience an end to the struggle. They no longer identify their existence with their separate, mortal fleshliness. They are liberated from the struggle; liberated from sin. They are but a few but their expectation is that Christ will return and appear to all so that all humankind may come to this liberation. This adult state is not the end of created, fleshly existence but rather its surrounding with the life of the Spirit, so that life on earth is transformed; this is 'heaven on earth'.

5. A future hope gives purpose to this childhood of humanity. One example of that hope is the expectant waiting of the Jewish people for the deliverer - the Messiah or Christ. For Paul, Jesus is the longed-for Christ. In Paul's understanding, humankind is unable to effect a liberation from sin; only a new beginning, a new creation, can bring this about. Jesus dies in place of humankind, dies identified with humankind's separation from God, and by appearing to a few witnesses after his death, an effective break with the fallen past is effected. It is to be completed when he appears to all and all are liberated from sin. Now the whole of humankind lives the kind of life that Jesus lived; there is no separation from God; all are 'in Christ'.

6. In this intimacy with God of the adult state, God guides all the actions of humanity without undermining freedom. This is the same life of faith that Jesus lived and it means that an external law, mediated through others, is no longer required.

7. The life of Jesus is the first incarnation of God. The risen Christ encounters just a few whose witness is preserved in the Christian Scriptures and in the church. In the encounter with all people that Paul expects in the future, all of humanity will become the incarnation of God.

Postscript: the church in the time of 'adolescence'

Most of what I want to say in this following section is informed by my experience of the Roman Catholic church. Not all of it is easily applicable to other mainstream churches but it aims to make some brief theological points about the church which connect with the theology of Paul that we have been considering.

A first point can be made. We have just been looking at the importance of the apostles. One thing that joins the Protestant and Catholic views of the church is the concern to be connected to the experience and witness of the apostles, although in different ways. On the one hand, the Protestant churches connect themselves to that apostolic witness through the primacy that they give to the authority of Scripture. From a Protestant point of view, it is Scripture that contains the apostolic word, so it is Scripture to which the contemporary Christian must look in order to be correctly guided by God. The Catholic church similarly emphasises the importance of the apostolic witness but in a different way. In the Catholic church the bishops are seen as successors of the apostles. Quite specifically, it is taught that one called to be a bishop must be a witness of the resurrection. And so as well as turning to Scripture for authority, within the Catholic church there is a turning to the bishops as those who are successors of the apostles, able to exercise their authority. So this connection with the apostles is seen as vital for the mainstream churches but in different ways.

Thirty years ago, the Catholic church went through an enormous upheaval. Many elements of that upheaval were similar to changes going on in other churches but we will focus on a couple of aspects of what happened in the Catholic church. The Second Vatican Council, a gathering of the bishops from all over the world, met in Rome, on and off over a period of three years. Every area of the church's life was touched by their deliberations. Part of what they were doing was in response to the changing situation of the modern world. But a significant influence on their thought was the recovery of the sense, particularly through biblical scholarship, of the centrality in the teaching of Jesus, and indeed in the whole of the Christian

Scriptures, of a looking towards the coming of the kingdom of God in power: Jesus, proclaiming that the kingdom of God, the rule of God is close, saying 'make yourselves ready'. It was a recovery of the theme at which we have spent so much time in looking at Paul.

Where the Second Vatican Council had the most immediate impact was in the worship of the church, its liturgy. It was after the Council that Catholic priests no longer led the celebration of the mass with their backs to the people, looking up to heaven, in a kind of intermediary role. Instead they stood behind the altar, in the role of one presiding at a meal with the community gathered around the table. There were many other ways in which the communitarian dimensions of the liturgy were restored and strengthened, worship having become rather individual and cerebral. But along with this change was a renewed sense of the church in waiting, recalling the great events which brought it into existence - the events of the Bible - looking forward to the fulfilment of those events in the future.

This change of perspective was not new teaching but a restoration of the understanding that Paul was relaying in the letters. When he gives instructions on the eucharist, he recalls the night that Jesus was betrayed, the words that Jesus said when he broke the bread - 'Do this in remembrance of me' - and the same with the cup, and then Paul says:

> For as often as you eat this bread and drink this cup, you proclaim the Lord's death until he comes (1 Cor 11:26).

This is very precise. In participating in the eucharist, people are recalling the death of Jesus, a historical event, aware that this is an interim time, looking forward to the time when the effects of that death are realised, and then there is an implication that this ritual of remembrance will no longer be required. This is traditional theology, but it is extremely difficult to keep hold of. What has happened at various stages in the history of the church is that, at least in popular understanding, the church and its worship becomes identified with the kingdom. There is a good example of this process going on in the present Roman Catholic mass. Just before the point in the mass where people come up to communion the priest holds up the consecrated bread and wine and quotes two passages from Scripture. This is the RSV translation:

> Behold, the Lamb of God, who takes away the sin of the world! Blessed are those who are invited to the marriage supper of the Lamb.

Or that is what the priest should say. The first sentence is from the gospel of John (1:29). The second sentence is a very clear reference to the transformation at the end of time. It is a quotation from the book of Revelation where the image of marriage is used to indicate the restored intimacy between God and humankind (Rev 19:9, cf. 21:2).

In fact, because a prosaic translation of the Scriptures was used at this point in the liturgy, the words the priest uses are these:

> This is the Lamb of God who takes away the sins of the world. Happy are those who are called to his supper (*The Roman Missal* 1975:510).

Partly because of this unclear translation of the text, what has happened in the minds of many priests and people is that the invitation is not seen as a reminder of the invitation that will be made to all at the end of time but as an invitation to receive the bread and wine at the particular mass that is being celebrated. It is not uncommon for priests to change the words still further away from their intended sense: 'Happy are those who are called to receive the body and blood of Christ.' With these words the particular sense of this biblical passage being quoted has gone altogether. Instead of being reminded that although this eucharist is the centre of the church's life it is only a foretaste of the feast to come, the future dimension is lost. The centre of the Christian life then simply becomes the sacraments without their essential connection with this promised future.

So this understanding of the church standing in an interim time - in our presentation, an adolescence - is there but it is fragile. It is a focus that is easily lost. Given the importance that is placed on the sacraments, particularly in a Catholic context, these can become the whole story instead of a remembrance of the past and a pointer to a glorious future still to come.

Yet the theology of the Catholic church, reiterated in the Second Vatican Council, is unequivocal. Here is how the Council document on the church, *Lumen Gentium*, describes this relationship between what has already been received and what is to come in the future:

> Already the final age of the world is with us (cf. 1 Cor 10:11) and the renewal of the world is irrevocably under way; it is even now anticipated in a certain real way, for the Church on earth is endowed already with a sanctity that is real though imperfect. However, until there be realized new heavens and a new earth in which justice dwells (cf. 2 Pet 3:13) the pilgrim Church, in its sacraments and institutions, which belong to this present age, carries the mark of this world which will pass...(Flannery 1975:408).

The church, specifically in its sacraments and institutions - those things which are so central to the life of the church - is itself part of the present age and carries the mark of this world which will pass.

Part Two:

Early Friends and the Second Coming

Chapter Eight

Come again?
early Friends as an apocalyptic movement

Douglas Gwyn

The Quaker movement arose in a moment of major crisis in English society. It was the cumulative moment of the English Reformation, the moment of Puritanism's crowning glory – and its undoing. It was the moment when England decisively broke with the long tradition of feudal social organisation and groped toward a new basis. These were booming times of new commercial vitality, moving toward capitalism, yet only half-consciously and often self-defeatingly. Mid-seventeenth century English society muddled through one of the privileged moments in history, making choices that exerted enormous impact upon the future of western culture – for better and for worse. Many inspired individuals and groups emerged during that fateful period, offering visionary programs for the future. Early Friends embodied one of the most powerfully integrative visions of that exciting period. Their covenantal vision for modern society stands as a compelling 'path not taken'.

Tim Peat has already led us (in Chapter 5) to consider Paul's tortured words in Romans 7:15-24. It would be useful to revisit them here:

> I do not understand my own actions. For I do not do what I want, but I do the very thing I hate. Now if I do what I do not want, I agree that the law is good. But in fact it is no longer I that do it, but sin that dwells within me. For I know that nothing

> good dwells within me, that is, in my flesh. I can will what is right but I cannot do it... For I delight in the law of God in my inmost self, but I see in my members another law at war with the law of my mind, making me captive to the law of sin that dwells in my members. Wretched man that I am! Who will rescue me from this body of death? (NRSV translation here is somewhat different from Tim's).

This agonised statement fits very well the dilemma of Puritanism, both in its anxious spirituality and in its self-defeating politics during the English Civil War and Commonwealth periods (roughly 1640-1660). We must examine both aspects of the Puritan double-bind in order to understand the meaning of early Quaker witness.

Why early Friends?

Why study early Friends? Should the faith and action of Quakers living three and a half centuries before us have bearing on our faith and action today? It is a paradox of modern Quakerism that we profess to live by the light of our own experience, free of human traditions; yet we often resort to a good example or quotation from George Fox or other early Friends to strengthen a particular viewpoint. Evangelical Friends see early Quakers as vibrant evangelists. Liberal Friends sometimes view them as early activists. There is truth in both of these interpretations. But both are caricatures that ultimately do not capture the enduring power of early Quaker witness.

The abiding fascination with early Friends may have to do with their place in history. They lived just at the dawn of our modern era. Their way of thinking and manner of expression are just familiar enough to engage us, and yet not fully conformed to the boundaries that constrict our modern consciousness. So they fit only half-way into the categories we can provide for them. But if we keep listening to them, they may help us find a way out of the impasses that modern consciousness imposes on us. It is not that early Friends have 'the answer' for the Quakerism of today or tomorrow. But if we allow ourselves to be challenged by their prophetic witness, the right questions may occur. From there, God can begin to work with us.

The political rise of Puritanism

Puritanism emerged in the later sixteenth century as a movement to reform the English national church beyond the modest and self-serving aims of Henry VIII in the 1530s. Puritans were inspired by the more thorough-going reformations on the Continent, particularly in Calvin's Geneva and Zwingli's Zürich. Puritan concern stimulated growing vitality in Bible study and biblical preaching in English religious life, but these growth points were in tension with the conservative policies of the Crown-appointed episcopal hierarchy. In particular, Puritan sensibilities were at variance with official liturgical guidelines, which de-emphasised the role of preaching, maintained a more sacerdotal style of clerical leadership, and seemed more Roman than Genevan.

But while Puritanism was religious in focus and intention, it represented a larger shift in English life. Economically, Puritan leadership tended to arise from the lower gentry and the new wealth of the commercial revolution in England. Their zeal for creative investment, hard work and social betterment placed Puritans at odds with the old, landed wealth of the aristocracy and the Crown. New Puritan wealth found increasing political representation in Parliament, where calls for free trade and social reform began to be aired. But most of all, Puritans wanted to restructure the national church according to a Presbyterian order of government, in which Crown-appointed Bishops would be replaced by Parliament-nominated Presbyters. Elizabeth I and the Stuarts, James I and Charles I, were unanimous in rejecting this plan, which they recognised would rob the Crown of much social influence. 'No Bishop, no King,' quipped James I.

Covenant was the centrepiece of Puritan theology. Borrowed from the Reformed tradition of Calvin, Zwingli, and Bullinger, the covenantal, or federal, theology of the Puritans rediscovered the centrality of covenant in the biblical saga. Reformed covenantal theology was grounded in a firm belief in predestination, God's election of only some souls for salvation. To be among the elect was to be in included in God's covenant of grace through Jesus

Christ. Calvin and Zwingli had taught that through a sweeping reformation of the church, God's elect would naturally emerge into the forefront of religious life, purifying the church of its old Roman corruptions, instilling new voluntarism among the faithful, in place of the old medieval passivity. This purification of the church would renew the marriage of church and state. The influence of the reformed church would work for an honest, disinterested Christian magistracy to rule with justice and equity. At the same time, the elect would be expected to rise to the fore of commerce through honesty, hard work and God's favour. A free-market economy would naturally allow the elect to emerge as leaders of a new economic era. So the covenant of grace would consolidate all realms of society into a godly order. The idea of covenant replaced static, hierarchical models of social thought, such as Thomas Aquinas' Great Chain of Being, that had dominated medievalism.

Hence, covenant served as a biblical concept to aid in rethinking not only religion but also politics and economics. The elect, those in God's predestined covenant, were the vanguard of a new society. They would become the benevolent elite of a truly Christian England. Covenantal consciousness became an important tool for imagining a market economy based in contractual rather than naturalistic relations. Covenant became an important theme in imagining a political society that was still monarchical but led by parliamentary policy-making. (In the long run, covenantal theologies made their most lasting contribution in helping influence later liberal thought, specifically contractarian political philosophy, which views human societies as comprised of implicit and explicit social contracts.) Finally, covenant undergirded the new, voluntaristic sense of church membership. Though classical Puritanism continued to insist upon a parish-based state church structure, covenantal faith led many to conclude that a truly voluntaristic church must be independent of state control and its corrupting influences. The Independent party within Puritanism renounced the traditional parish system for a decentralised structure of freely covenanted congregations. Thus, covenant was a key term in helping to conceive a separation of church and state, as well as religious freedom and plurality.

If these progressive social forces could have worked in tandem with an enlightened Stuart monarchy, the seventeenth century would surely have taken a different course. Unfortunately, Puritan reformism elicited an imperious absolutism from both James and Charles, who answered Puritan initiatives with an archaic theology of the divine right of kings. The Puritan coalition never dreamed of overthrowing the Stuarts. Nevertheless, by 1642 they found themselves in a civil war against Charles. Hoping merely to batter Charles into a negotiating position, Parliament fought a fitful, ambivalent war in the first phases. However, as time dragged on, the Presbyterian majority in Parliament lost control of their situation. They found themselves in competition with a burgeoning Independent party that resisted the Presbyterian plan for a national English church. Moreover, the Independent Oliver Cromwell took control of the Army and turned it into a serious military force, whose ranks were now swelled by men set on deposing Charles permanently and establishing a radically utopian society in England.

At this point, the Puritan coalition began to self-destruct. It was split internally by the Presbyterian-Independent struggle over the direction of both church and state. It was also beset by growing numbers of Baptists and Spiritualist groups rapidly moving beyond the pale of Calvinist Puritanism. By 1647, as Charles was defeated and captured, the Independent-controlled Army became the decisive political actor in England. Yet the Army's officers themselves were barely in control of their men. The Army had become a 'many-headed monster'. Many soldiers espoused republican politics and various prophetic ideas of the kingdom of God on earth, the new age of the Spirit and the return of Christ. As in Paul's tormented self-description, the Puritan-led Parliament and Army had become bodies whose heads willed one thing and whose members did quite another thing.

The Puritan spirituality of anxiety

The enormous religious, social, economic, and political energies aroused by Puritanism were the outgrowth of its anxiety-driven spirituality. As noted earlier, the Puritan covenant of grace centred upon the doctrine of predestination. God had elected only some souls for salvation, a decision made before the foundation of the world. By implication, then, the Puritan spiritual quest was grounded in the struggle to ascertain one's predestined fate. Naturally, one hoped to be destined for eternal salvation rather than damnation. In this-worldly terms, one also wished to be among the elect as God's vanguard on earth, leading the way toward a purified church, economic growth and a just society.

Adolescent and young adult Puritans were typically caught up in an identity crisis: am I among the elect or not? This was a vexed question: it suggested that one must *infer* a relationship with God, rather than *experience* it. It had to do with an event before the beginning of time, rather than the present. Puritan clergy had developed a form of pastoral counsel that helped the young search for signs that God's grace was working in them. A self-loathing for sin, a desire to be without sin, a love of hearing sermons, an esteem for those counted among the righteous – these were taken as signs of one's election, signs of belonging in the covenant of grace. Moreover, in less overtly religious realms of life, industrious hard work, success in business and good citizenship could also be viewed as signs of grace. Now, Puritan clergy were not trying to drive people mad, but to encourage religious life and model citizenship, as well as give assurance to anxious young souls. Indeed, such counsel set many young people on a path toward faithful church involvement, productive work habits and responsible adulthood.

But there were some, particularly the most morally scrupulous and introspective young idealists, for whom such counsel was truly maddening. For these, every momentary assurance of salvation turned sour, since every such inference could be suspected as a self-serving delusion. It was particularly such young hyper-Puritans who found themselves caught in Paul's agonised dilemma. For example, the young William Dewsbury was encouraged to find God's grace working in him, to 'apply the promises' to his condition. But the only thing he felt working in him was God's wrath. He could not find himself among the elect, but neither could he resign himself to damnation. Young Puritans like Dewsbury tended to pass through

Presbyterian and Independent forms of Puritanism and then drop out, first into the Baptist sectarian movement, then out of all church fellowship.

The Seeker scene

By the early 1640s, these drop-outs were dubbed 'Seekers'. They were not a new church, creed or political agenda. They were not even a coherent movement. They were a growing phenomenon of isolated individuals, small prayer groups, and occasional massed gatherings, sharing the perception that there were no legitimate churches, clergy or sacraments. They opted to wait for the appearance of a new, authentic church to be revealed. Seekers rejected Puritan predestination, tending to believe (along with General Baptists) that Christ died for all souls. They tended toward a greater emphasis upon the Holy Spirit, a spirituality of experience rather than inference. Many emphasised the indwelling of Christ. They strongly rejected the Presbyterian attempt to reimpose a national church. Many supported the republican political reforms proposed by the Levellers in 1647, which would have guaranteed religious freedom, enlarged the electoral franchise and pressed wide-ranging legal reforms. So religiously and politically, Seekers were well outside the Puritan consensus.

By the latter 1640s, two basic types of Seekers were recognised. The first Seekers (Type A, let us say) clung to the traditional Reformation dream of a return to a pure New Testament faith and practice. They looked for new apostles to show the way forward, cutting through the array of competing creeds, sacramental practices and clergies, teaching right doctrine and practice. Their new revelation would need to be beyond question; hence the new apostles would perform signs and wonders like those recorded in the Book of Acts. Nothing less would propel English society beyond the self-defeating politics and paralysing *angst* that had overcome the Puritan Reformation.

But a second type of Seeker (whom we shall call Type B) questioned the logic of the first, classic Seeker position. Why should God take

England back to a New Testament church, which Seekers generally agreed had been corrupted by the end of the first century? That would be a futile enterprise. God's people must move *forward* in history, not backward. A new Pentecost, inducing a new Age of the Spirit, was necessary. Type B Seekers (especially those in Parliament's Army) believed it was already starting to break in upon their worship groups. This was the dawn of a new dispensation, in which outward sacraments and liturgies, as well as a regularised clergy, would be swallowed up into a more totally inward and immediate experience. Christ within would reveal all to the heart, or conscience, of the new 'spiritual Christian'. This new age of internalised, spiritual faith would soon sweep over all England and the world.

We see two basic tendencies among these two Seeker positions. The Type A position maintained a Protestant outlook, still holding out for 'primitive Christianity revived'. Type A Seekers were conservatives driven to radical conclusions by the self-defeating religion and politics of Puritanism. The Type B position manifested a proto-liberal tendency. History was seen as a sequence of progressive revelations, or dispensations: Law, Gospel, and Spirit. Each new dispensation took away another veil from the truth, allowed the light to shine more brightly. These Seekers believed they were standing at the threshold of the final, climactic phase of world history, the Age of the Spirit. In the writings of Seeker John Saltmarsh, this new spiritual Christianity linked confidently with scientific inquiry, human reason, democratic politics and religious freedom.

Type A and Type B Seekers

A close study of the English Seekers of the 1640s and '50s reveals that there were two basic types, which we will call A and B. Type A seeking still operated essentially upon Protestant assumptions. It was a search for the restoration of the true church, based on the New Testament example. Thus, 'primitive Christianity revived' was its Reformation ideal. A different strain of seeking also flourished during this period. What we might call Type B seeking concluded that God would not take seventeenth century Christians back to a first century faith. God would take them forward into a new dispensation, a new age of the Spirit. In that new order, all the realities of Christian faith that had been mediated through outward sacraments, clergy, books, institutions etc. would be known inwardly, without mediation. A mystical communion with Christ, an inner 'land of rest', was the ideal of Type B seeking. Type B seeking was often allied with proto-liberal ideas of progressive revelation, democratic politics, and the new sciences.

Few Seekers would have fitted these pure types, but many would have exhibited tendencies in one direction or another. The Type A tendency probably emerged first, by the early 1640s, and probably flourished all over England, but especially among northern Seekers. The Type B tendency emerged later, but certainly by 1647. It seems to have predominated more in the South, especially London, and among the ranks of the New Model Army. Early Quaker preaching appears to have provided a synthesis of both types. It combined the inward, mystical tendencies of Type B seeking and the Anabaptist-style passion for a true, visible church inherent in the Type A position.

Many different predictions of divine intervention and schemes of salvation history proliferated during this period. Some looked for new apostles, others for a new Age of the Spirit. Some for the physical return of Christ, others for a 'rule of the saints', a radical coalition of religious leaders to rule England for Christ. Some predictions of England's transformation envisioned abrupt and supernatural acts of God. Others were more humanistic and gradualist in their expectation. In various ways, all of them may be seen as eschatological, for they all saw an end to the world as they had known it. And whether they saw the Second Coming in terms of Christ's physical return, the Age of the Spirit, or a new regime mediated by new apostles or the saints, all shared a sense that biblical history and English history were becoming one.

But by the end of the 1640s, as Oliver Cromwell began to consolidate power and search for a political centre, seeking people of all varieties entered a state of disillusion and despair of the kingdom of God on earth. Some Seekers, particularly the Type A variety, began to settle in for a longer struggle, feeling lost in a wilderness. They had been delivered from the spiritual Egypt of Puritanism, but they were still far from the Promised Land of rest. Others, often of Type B persuasion, were so acutely disappointed in their new-age optimism and political activism that they revolted in outrage against the Puritan regime. That moment of nihilistic abandon coalesced in the Ranter scene, which first exploded in London over the summer of 1649, but continued to simmer in many places across the country throughout the 1650s.

The Quaker emergence

Somewhere in the mix of all this Seeker exploration, young George Fox roamed the Midlands. He had left home at age nineteen in acute despair. He was scandalised by the pallid and hypocritical Christianity in his local parish church in Leicestershire. He went to several Puritan divines, hoping to find insight and a way out of his condition. Though some honestly tried to help, it was impossible to reach his condition through the typical Puritan counselling that searched for signs of God's grace. Young Fox began to visit more radical, Separatist teachers and congregations, still without relief. It was only as he abandoned this lateral seeking from place to place that he heard a voice saying, 'There is one, even Christ Jesus, that can speak to thy condition' (Nickalls 1952:11). That breakthrough experience shifted Fox from seeking to what he would later describe as *standing still* in the light of Christ (see, for example, Fox 1831:7:20f).

Following Jesus' teaching, Fox came to understand the experience of the light as Judgment Day, the Day of the Lord revealed ('apocalypsed') within (see John 3:19-21: 'this is the judgment, that the light has come into the world... those who do what is true come to the light, so that it may be clearly seen that their deeds have been done in God'). The light showed Fox that he was living in alienation from God. But as he stood still and submitted to that painful revelation, it began to awaken a new sense of God's presence, guidance and empowerment. This was a Christian approach very different from Puritan teaching, for it was based upon a clear, even visceral *experience* of God, rather than upon mental inferences. It was not a spirituality of anxiety but of desolation, because it was attained only through radical surrender to God's active work within.

But this was also different from Seeker approaches. It shared much in common with the Type B Seeker teaching that Christ reveals all within, without the outward mediations of sacraments, human teachers, etc. But Fox's approach generated a new kind of moral empowerment. Those convinced by early Quaker preaching consistently described an acute sense of knowing God's will and being empowered to do it. This was the kingdom of God coming in *power*, not merely in words. The realities Seekers had prophesied as *imminent* were discovered as *an unfolding present*. (See the similar shift between John the Baptist and Jesus of Nazareth treated in the Excursus, p. 246.)

Fox employed many apocalyptic images to describe the changes he experienced in those early years. He echoed the language of Isaiah 40 to describe the purifying and transforming power of the light as 'mountains burning up and the rubbish, and the rough and crooked ways and places made smooth and plain that the Lord might come into his tabernacle. These things are to be found in a man's heart' (Nickalls 1952:16). Thus, apocalyptic images of cosmic conflagration were to be fulfilled inwardly by experience. As his personal transformation culminated, Fox saw himself passing through the flaming sword into Eden, where he experienced the purity and wholeness of creation (Nickalls 1952:27). The creation around Fox thus became the new creation to his eyes.

This is a fully apocalyptic spirituality (again, see the treatment of apocalypse in the Excursus). Fox described a spiritual transformation that recapitulated the entire biblical *history of salvation* in the *mystery of personal experience*. But the word 'mystic' does not adequately describe Fox, for these experiences did not remain private or other-worldly. They were grounded in a radical moral and social practice. They sent him into the world with a prophetic message to preach (see Benson 1968). Moreover, he experienced an apostolic calling to gather a new people of God into this new apocalyptic faith. Indeed, Fox's uncanny powers of spiritual discernment and occasional faith healings convinced some Seekers of the Type A tendency that this was the new apostle they had awaited.

Apocalypse

'Apocalypse' is a noun used loosely in our culture to characterise cataclysmic events of many kinds. 'Apocalyptic' is an adjective often used to describe religious groups and teachings that emphasise the end of the world, the Second Coming of Christ, and other eschatological themes. The word is a derives from the Greek word *apokalypsis*, which means 'revelation', or 'taking away the veil'. Hence, the Book of Revelation is alternatively titled the Apocalypse of John. John (either the disciple of Jesus or another early Christian) had a series of revelations from Christ while imprisoned on the Isle of Patmos. For another example, Paul insists that he received his understanding of the gospel by a direct revelation (*apokalypsis*) of Jesus Christ.

Thus, in the root sense of the word, an apocalypse is a revelation, an unveiling of reality. The revelations of John unveiled the demonic nature of the Roman Empire and the cosmic significance of the early church's resistance to the worship of Caesar as lord. Paul's revelation from/of Christ laid bare the turn of the ages that had been effected by the crucifixion and resurrection. Within a biblical worldview, in which reality is most basically temporal, unfolding in time, the revelation of ultimate truth is logically a revelation of the end, the outcome and destiny, of the universe, and of its true Lord.

By 1646, Fox was travelling with a message that shared much in common with other Seeker preaching, but with a particular moral rigour and down-to-earth realism. It tended to cool the fevered brows of enthusiasts, grounding their spiritual experience in a more sober life. While Fox himself remained an itinerant preacher much of his life, his message strongly encouraged settled domestic life, another aspect of 'standing still' (see Levy 1988). By the end of the 1640s, he was the central figure in growing network of Midlands groups calling themselves 'Children of the Light'. But in the latter 1640s, most Seekers were not yet ready to be settled. Religiously, they still looked outwardly for the coming salvation; politically, they still hoped that the Army or Oliver Cromwell would achieve their liberation.

It was only in late 1651, after the political disillusionment of Seekers and a year spent by Fox incarcerated at Derby, that his message began to connect powerfully with large numbers of Seekers. The breakthrough occurred in the North, moving from the West Riding of Yorkshire westward into Westmorland, Lancashire, and Cumberland. A number of ex-soldiers and gifted Seeker leaders quickly gathered around Fox's message and began to spread around the countryside, multiplying its effects. Fox's *Journal* indicates that he was preaching repentance and the Day of the Lord in the steeplehouses, marketplaces and streets of northern towns. The sensational effects of his preaching are hard to fathom, unless we take seriously the apocalyptic import of his key refrain that 'Christ is come to teach his people himself.'

This was a clear Second-Coming message. Fox preached that the light in people's consciences was nothing less than the presence of the risen and returned Christ, the ultimate authority on earth. That authority, if turned to (repentance) and followed (obedience) was sufficient to guide the individual into a righteous life. It was sufficient to gather groups into the true church that materialises Christ's body on earth. Through the proliferation of gathered communities of men and women under Christ's direct teaching, this authority was sufficient to transform all society into the covenantal harmony and peace of God's kingdom on earth.

To those who had lived on the edge between hope and despair for the past ten years, hungering to the point of faintness for true righteousness and justice, this message had explosive power. It confirmed the hopes of many Type A Seekers in that Quaker worship and ministry seemed to move beyond the endless formal inventions of Protestantism. The power of Quaker silent worship shook them to their foundations. Quaker ministers travelled like the prophets and apostles of New Testament times, exercising an authority that relied not upon office but pure spiritual charism. Yet these new apostles did not re-establish the sacraments and other 'ordinances' of traditional Christianity. Like the Type B Seekers, Friends preached the inwardness of the sacraments in personal experience.

Quaker witness came in many ways closer to the Type B position, except that it denied the dispensational doctrine of the three ages, in which the new age of the Spirit supposedly bestowed a new level of inspiration. The light of Christ's apocalyptic revelation was the same light that Paul (2 Cor 4:6) and John (Jn 1:19) had witnessed in New Testament times, and that David had witnessed in the Psalms (Ps 119:105). So in one sense, there was nothing new about this apocalypse, this revelation of the light within: it was timeless and universal. But at the same time, the light was doing something new and earth-shaking at that historic juncture.

The earth that was shaken was the 'earth' in people's hearts, Fox emphasised. It was their 'grounding', we might say, in a socially constructed self, a particular niche in society. When that grounding was shaken, the constructed self came down. This was a 'consciousness raising' experience, opening the way for a new self to be constructed by the direct guidance of the light and the nurture of others struggling through the same experience. But this inward apocalypse did not remain a private phenomenon. Quaker convincement quickly moved into outward behaviours (particularly plain speech, dress and demeanour) which jarred the mannered social codes of English society. So *the inner apocalypse soon became a social apocalypse*. The confrontation unfolded in steeplehouses (against the falsely assumed authority of the clergy), in marketplaces (against deceitful forms of mercantilism), in the streets (against fawning conventions of social deference), and in courtrooms (as Friends were brought before magistrates for various forms of resistance). As Fox commented in his *Journal*, 'the Lord said unto me if I did but set up one in the same spirit the prophets and apostles were in that gave forth the Scriptures, he or she should shake all the country in their profession ten miles around them' (Nickalls 1952:103).

In those first years, Friends called their movement the Lamb's War, because it was a struggle against alienated social conventions at all levels. It amounted to a nonviolent cultural revolution, aimed to 'stop the world' of immoral and unjust social norms. The conscience is the place in the self where 'received' ideas and habits are melded together into some coherent sense of the world and one's place in it. But the light, the 'witness' awakened within the conscience by Quaker preaching, offered a fundamentally different way of being in the world. The light *revealed* the world around the individual in a disturbingly new way, laying bare its inequities and hypocrisies. More disturbingly, it revealed the individual's deceitful, inauthentic way of being and acting in the world. The *sham* of worldly convention and the *shame* of one's part in it were the painful apocalyptic revelation of the light in early Quaker experience.

A 1655 statement by Edward Burrough asserts the Second-Coming perspective of early Friends succinctly. In *A Trumpet of the Lord Sounded Forth in Sion*, Burrough criticised those who had hoped for the physical return of Christ in glory. Their hope had not been fulfilled because the:

> Way of his coming is not prepared, but Rocks and Mountains are standing, and Valleys are not filled up, and rough and crooked is your present way... for your hope of his coming hath no whit purified you, as he is pure; for you are in the flesh, and in the liberty of it, which is Rebellion to his Reign; and Christ is kept in Prison, in exile with that mind... and to you, what purpose is it to desire the day of his coming? for with wrath will he come, and with vengeance will he appear, and will break your Kingdom like a Potter's vessel.... Your high nature stands, and Satan is not bound...your minds are outward, and they are your thoughts, which are vain.... The Sufferings of Christ must you know, before you can see him Reign; and through his War you must strive before you obtain his Victory (Gwyn 1995:104).

Christ's return is not a science-fiction epic to sit back and watch, while expecting to be vindicated and saved from the transforming fire. To see Christ come to *earth* is to find the apocalyptic visions from Isaiah to Revelation fulfilled *within*. Again, the Second Coming, expected as an event in history, steals into the world through the mystery of personal experience. But as men and women unite in turning to and following that powerful revelation, the mystery becomes a socially dynamic movement, and the Second Coming becomes a historical phenomenon.

We have seen the impasse of the Puritan covenant of grace at all levels: personal spirituality, church reform, and politics. We have also seen the proliferation of alternative spiritualities and politics, and their failure by 1650. Finally, we have begun to glimpse the strange, disturbing grassroots movement that was dubbed 'Quaker' by 1650. The bold Quaker announcement of the Day of the Lord

The Book of Revelation and George Fox

It comes as a surprise (if not a shock) to many Friends today to find that George Fox read and used the Book of Revelation (the Apocalypse of John) extensively. He reports in his *Journal* that by age twenty-three he was having great openings regarding that most mysterious and forbidding of New Testament books. The clergy advised him to stay out of it, but he would not. He reasoned that while the New Testament epistles were written to the saints of ancient times, Revelation addressed the struggles of future generations (Nickalls 1952:8). Revelation is the subject of Fox's only extensive piece of biblical commentary (Fox 1831, vol. 5:127-141). Of course, the entire Reformation period had been taken up with various interpretations of Revelation, in which the Papacy was typically identified with the Beast.

But Fox's interpretations were unusual in identifying all the established churches with Babylon and the Beast. Any church that relied upon state support and enforcement of its worship and clergy was antichristian. For Fox, Revelation was a book not for use in predicting the future but in interpreting the present. Accordingly, what it says about the world 'out there' must be interpreted by the light's revelation within. So the Lamb in Revelation that breaks the seals on the scroll is the light of Christ, who breaks the seals on the human heart. The Lamb's War language of the early Quaker movement derives from the Book of Revelation, in which those who follow the Lamb are locked in struggle against the forces of the Dragon. The demonic power of the Dragon consists in keeping humanity in alienation and distraction from the power of God within.

and the relentless Quaker confrontation with the Puritan establishment ripped through the social fabric of Puritan society with alarming speed in the 1650s. We have suggested some of its apocalyptic, disruptive dynamics. In the next chapter, Tim Peat will compare these dynamics with the writings of Paul. Then we will move on to examine the covenantal principles of coherence that made the Quaker movement the great survivor among English radical groups of the Commonwealth period.

Eschatology

'Eschatology' is a word characterising any belief or theory pertaining to the end of time, the end of the world or the end of life. For example, any belief regarding what happens to the individual after death is eschatological. The word derives from the Greek word *eschatos,* meaning 'end'. But the word is most typically used to describe doctrines about the end of the world, the destiny of the human race, the Second Coming of Christ, the resurrection of the dead, the Last Judgment, the new creation, etc.. Eschatology can easily lead to a fantasy world, part biblical proof texts, part science fiction. But any outlook, religious or scientific, that contemplates the origins of things (protology) must also ponder their end. The strength of early Quaker eschatology was to keep all questions about the future grounded rigorously in the present, just as it kept all questions of theology and politics grounded tenaciously in practical terms. Eschatologies that emphasise present realisation are sometimes classified as 'realised eschatologies'. 'Realising' is probably a more apt description in the early Quaker case, since Friends viewed present realisation as part of a larger, unfolding reality, neither totally present nor totally future.

(This chapter has distilled previous work, *Apocalypse of the Word* (Gwyn 1986) and *The Covenant Crucified* (Gwyn 1995), as well as a forthcoming study of the early Seekers and Quakers.)

Chapter Nine

Paul's vision fulfilled

Timothy Peat

As demonstrated in the first part of the book, Paul had an expectation that in the future there would be a transformation for all humankind - that all would be liberated from wrongdoing, that all would be guided directly by God without the need for any mediation of that guidance. This transformation was connected with the idea that Christ would come again and the kingdom of God would be established upon earth. By seeing how the various elements of Paul's thinking interconnect it is possible to see how a future transformation for all humankind, the Second Coming and the kingdom of God are integrated in Paul's thinking. Paul associates a transformation in his own life with the appearance to him of the risen Christ. It is this that not only gives Paul new information about God and God's purposes but, more importantly, brings about a transformation by which he and others encountered by the risen Jesus become ambassadors for Christ in the world. His claim is that this group now act in the place of Christ, live by the same faith that he lived, have in themselves the same 'word of reconciliation' from God as was in Jesus and live free from sin. As Paul expresses it, just as Jesus was 'the righteousness of God' (1 Cor 1:30), showing God's right action in the world, so those who have witnessed the risen Jesus themselves become 'the righteousness of God' (2 Cor 5:21). Paul's expectation is that what is experienced by the few who encounter the risen Jesus in the earliest days of the Christian movement will be the possibility for all humankind when Christ returns in glory, to be witnessed by all. This is the Second Coming; Christ's appearing is essentially bound up with the transformation of those to whom he appears.

It is easier to see how this transformation can be expressed in different terms as the kingdom of God, when it is remembered that 'kingdom' is a misleading translation. The Greek word *basileia* is not something concrete but abstract: it is the activity of 'ruling' or 'reigning' or 'having dominion'. When Paul speaks of inheriting the kingdom, this is to be understood as the inheritance of a *way of acting* rather than an object. This is the point of linkage between the Second Coming and the kingdom of God in Paul's thinking: they are both ways of describing a transformed human condition in which humanity is free of selfishness and where the will of God and human desire are united.

In the time of early Friends, expectation of dramatic change was rife. Political and religious upheaval provided an environment in which ideas of the Second Coming of Christ and the imminent coming of the kingdom could flourish. There was a range of views of what might be about to occur (see Chapter 8, p. 97f). The expression of those expectations used traditional language about the Second Coming and the kingdom of God. George Fox and the early Friends used much biblical language in speaking of what was happening among them. The book of Revelation was a popular source of this biblical material. In that book, the vision of the future transformation is expressed in mythological and poetic language. It can be read in such a way that the sense of a transformation of humankind can be obscured by the extraordinary nature of the language that is used. But Friends also sought to describe what was happening to them in language that was fit to relay their actual experience. What these ways of speaking reveal is how close their experience was to what Paul was suggesting would take place at the Second Coming: immediacy of relationship with God and liberation from sin are central to their experience; other parallels come through too. To reveal the range of connection, the different aspects need looking at in sequence.

1. Christ is now come

In 1671, George Fox and several other Friends wrote to the governor of Barbados in order to persuade him that Friends were not seeking to undermine traditional Christian belief. They do this by offering a statement of belief which includes many phrases from traditional creeds.

> To the Governor and Assembly at Barbados, 1671.
> That God who is the only wise, omnipotent, and everlasting God we do own and believe in... And that Jesus Christ is his beloved and only begotten son... in whom we have redemption, through his blood even the forgiveness of sins... (Nickalls, 1952:602).

A belief in God; belief in Jesus Christ his only son; a traditional understanding of the atonement, that through the blood of Jesus Christ, sins are forgiven; all these come through in these brief extracts. But this apparently traditional credal setting serves to highlight very well the dramatic claim that Friends were continuing to make. Even though these words were written long after the extraordinary experiences of the early Friends in the 1650s there is a vital connection with their experience at that time. At the very point where the traditional creed includes the belief that Jesus Christ will come *in the future* to judge the living and the dead, Fox and the others say instead:

> *[Jesus] it is that is now come* and hath given us an understanding that we may know him that is true... (Nickalls, 1952:603) [italics added].

There was an understanding among the early Friends that they were caught up in the Second Coming of Christ, that it was happening among them. It is important to note that in speaking in this way they were not speaking of a Second Coming of Jesus appearing out of the clouds of heaven but rather of a transforming experience which brought them into a new relationship with God.

2. Liberation from sin

An essential part of the transformation that Fox describes is a sense of being fully liberated from sin:

> The priest said, there might be a perfection, as Adam had, and a falling from it. But I told him, "There is a perfection in Christ, above Adam and beyond falling; and that it was the work of the ministers of Christ to present every man perfect in Christ; and for the perfecting of whom they had their gifts from Christ; therefore, they that denied perfection denied the work of the ministry, and the gifts which Christ gave for the perfecting of the saints." The priest said, we must be always striving. But I told him it was a sad and comfortless sort of striving, to strive with a belief that we should never overcome... (Nickalls 1952: 688).

The claim was that this was a liberation leading to a perfection that was not just a restoration of the state of Adam but 'a perfection in Christ, above Adam and beyond falling.' The passage above makes the issue as clear as it could be. The priest with whom Fox is debating makes the thoroughly reasonable point that there is a perfection, but one from which we keep falling so that 'we must be always striving'. Fox is unequivocal in his rejection of this view. There is no sense in striving when there is no chance of success; a perfection beyond falling is possible.

3. The inner voice or word

In Fox's understanding the Second Coming involved a restored intimacy with God such that it was now possible for people to discover the Spirit of God in themselves and to be taught directly by Christ:

> And I brought them all to the spirit of God in themselves, by which they might know God and Christ and the Scriptures and to have heavenly fellowship in the spirit... [N]ow the everlasting Gospel was preached again that brought life and immortality to light, and the day of the Lord was come, and Christ was come to teach his people himself and how they might find their teacher within, when they were in their labours and in their beds (Nickalls 1952:155).

There are many such descriptions in the writings of the early Friends. Their experience, they claim, brings them to a point where no outward teacher is needed. They are directly guided by God who is experienced as a voice speaking within them. In this respect, there are direct parallels with the claims that were made in the first part of the book, that central to the life of the early Christians was their experience of an inner voice or word from God guiding them in a direct way rather than through guidance mediated through the law.

4. The light exposing wrongdoing

Just as in Paul's understanding the Second Coming is a time of judgment, so for Fox. The divine light of Christ exposes the evil thoughts, words and actions of those to whom it comes (see Chapter 8, p. 98f). If what the light shows is accepted then the person may continue in the light which eventually leads to their liberation; rejecting what the light shows and the person brings their own condemnation:

> As I was walking I heard old people and workpeople to say, 'He is such a man as never was, he knows people's thoughts', for I turned them to the divine light of Christ and his spirit that let them see all their thoughts, words, and actions, that were evil, that they had thought (or spoken) or acted; with which light they might see their sins and with the same light they might see their saviour, Christ Jesus, to save them from their sins, and that there was their first step to peace - to stand still in the light that showed their sin and transgressions and showed them how they were strangers to the covenant of promise, without God in the world, and in the Fall of old Adam, and in the darkness and death; and with the same light they may see Christ that died for them, who is their way to God and their redeemer and saviour (Nickalls 1952:117).

Note that it is not only particular sins which the light reveals; it is also a more fundamental 'state of sin' which Fox describes in this passage as being 'strangers to the covenant of promise, without God in the world, and in the Fall of the old Adam, and in the darkness and death.' Particular sins are only manifestations of this more fundamental state of darkness and separation from God.

Paul's letter to the Corinthians includes a unique account of what happens when someone enters the community that is acting and speaking from:

> But if all prophesy, an unbeliever or outsider who enters is reproved by all and called to account by all. After the secrets of the unbeliever's heart are disclosed, that person will bow down before God and worship him, declaring, 'God is really among you' (1 Cor 14:23-25).

There is a similar sense here of the outsider coming to an experience of what it is in them that is wrong, a realisation that they did not previously have.

It has for some time been recognised by scholars that Paul's thinking moves 'from solution to plight', that is, there is an event in his life in which he experiences a liberation from his previous condition. It is only from that experience of liberation, this 'solution', that he comes to name 'the plight' from which this event has freed him (Sanders 1977:474-97). It is only as he comes to liberation that he understands that he was previously in a kind of slavery. Part of the 'plight' is that he does not recognise that he is in it. There is an interesting clue in the two texts above as to why Paul's thinking might move in this way. In both texts, recognition by a person of the plight that he or she is in is an essential part of the liberation from that plight; coming to the solution and recognising the plight are bound up together. This essential state of sin, of, as Fox puts it, being 'without God in the world,... in the darkness and death' is not seen for what it is. It is only from the experience of liberation that the previous state is recognised as a kind of slavery.

5. Conflict

It is readily acknowledged that early Friends were provocative in what they said. They challenged the tithing system of the time where a significant amount of income went to support the church. In this and other ways they challenged the church of the time. They were strident in their claims for the possibility of coming to a state of sinlessness. They challenged the church's reliance on 'externals', priest, sacraments, Scripture, saying that reliance on these was an obstacle to coming to unmediated guidance from God. All that said, there is one important source of conflict that should not be missed. It connects with our last section. To be placed in a situation where sin was being exposed, even if inwardly rather than publicly, might lead to repentance and contrition but it could also arouse acute hostility. Time and again Fox arouses a strength of feeling that seems inordinate when put alongside the content of what he says. The quotation that follows gives a sense of the dramatic impact that Fox could have, bringing a crisis in the individual that demands a response. Here he is addressing a Colonel Rous, a man Fox describes as being 'as full of words and talk as ever I heard a man in my life':

> And the light was spoken of to him (which let him see his sinful life that he had lived in and his words and his ways), that would be his teacher to lead him from them, if he minded it, and his condemnation if he acted against it... And he was stricken dumb and his mouth was shut, and he cast his head up and down and his face swelled, and he could not speak for a good space. His face was as red as a turkey. And his lips rent and he mumbled, and the people thought he would have fallen down (Nickalls 1952:251).

It seems that Paul and the early apostles aroused a similar strength of feeling (Acts 5:33; 7:54; 13:50; 18:6; 21:30). The reason given in these passages for the hostility to the apostles is the challenge that they are perceived to present to the Jewish law and temple. But this was not the only source of resistance. Paul records how even a Gentile audience could react with hostility:

> For you, brothers and sisters, became imitators of the churches of God in Christ Jesus that are in Judea, for you suffered the same things from your own compatriots as they did from the Jews... (1 Thess 2:14).

One way of understanding the strength of this reaction is if their words and presence had a direct effect on their hearers, exposing any selfishness in them. This could lead to acceptance of what was revealed and consequently to contrition and a desire for change but it could also lead to hostile and violent resistance. Just as Fox speaks often of 'the Lamb's war' for this activity of the early Friends, Paul too uses the language of warfare:

> Indeed, we live as human beings, but we do not wage war according to human standards; for the weapons of our warfare are not merely human, but they have divine power to destroy strongholds. We destroy arguments and every proud obstacle raised up against the knowledge of God, and we take every thought captive to obey Christ (2 Cor 10:3-5).

Conclusion

The early Friends were claiming that the Second Coming was happening among them. Their perception of this was not of a return of Jesus through the clouds of heaven but as a Word guiding them and a Light revealing sin and bringing them to liberation. In Paul's vision this is not a liberation that remains an individual matter. As 'the sin' is exposed and ended so there is a new community formed; individuals no longer feel separate from each other. While each one is different, Paul uses the image of the body to suggest how there is now an organic unity among them:

> For just as the body is one and has many members, and all members of the body, though many, are one body, so it is with Christ. For in the one Spirit we were all baptized into one body - Jews or Greeks, slaves or free - and we were all made to drink of one Spirit (1 Cor 12:12).

There is the same sense among the early Friends:

> And from that day forward, our hearts were knit unto the Lord and one unto another in true and fervent love, in the covenant of Life with God; and that was a strong obligation or bond upon

> all our spirits, which united us one unto another (Francis Howgill [*Quaker Faith and Practice*, 1995:19.08]).

In the first part of the book, about Paul's vision, it was suggested that the liberation he describes is an ending of the ego, an ending of a divisive assertiveness. We can read both these texts as simply idealised pictures to serve as words of encouragement, but they are not presented in that way. They are presented not as exhortation but as description, recording the reality of a new kind of life. They are consistent with Paul's understanding of the life of faith as involving a death of the ego and a real and lasting liberation from wrongdoing.

Chapter Ten

The covenant of light:
the early Quaker vision for a new creation

Douglas Gwyn

We have examined the apocalyptic power of the light, its disruptive, unmasking, jarring effects upon individuals and societies, even history. The light's revelation was 'the end of the world' as early Seekers had known it. It unmasked all, high and low, male and female, human and other, as God's creation. It demanded that one encounter all God's creatures in the light that created them. The desolating power of the light humbled the old self. Yet where it was followed obediently, the light filled all things with a grandeur never visible to the old self.

Covenant and community

We are now ready to explore the creative dynamics of the light's apocalyptic revelation. The apocalypse not only shakes heaven and earth; it also produces a new heaven and earth (see the development of apocalyptic faith in our Excursus on the biblical understanding of history, p. 245). The light's power to forge a new and vital coherence is witnessed most acutely in the covenantal language of early Friends. They experienced the light healing them, binding them into new solidarity, helping them to live more healthily and simply in God's creation. Early Friends wrote often of the 'covenant of light'. Francis Howgill, a Westmorland Seeker turned Quaker in 1652, witnessed to Christ, saying 'He who is the Light is the Covenant, and he who is the Covenant is the Light, for they are one in him' (Gwyn 1995:100).

The ultimate aim of the Lamb's War was not simply iconoclasm and rebellion. The apocalypse of Christ's light initiated new patterns of personal morality and social order. What was the covenantal vision of early Friends? How did it differ from and conflict with the Puritan covenant of grace, as we reviewed it in Chapter 8?

Covenant abides most fundamentally as the 'assumption into a life-relationship', according to Martin Buber (Buber 1946:103; see also Gwyn 1995:6). It is the dynamic of healthy, mutualistic relationships, expressed in qualities of trust, dependability, flexibility, love, patience, and forgiveness. Marriage and family relations are those most commonly associated with covenant. The vows exchanged by a couple at marriage enact an explicitly covenantal moment. Through simple but sweeping promises made to each other, both parties step into an all-embracing relationship of trust and accountability. Covenant is a relationship lived in the light of some transcendent perspective. The transcendent frame of reference may be God, nature, or a set of shared values held to be universal and inviolable. But it is something larger than its human participants. The covenant is seen to embody and be undergirded by that transcendent point of reference.

Covenant

Covenant is the hidden, binding force of the universe. It is God's covenantal faithfulness that holds things together, from the laws of physics to the intimate realms of human relationship. Of course, there is plenty of chaos in the universe. But in the tradition of biblical faith, covenant continues to exert a benign order amidst the forces of chaos, rebellion, and sin. When a human being chooses to live in conscious, faithful, covenantal relationship with God, the edifying power of God's love gains ground on chaos and sin in that person's life. When communities of faithful individuals live in covenant with one another under God, they dedicate themselves to being a 'city set upon a hill', a 'light to the world' that models peaceful, just and loving relationships.

Friendship

Friendship is a privileged form of covenant. Even marriage cannot thrive without friendship. There is a polymorphous quality to friendship that can permeate any social situation, often subverting official oppositions and hierarchies. Between natural allies or ostensible enemies, friendship opens up new possibilities for cooperation and mutual trust. In Jesus' final conversation with his disciples, cementing his covenantal bond with them, he no longer called them servants but his friends (Jn 15:15). He compared his intimacy with his friends to his intimacy with God.

Covenantal community is crucial to the biblical faith: it mediates between the intimacy of personal experience and the social and cosmic totality encompassed by God. That is, as we saw the apocalyptic experience of the light bridging between biblical history and the mystery of personal experience, so the covenant of light was the early Quaker solidarity that mediated between the immanence of the light within and the transcendence of God as Lord of all history, all reality. Without a community of shared understanding and obedience, the transformed personal morality of early Friends would have remained a private phenomenon. The covenantal faith they exhibited by their unified morality and social witness made their testimonies prophetic, social, historic. Without a covenantal community, the Second Coming would be nothing more than a private apocalypse or a spectator event. (See the comments on covenantal community in the Excursus, p. 242).

The early Quaker movement adopted the name Friends, or 'Friends in the Truth'. The name evoked the intimacy with Christ and with one another they had found in the light. It was also thematic of the movement's ability to cut across boundaries of gender, religious authority, social status, and economic class – subverting all of them. The familiar form, 'thee' and 'thou,' with which early Friends addressed everyone, even Oliver Cromwell or Charles II, scandalised many. Friends said many harsh things to religious, social and political authorities, yet they often prefaced their words with the address, 'Friend...'. The apocalyptic spirituality of early Friends combined the intimate and the ultimate in new ways. The disorienting intimacy of their language invited strangers to confront ultimate reality as never before. The Quakers' every nuance of language and gesture aimed to end the self-evident hierarchies and assumed privileges of their world, and to introduce a new, universal mutuality in the light.

Early Friends seemed puzzlingly eccentric to their contemporaries. They spoke in stilted, biblical language. They dressed and conversed with stark simplicity. Yet in spite of their severity of manner, these Friends could be surprisingly open, forgiving and inclusive. The bizarre, off-putting quality of early Quaker demeanour should not be too surprising; these men and women looked at the world through a profoundly altered perspective, the light of Christ within. The Lamb's War, the conflict between them and their Puritan neighbours, was essentially a conflict between two profoundly different sensibilities, two forms of covenantal consciousness.

Covenantal conflict between Puritans and Quakers

We have previously noted the Puritan covenant of grace and its grounding in the doctrine of predestination. Its spirituality of anxiety grew out of the individual's desire to know if he or she was one of God's elect. Religiously, the elect were leaders of a reformed, purified church. They were taught by an enfranchised clerical ruling class. This men-only elite was academically trained in the Bible, rhetoric, and philosophy. These experts were qualified to preach from the Bible, catechise Christian doctrine, counsel seeking souls, and nurture a voluntaristic church membership. Supporting them were vibrant new lay leaders (early Friends usually referred to them as 'professors'), who were often upwardly mobile. These exerted their influence in the community to encourage greater church involvement and moral regeneration. The Puritan clergy's alliance with the local gentry and commercial leaders was an important dimension of the covenant of grace. It combined the interests of ecclesiastical, social and economic leadership. This union found expression in a Puritan political establishment, through the election of godly men to Parliament and the appointment of solid Christians to the magistracy.

Thus, the Puritan covenant of grace was a multidimensional vision for a reformed English church and society. It tended to enfranchise new ruling classes in ecclesiastical, economic, and political relations. During the 1650s, the new Puritan establishment sought to consolidate its victory over the backward and recalcitrant forces of the Stuart throne. But this closure was frustrated by the emergence of the Quaker movement and its alternative covenantal vision. The Quaker covenant of light was founded upon a different spiritual sensibility, a *spirituality of desolation*. In contrast to the Puritan seeking to *infer* his or her election according to psychological symptoms, the newly convinced Friend was immersed in a harrowing *experience* of the light. The light deconstructed the constructed self, melted the alienated heart, broke up the hard 'earth' within, in order that God's seed, a new self, might rise to life. The struggle was to *stand still*, to *surrender* to this desolating power, rather than flee from it.

As the Quaker came through this experience, she or he came into a new kind of covenantal solidarity. Consequently, *the covenant of light tended to reopen all the closed circles of the Puritan franchise.* It opened up an *indeterminate* relationship with God through the assertion of Christ's light present in all people. It opened up spiritual authority and leadership in all directions, since Christ could speak and act through anyone in any given moment. Spiritual authority and power were dependent not upon expertise but upon submission to the divine power within. By implication, the covenant of light also opened up indeterminate social relations in all directions. If the light empowered a woman to speak in church, what else might it lead her to do? The dynamics of Christian spiritual friendship opened up indeterminate possibilities between men and women, between rich and poor, and (as the movement spread beyond England) between Christian, Jew, Turk, and pagan.

Even the creation itself was part of this new covenant. The Puritan relationship with nature tended to be instrumentalist, or utilitarian. It aligned with the imperatives of the new capitalistic and scientific enterprises. The Quaker by contrast tended to sense some dialogical rapport with the creation. Fox taught that not only did the rich exploit the poor but they also 'devoured the creatures' through conspicuous consumption. Hence, the imperative to a simple lifestyle was a call to solidarity with the earth as well as fellow humanity. Certainly, the Quaker movement was friendly toward the new currents of capitalist enterprise, scientific exploration, and technological advancement. Friends would soon become leading innovators in all these areas.

But they tended to view these within a holistic vision of covenantal faithfulness to God, humanity, and the created order.

The radical impetus of the Quaker vision would have produced nothing but a large collection of public confrontations and lively, Spirit-infused meetings were it not for the strong domestic ethic of early Friends. All the itinerant ministry, steeplehouse incidents, and heroic suffering under persecution would have led quickly to fragmentation without the grounding the movement maintained in marriage and family life. Here political and social radicalism stood in paradoxical tension with a rather conservative and everyday quality of Quakerism. Much like the tribal confederation of Israel's first two hundred years without a state apparatus, or like early Christianity's international network of house churches, early Friends understood that the primal covenant of creation must steady the feet of a people challenging the entire social superstructure around them. The new creation of a transformed social order must reconcile with the original blessing of the old creation.

No covenant persists or develops through time without elaborating specific terms of shared understanding and practice. The covenant of light incorporated disciplines of group worship and group spiritual discernment, as well as rigorous moral codes, record-keeping and financial arrangements. As early as 1653, letters from leaders to the first Quaker groups in the North evince a strong concern for regular meetings, moral accountability and procedures to heal internal rifts. From the first, the Quaker movement thus exhibited both *orthodox* and *orthopractic* tendencies, concerns for both right doctrine and right order. While they adamantly resisted any credal distillation of their faith, there was definitely a clear shape to early Quaker Christian belief. At the same time, that belief structure was strongly tied to definite codes for individual behaviour and group process. Contrary to nineteenth century evangelical and twentieth century liberal tendencies among Friends, the early and classical periods of Quakerism refused to choose between orthodoxy and orthopraxis. So while the first Friends went as far into indeterminacy as any movement is likely to proceed and still be identifiable and viable, there was also a process of definition underway from the start. After all, the Second Coming, the kingdom of God on earth, the new creation, cannot be simply a private experience or a warm feeling. The early Quaker movement went about not only to *proclaim* the Day of the Lord and return of Christ; they also sought to *enact* the new order that Christ brings.

Again, the covenantal community of faith stands as the mediating factor between individual experience and the social whole. On one side, it must nurture and shape the spiritual and moral life of its participants. On the other side, their consistent, identifiable words and behaviours in the world must have a prophetic edge of nonconformity that challenges unjust norms and policies. So these 'Friends of Truth' had a concern for 'the reputation of Truth'. They sought to exhibit a consistently high standard of individual morality, business ethics, and social carriage before all. This would not only attract those of tender conscience to the movement; it would also continue to challenge the jaded and arrogant attitudes of society's alienated citizens.

Covenant and testimony

As a mediating community manifesting the covenant of light in the world, the Quaker community took shape through its *testimonies*. Testimony is a term with both religious and legal meanings deriving from covenantal premises. In legal terms, for example, testimony given in a court of law is one's testimony to the truth of some matter. The court seeks to apply that testimony within a constitutional framework of laws and rights to obtain justice for all parties. Most constitutions are framed in covenantal terms, since some kind of transcendent reference point is usually invoked, whether it be God, universal values, or a larger-than-life sense of 'the people'. In religious terms, one's testimony is one's statement of belief, based upon lived experience. It is a testimony to God's reality, presence, and goodness. Just as the citizen is legally bound to give testimony to relevant questions of a given case of law, so one who has experienced something of God is covenantally obligated to give evidence of it to the world.

So the Quaker testimonies evolved as ways of speaking and acting that testified to the lordship of Christ in their lives. Thus, testimonies replaced creeds in the covenant of light. The early Quaker maxim was the *possession* of the Truth in life, not simply *profession* in words. Today, we tend to think of the Quaker testimonies as a set of abstract values: simplicity, peace, community, harmony. But to early Friends there was *only one testimony, to Christ, and it was everything one did.* From the way they worshipped to the way they walked down the street, to the way they dealt with the local church establishment, to the way they died – all these were a testimony in life to the true authority of Christ, returned to earth and ruling in the bodies of his faithful friends. Ultimately, all human authorities will align with this authority or pass away. This total sense of life as a testimony is largely lost among Friends of all varieties today. An abstract set of liberal social values comes no closer to the concrete sense of early Quaker testimony than does a Protestant creed.

Quaker discipline remained localist and *ad hoc* through the movement's early years, but over time, several factors led to the standardisation of procedures among Friends. First, the imprisonments and deaths of Quaker leaders diminished their ability to coordinate and nurture the movement through constant travel and consultation. Second, the desire for even-handed treatment of all participants inevitably led to a set of normative procedures, first in the North, then nationally. Third, while women were often the most courageous torchbearers in prophetic public witness, their charism had not yet found expression in regularised spiritual leadership within the movement. Starting in the latter 1660s, George Fox, Margaret Fell and others began a concerted and sustained effort to organise English Friends into a national system of men's and women's meetings for business, differentiated on monthly, quarterly, and yearly levels of frequency and geographical inclusion. Thus, the Quaker movement as a utopian covenantal initiative reached its constitutional moment of definition.

We have seen how the Quaker covenant of light emerged out of the self-defeating contradictions of the Puritan covenant of grace. It emerged from the desolating disappointments English radicals experienced as they saw their leaders appropriate the victories of the Civil War for personal power, wealth and the consolidation of a new ruling class. It was refined in the crucible of a spirituality of desolation that left no human design, hope or righteousness standing. The Lamb's War of the 1650s was a covenantal conflict between two fundamentally different visions for the future of English society. But as the Puritan regime succumbed to its internal contradictions, hastened by the onslaught of the Quaker offensive, Friends had to face a still more serious adversary. At least the Puritans had a vision with which to engage and argue. There was little in the way of vision among the powers that reclaimed control in 1660 with the Restoration of monarchy and state religion. They consolidated political resolve chiefly by wreaking vengeance upon the radical groups that had made it impossible for wealth and power to rule over the past two decades.

Among those groups, Quakers were the most successful, resilient and truculent. They posed the most inviting foil for the vindictive mood of the new Cavalier Parliament. Friends responded to this brute malevolence with sheer willingness to suffer for their witness. The heroism of Quaker suffering under persecution continued to draw large numbers of tender souls to the movement. But as the Restoration became more secure and moved toward a coherent liberal political settlement, Friends faced a nemesis more subtly formidable than either the Puritans or the Cavaliers. The emergence of a liberal political philosophy, which bracketed covenantal questions of divine will and ultimate truth for the sake of pragmatic, contractual arrangements between self-interested parties, offered no clear counterpart to the covenant of light. Anything as grandly utopian and covenantal as the Quaker movement became odious and anachronistic to a new regime bent on making the most of the strong updrafts of capitalist expansion. (The political logic of that period can be compared to the conservative and reactionary entrenchment of our own recent Thatcher and Reagan era, in which utopian politics were scornfully repudiated.) What appropriate counter-cultural response could Friends offer to a society held captive within a system of relative truths and self-serving pragmatism?

[This chapter summarises material from *Apocalypse of the Word* (Gwyn 1986) and the first half of *The Covenant Crucified* (Gwyn 1995).]

Chapter Eleven

From covenant to contract:
the Quaker counter-restoration

Douglas Gwyn

The undeniable problem with apocalyptic movements is that history always seems to prove them wrong. They declare the imminent end of the world, but it does not come. It is true that many *so-called* apocalyptic movements, those caught up in the business of predicting the end and waiting for it to happen, *are* proven wrong. I prefer to classify these false apocalyptic movements with the more general sociological term, 'millennialist'. Such groups do not embody the root sense of the Greek word, *apokalypsis*, which means 'revelation'. There is a profound difference between those who have *seen* the end of the world revealed and those who simply *desire* it. The latter *hate* the world and draw back to await its destruction; the former *love* the world as God does and reach out to reconcile the world to God's coming realm of justice and peace.

The true apocalyptic tradition, as we find it in Jesus, Paul and the early Friends, is centred in an experience of God as a revealing *presence*; it discovers the kingdom of heaven to be an unfolding *present*. It *enacts* the kingdom of God and *invites* others into it; it moves from inward experience to outward action. The apocalyptic spirituality manifested by Paul and by early Friends generates conflict with the people it confronts, but is consistently nonviolent in its tactics. True apocalyptic consciousness knows that only the power of God can end the world and bring justice. And it knows from personal experience and transformation just how present that power is. True apocalyptic movements not only *expect* the end of the world; they act in ways that *anticipate* the reality of heaven on earth now.

But the problem with apocalyptic movements remains: their participants expect the entire world to be overcome soon by the same power that has overwhelmed them. What does it mean when the world remains largely unmoved? An apocalyptic prophet like Paul clearly believed that the whole world would come to an end shortly. Was he wrong? I don't think so. Insofar as he and those who shared his experience *lived* the end of the world, *they were right* and exerted a powerful influence. They precipitated one of the great historic cultural shifts in history. It was not Paul but the world that was wrong. Insofar as the world refused to hear, but responded to the Christian message with brute repression, utter indifference or pragmatic compromises, the world was wrong. Over time, and in small, incremental steps, the church accommodated itself to the intransigent powers of the world. To the extent that the church compromised with the world, it collaborated in putting off the kingdom of God on earth. Departing from an end-time vision, the church reframed itself for the meantime. And what a long, mean time it has been.

We confront here the terrible underside of human freedom. People often look at the horrific disasters of history (the atomic bomb and Nazi Holocaust, for example) and ask how a loving God would allow these to occur. But God lets us choose. The knowledge of good and evil was there within reach in Eden. Sticks and stones were there in the field for Cain to pick up and use against Abel. God does not let us make only small mistakes. We tend to celebrate human freedom as something unquestionably good. We like it because it freezes God and gives us all the options. It is our world. *Only when we are willing to give the freedom back to God can we enter God's world, discover the kingdom of God on earth.*

In *A Trumpet of the Lord* (1655), Edward Burrough wrote to the 'Free-Willers', those who believed salvation was their choice to accept or reject:

> Herein you affirm that whereof you are ignorant, which may be true in Christ, but a Lye unto you; for you are not dead with Christ from the Rudiments of the World, but are alive against him in the World; they for whom he died, are dead, and they who yet live put him to death. Free-will unto the wayes and fashions, and vanities of the World stands in you, and you know not the daily Cross of Christ, which is unto man's will; nor what it is to follow Christ, and to obey him, which is contrary to a man's will... There are some true desires among you, but your minds are not truly informed, to the fulfilling of your desires (Gwyn 1995:103).

Those who believe they can choose to accept Christ will never do so, but instead end up crucifying him. The only way to 'choose' Christ is to surrender to his way of the cross as it is revealed. Likewise, the end of the world and the new creation are realities known among those who die and rise with Christ.

It is in this light that we must look at the failure of the early Quaker Lamb's War, the defeat of the nonviolent cultural revolution that grew so phenomenally in its first five years. It is in this light we must contemplate the recontainment of the Quaker movement within the new regime of nascent capitalism, and the revised position Friends themselves finally took as a tolerable sect within the new order. Early Friends were not wrong about the end of the world. The world was not willing to follow them through the opening into God's realm. Indeed, we contemplate here the closing of one of the most wide-open doors any society in history has ever encountered. In the process of society's belligerent rejection of the covenant of light (a feat of free human will) the Quaker movement was eventually transformed from a confrontational, covenantal initiative to an embattled, beaten people ready to strike a bargain with England's new rulers.

Three decisive moments
There are three major transitional moments marking key shifts in the early Quaker movement. These are the Nayler incident of 1656, the Restoration of the Stuart throne in 1660, and the gospel order initiative of 1666.

The year 1656 was the high water mark of the fully apocalyptic Quaker movement. Quaker convincements grew exponentially up to that year, and though Puritan authorities responded with increasing persecution, they were kept off-balance by the wild-fire spread of the movement, which had begun moving southward in 1654, gaining major urban strongholds in Bristol and London. Cromwell's early inclination to tolerate the movement was bolstered by Fox's unambiguous statement of pacifism in 1655.

But even Cromwell's good will was evaporating by the summer of 1656. That was a year of fever-pitch Quaker activity, a year many radicals expected to be the year of Christ's return, or an end-time transformation of some kind. But the forces of reaction and repression were galvanised most decisively in October when James Nayler and a group of his followers enacted in the streets of Bristol a sign of Christ's entry into Jerusalem. Nayler understood the act as symbolic of Christ's coming in the flesh of common people like himself. But Parliament was able to use the confusion of his adoring followers to accuse Nayler of messianic delusions. The high theatre of Parliament's trial and Nayler's barbaric punishment were effective in catalysing public opinion against Quakers. Escalating official persecution was seconded by widespread mob violence against Friends. From that point onward, the Lamb's War was on the defensive.

Still, the all-embracing apocalyptic dimensions of the movement were far from collapsing. The remainder of the decade saw vigorous Quaker activity on many fronts, aggressive prophetic witness against the hardening Protectorate military regime and its Puritan social base, and large Quaker gains in both territory and numbers. The eventual collapse of the English Commonwealth in 1659 was accompanied by many eloquent Quaker reflections upon the hollow victories of the Civil War, the self-serving motives of those who had led it and the historic judgments of God made visible in the self-defeating politics of Puritanism. Because apocalyptic consciousness is extremely pessimistic of the human condition on its own terms, yet brazenly optimistic of what God can do in the world, Friends greeted the Restoration with surprising equanimity. The apocalyptic outlook is supremely ironic. Friends were willing to consider Charles II a potentially better ally than Oliver Cromwell had proven. Charles had in fact made significant statements of his desire to effect religious toleration in England. Friends were ready to work with him.

But the Restoration period was defined not by Stuart sentiments but by the vengeful policies of the Clarendon administration against radicals of all varieties. Quakers bore the worst brunt of the Cavalier vendetta (though Baptists also suffered greatly for their unwillingness to hide from the new regime). The politics of martyrdom dominated the Quaker movement of the 1660s, much as they defined the early church from the end of the first century for many years to come. Slowly, we begin to hear Quaker arguments for toleration become more apologetic, sometimes bracketing prophetic rhetoric of God's will in order to argue that toleration would serve the best interests of the persecuting establishment. Yet the apocalyptic outlook still predominated. The Book of Revelation provided rhetorical support for the stubborn Quaker willingness to suffer mob attacks, militia violence, miserable prison conditions and many deaths. Friends prophesied God would soon act in judgment against the Restoration regime, if the latter did not repent soon.

It has become fashionable among historians (Hill 1985:129-69 and to a lesser extent Reay 1985:103-22) to speak of the acquiescence of the Quaker movement after 1660. The major statement of Quaker pacifism to Charles II in January of 1661 has been used to argue that Friends were not pacifists in the 1650s, and that they became cringing, pragmatic pacifists after 1660, when there was nothing left to gain by violent options. Both assertions are wrong. The tactics of the Lamb's War in the 1650s were consistently nonviolent.

(A few Quakers were drawn into armed insurrection in 1659, but many more enlisted in our century's two world wars. Pacifism is always vulnerable to a good cause.) When Friends did become more programmatically pacifist in the 1660s, they argued their case on the merits of their behaviour during the 1650s. They were unwilling to fight for or against any regime, and ready to suffer under all of them. The larger eschatological horizon of early Quaker pacifism is revealed by a central section of the Declaration of 1661:

> We do earnestly desire and wait, that by the Word of God's power and its effectual operation of in the hearts of men, the kingdoms of this world may become the kingdoms of the Lord [cf. Rev 11:15] (Nickalls 1952:400).

It is all too easy for today's privileged academics to make belittling suggestions regarding the political motives of a people who suffered such widespread violence against themselves in the 1660s. Such misinterpretations begin with the failure to understand their apocalyptic outlook.

The outbreak of plague in 1665, the botched attempt to seize Hispaniola, the new Dutch War and finally the Great Fire of London in 1666 all seemed to confirm Quaker prophecies against the Restoration. The political mood turned so sour that Clarendon fled into exile in 1667. So the initial administration of the Restoration was indeed overturned. However, the economic prosperity and political resiliency of the Restoration settlement were also abundantly clear by 1666. The English people did not want to re-enter the political chaos of the previous two decades.

That brings us to the third and decisive transition of the early Quaker movement. The evident hardening of the powers into a new structure of alienated arrangements, the decimation of the ranks of early Quaker prophets through persecution and the need to institute a corporate form of spiritual authority in their place were compelling forces toward consolidation of the movement. The remaining leaders, pre-eminently Richard Farnworth, George Fox and Margaret Fell, began to standardise Quaker organisation, enabling Friends to sustain a more long-term minority position in English society.

Gospel order

Richard Farnworth led off with an epistle in May of 1666, a sweeping statement of the primacy of corporate Quaker authority over individual spiritual leadings, signed by twelve leading (male) Friends. But he died of a fever just a month later, and could not build upon his initial position statement. Margaret Fell remained imprisoned at Lancaster until 1668. Fox was released in September 1666 from two years of imprisonment that had nearly killed him. He quickly launched the huge project to articulate an organisational plan and to convince Friends, group by group, to adopt it. The theme of this important new phase was 'gospel order'. Fox repeatedly reminded Friends of the gospel they had received so joyfully in previous years. Now it was time to come into the 'comely order' of that gospel. The system of men's and women's meetings Fox proposed was not itself gospel order. *Christ's direct government* among God's people by the Spirit was gospel order. The system Fox promoted was simply the *regimen* of eldership, meetings and group spiritual discernment that *created the space* for Christ to lead.

The gospel order initiative was a decisive end to the apocalyptic fervour of the Lamb's War for three related reasons. *First*, it was the *constitutional moment* of Quakerism, in which the experience and experiments of the previous twenty years culminated in a full formulation of Quaker faith and practice, in which the molten dynamics of the covenant of light hardened into a reproducible set of relationships. While admirably maintaining the spiritual 'breathing space' for true *covenantal* faith to continue, gospel ordering introduced a set of definite *contractual* understandings and obligations among Friends. *Second*, while faithful to the apocalyptic ferment and intent of the early movement, gospel ordering nevertheless signalled a shift from an all-embracing, confrontational movement for the total transformation of English society, toward a fully demarcated, defined, and self-sustaining *model* of the kingdom of God on earth. This self-contained modelling logic exhibited a *microcosmic* eschatology, rather than apocalyptic eschatology. Fox often wrote of gospel order making Friends a city set upon a hill, a light unto the world: that is, a 'peculiar people' whose ways exemplify God's order. The alienated world in general might find Friends eccentric or irrelevant, but some tender souls would gravitate to this beacon of covenantal community.

Third, by the latter 1670s and early 1680s, this new logic began to express itself in a decidedly different political posture. An apologetic campaign, led by Fox, William Penn and Robert Barclay, restyled Quakers as eminently stable, sane, dependable citizens and the finest, fullest fruits of the Protestant Reformation. This was a self-presentation startlingly different from that of the early period. Early Friends had posed as social pariahs, heralds of the Day of the Lord, almost a new race of humanity, emerging through the desolating apocalypse of the light. Now they posed as England's favourite sons and daughters, the most thoroughly reformed Protestants, whose prodigal status was only obliquely left to inference.

It is in this third sense only that we may speak of Quakers striking a bargain with the world, of covenant becoming a contract in the pejorative sense. The first two aspects of contractual expression were inevitable to any movement that would survive. This was an extremely creative moment in Quaker history. Anyone who feels gratitude at inheriting the Quaker spiritual tradition must affirm early Friends for taking this step; otherwise, no tradition would have survived for us to inherit, and the early Quakers would have been simply one more of those colourful groups who came and went during that tumultuous period. In particular, Quaker organisation created a resilient counter-cultural model of spiritual formation and social relations. Phyllis Mack (1992) has amply shown how this organisational phase instituted the lasting contribution of Friends as an alternative model of gender relations and as a seedbed for later feminist developments.

Even in this post-apocalyptic phase, Fox displayed an enduring utopian and eschatological vision. He portrayed men's and women's meetings as an embodiment of the primeval man and woman, reliving the original, mutualistic relations in Eden before the Fall. This was Christ's government, he argued, which was *before* 'the devil's government', the alienated structures of human society, began. This government would still stand *after* the last version of the devil's government had fallen, no matter how long that might take. The End, even if it subsists only as a microcosm within a hostile world, is in some aspects a return to the Beginning. Fox's keen sense of the counter-cultural meaning of the gospel was undiminished. In the face of the cynical power arrangements of the English Restoration regime, Fox sounded the theme of gospel order as the *restoration* of the holistic relations of Eden.

The Quaker counter-restoration, a cumulative expression of the collective Quaker genius and an apt response to the new political realities surrounding Friends, nevertheless could not exert the same contagious social energies that the Lamb's War had exhibited. By the end of the seventeenth century, it became clear that Quaker utopianism could subsist only as a rigorously self-contained phenomenon. In society at large, the pragmatism of the limited contract had replaced the idealism of covenantal vision, both Puritan and Quaker. The Church of England had been restored as the normative expression of religious life. The new ruling interests of nascent capitalism were well represented in Parliament. If people looked toward a 'new world', it was the New World of America or the new possibilities of a vigorously expanding English economy. But the numbers of desperately poor skyrocketed by the end of the seventeenth century; they found little sympathy from England's new rulers. The Religious Society of Friends floated upon these currents, maintaining a great deal of internal logic and integrity, but powerless to influence the larger tides of culture and politics.

Still, we are left with the abiding sense that Friends struck something of a 'deal' with an arrogant, alienated regime. In the face of an establishment that continued to scapegoat nonconforming groups even through the 1680s, Friends strove to re-present themselves as 'harmless' and 'innocent'. They had been pacifistic all along, but they had also threatened the entire social order. Now they sought to make themselves as inoffensive as possible, while still maintaining their own standards. Street preaching, political pamphlets, and unauthorised travels in ministry were strongly restrained by Quaker leadership. Friends convinced themselves of their tamed identity before they convinced the world and were granted official toleration in 1689.

Fox's new alliances

One key indicator of the changing style of the Quaker movement after 1666 is the new set of alliances Fox made from that point onward. He certainly retained his friendship with the core of northern leaders he had gathered in 1652, at least those still alive fifteen years later. But after 1666, Fox forged a new set of alliances with wealthier and better placed Friends. Of course, his deep friendship with Margaret Fell was well known from the time of their first meeting in 1652. But Fox's marriage to Fell in 1668 marked a new kind of alliance between the two. Fell's social status as part of the lower gentry was well above the Quaker norm. Her alliance with Fox in promoting the gospel order plan added social prestige to the project. Much further above the norm were two new converts to the movement in the mid-1660s, Robert Barclay and William Penn. Fox quickly took a mentoring role with both of these well born, highly educated young men. Not only did Barclay and Penn quickly ally with Fox and Fell in the gospel order scheme but they added their social clout to political efforts to gain toleration. They also applied their theological education to the work of defining Quakerism as a coherent and respectable doctrinal system. Fox supported Penn and Barclay with a fatherly, even uncritical nurture.

One final indicator of Fox's shifting alliances is his changing base of operations from north to south. London, the political, economic and social centre of England and its colonies, became the new centre of Quaker organisation and activity. Clearly, an effort was underway to fit the Quaker movement into the new cultural mainstream.

The new tone of Quakerism can be found most jarringly in the writings of Penn and Barclay. Barclay's *Apology for the True Christian*

Faith (1678) is a masterwork, creating doctrinal coherence out of the chaotic and occasional style of first-generation Quaker witness. It still stands as the major theological statement of Quaker belief. The problem is, when Barclay organised Quaker theology into fifteen propositions, he utilised the fifteen sections of the Westminster Shorter Confession (Freiday 1967:xix). Thus, he presented a Quaker theology within a Puritan framework. The idiomatic integrity of early Quakerism was lost in the process. *Most pointedly, the apocalyptic horizon, the Second Coming impetus of early Quaker witness, disappeared.* We might say that the operation was a success but the patient died, or at least was not the same person any longer.

Penn worked tirelessly for toleration during the 1670s. He gave his utmost to the cause, helping organise the Meeting for Sufferings to promote political efforts and coordinate relief to suffering Friends. But Penn tended to try any kind of argument for toleration he thought might succeed. For example, in *One Project for the Good of England* (1679) he argued on pragmatic grounds that dissenting groups like Friends were simply too important to England's commercial growth to be ruined with fines and imprisonments. Why, he pleaded, should we treat one another so cruelly over matters that 'concern another world'? (Gwyn 1995:325-27) Another world? Here eschatology becomes a matter of life-after-death, rather than the all-embracing question of the kingdom of God on earth, here and now. Earlier Friends would not have thought of such an argument.

Fox's own writings became more doctrinally systematic during the same period, though without the academic and philosophical flourishes of Penn and Barclay. His apologetics tended to emphasise Quakerism as the ultimate form of Protestantism. Such arguments did not occur in his early writings, where Friends were presented as the beginning of something profoundly new, not the final form of an older process. But these were different times. Fox accepted that the historic door of opportunity had closed. In 1659 and again in 1666, he had experienced severe depressions as he saw the apocalyptic moment pass. It is evidence of his deep faith that his genius was not only mercurial but resilient. He worked as tirelessly to organise a sustainable Religious Society of Friends as he earlier had worked to promote the original Lamb's War.

The vanishing mediator

Max Weber, the first sociologist of religion, theorised the role of the prophetic mediator in religious beginnings (Jameson 1988:3-34). New faiths coalesce around a charismatic figure who is able to synthesise new vision amid the religious and social contradictions of the age. That synthesis is achieved in some makeshift fashion, more intuitive than rational. The prophetic mediator gathers a new group around the new synthesis. Weber notes that such mediators typically vanish sooner or later. Either they are killed off or the are eclipsed by later generations of leadership that work the synthesis into a more rational system and organisation that can endure over time, even if some of the charismatic power is lost. This process seems to be inevitable to the viability of any faith over more than one generation.

George Fox offers an interesting example of the vanishing mediator. As the central, charismatic synthesiser of the movement, he could have been killed many times over the years, either by angry mobs or by unspeakable prison conditions. Yet somehow he survived. More intriguingly, he even served as the chief architect of the rationalised structure of organisation that eclipsed his own charismatic leadership. He succeeded in part by working in partnership with new leaders of a more rational variety, particularly Barclay and Penn. He also managed to preserve aspects of the original charismatic style of Quaker faith and practice. But all the while, he slowly worked himself out of the middle of the structure he helped devise. He was still a much respected and revered figure at his death in January of 1691. But he had divested himself of nearly all roles of leadership. As a result, Friends experienced a remarkably smooth transition after his death. The Quaker movement had made an amazing journey over four decades: from an apocalyptic movement living in the Day of the Lord, to a well-organised body, living by a rather full calendar of meetings.

Epilogue

I view this transformation not as a decline but as the maturation of a successful movement. It was impossible for Friends to remain as the kind of movement they had been in the 1650s. But it is also impossible for me to look at these developments without mixed feelings. The study of history is the experience of mixed feelings. There is much to celebrate about this history. These are the beginnings of a small but surprisingly influential religious society. Friends have made out very well in the world: in business, in science and technology, and in the professions. We have also been moral exemplars and exerted a prophetic conscience in society over the centuries. Friends are *winners* in the last three hundred years of British and American history.

But it would be a mistake for us to forget that Friends were also *losers* in the seventeenth century's great moment of truth, and that Friends (along with everyone else) have been carried along in the subsequent culture of capitalism as *captives*. That culture has broken down our prophetic consciousness, degraded our social vision and fragmented our spirituality, making us strangers to one another. As a result, Quaker Evangelicals and Liberals cannot recognise one another as Friends today, despite the important claims each makes upon the rootstock of our faith. One of the symptoms of living under an occupation is that subjugated groups are divided and conquered by the dominant ideology. They look at each other as the problem and cannot recognise the problem that has encompassed them both. To the extent that we have made a bargain with the dominant culture, to the extent we have traded quiescence for toleration, quaintness for respect, acculturation for renewal, we have traded a covenant for a contract.

The apocalyptic impulse of early Friends, a people who lived the Second Coming of Christ, still rattles the cages of modern Friends and other captives who read their amazing writings. Something of the earthquake that jolted them still jars us. Even when we do not understand their message, something in its deep structures resonates within us. It is a disturbing word, a subversive memory. We hear and remember it with pain and chagrin at our present captivity. But we forget it at our peril!

[This chapter is primarily a summary of the latter chapters of *The Covenant Crucified* (Gwyn 1995).]

Chapter Twelve

Face to faith: turned upside-down

Douglas Gwyn

This chapter is devoted to a more personal statement. What personal experience and concerns do I bring to my reading of early Quaker writings? What has my study of early Quakerism meant to me? When I write or teach about early Friends, I focus mainly on what I have found in my research. But I have never tried to hide the fact that I speak and write as a Christian and a modern Friend. I aim to be a responsible scholar, researching and interpreting early Friends as accurately as possible. But 'objectivity' is an illusion; we all interpret from some perspective or another. I read early Friends from the perspective of my faith and my life experience. At the same time, however, studying early Friends has been an important life experience that has reshaped my Christian faith. My encounter with early Friends has interpreted me to myself as much as I have interpreted them for today.

Early Friends and the Second Coming

Over the past twenty years, I have focused on the apocalyptic vision of George Fox and the 'Lamb's War' campaign of early Friends. When Fox preached repeatedly that 'Jesus Christ is come to teach his people himself', he proclaimed nothing less than the Second Coming of Christ. But this was not mere speculation upon a physical return somewhere, sometime. Fox directed people's attention to the inward revelation of Christ by the Spirit, the Light *within. Fox preached that to come to the fiery revelation of that light is to come to the Day of the Lord, the Last Judgment, the end of the world, the new creation, the kingdom of God on earth. So the reality of all Scripture, including its prophecies of the future, was to be found in the here and now, through the powerful experience of the light within. Early Friends experienced the light not as a warm, cuddly inner teddy-bear but as the risen Christ, the ultimate future, the destiny of the universe, breaking into the present. It was a jolting, desolating presence that melted the heart, shook the hardened earth within and allowed the seed of God, a new self, to arise. The* seed *was another image Fox used to describe Christ risen and returned, Christ speaking and acting through the lives of transformed men and women, Christ challenging the violent and unjust norms of an alienated society. Hence, the return of Christ through the light or seed within was not limited to a private, inward experience. It moved outward into society, into history, as men and women followed Christ in a new way of life.*

In other words, apocalypse now! *Early Friends became an* incendiary force *in society, setting fire to every individual, every religious convention, every social institution they confronted. The apocalyptic experience and message of the earliest Friends still challenges us today. It invites us to know the Second Coming of Christ here and now. I know this by experience: the apocalyptic message of early Friends has helped shake* me *loose from any easy formula of what it means to be a Quaker. For more than twenty years, I have moved back and forth between different Quaker worlds. Sometimes I have served among evangelical Quakers as a Friends' pastor. Other times I have taught, worshipped and moved among Liberal unprogrammed Friends. Over the years, I have found my home in different ways among both major streams of modern American Quakerism. I have tried to interpret them to each other. I have argued that each stream is faithful to certain aspects of the Quaker vision. But each also distorts or ignores other aspects. Thus, I find myself at home in either tradition – and at odds with both.*

Quaker bispirituality/errantry

Lately, I have come to describe this condition as bispirituality *(see 'Quaker Bispirituality Today', in Gwyn 1997a). As a bispiritual Friend, I find myself drawn to the different forms of Quaker spirituality on the basis of their different strengths. It may seem to Friends on one side of the Quaker 'great divide' that I am betraying them by spending time on the other side. But here I am, and I can't seem to help it. How can I choose between being Christian and being universalist? From its beginnings, Quakerism has been both radically Christ-centred in its identity and daringly universalist in its implications. I find myself caught in that paradox. I can sojourn among Friends on either side, but I can't seem to make my permanent home on either side. I have instead invited Friends to come with me to the uneasy centre of that paradox, where Quakerism began and where it continues to have its greatest vitality. Are we willing to live in the unbearable tension of a paradox which explodes every handy definition of who we are as Quakers, which refuses the choice between Christian and universalist, and forces us out of the comfortable enclaves of liberal and evangelical subcultures?*

I testify that there is a Quaker 'place' in the Spirit that is neither evangelical nor liberal, neither Christian nor universalist. It is the same 'place' that Paul described as neither male nor female, Jew nor Greek, slave nor free. This is the apocalyptic paradox that galvanised the first Christians and the first Friends. This paradoxical outlook sees that the cultural forms of this world are passing away. This paradoxical outlook refuses the standard categories, comfortable though they may be at times. It steps into an unmapped territory between the entrenched camps that define not only Friends but the wider culture as well. I find a growing number of Friends standing there with me today, refusing either-or opinions *in favour of the neither-nor state of* communion *with the One who has risen beyond all our categories.*

It might not be evident to Friends that petty squabbles between orthodox and progressive viewpoints are a major social problem today. Many problems seem much more serious: racism, sexism, militarism, environmental degradation, domestic violence, civil wars all over the globe. But the theological and moral stalemates we find among most religious bodies today (including Friends) are a major drain on the energies we would otherwise devote to addressing those more overt social problems. Our resolve is neutralised and our basis for concerted action is divided by the endless bickering and nay-saying that continues within our churches and meetings. These 'culture wars' are more obvious and pernicious in America, where conservatives and progressives do battle on many different issues today. But I have found some subtle versions of the same conflicts in Britain.

Nevertheless, I also find reasons for hope. In my travels and sojourns among American Friends and British Friends, among evangelical Friends and Liberal Friends, among social activist Friends and contemplative Friends, among 'Quaker process' enthusiasts and individual 'free spirits', I am often struck by the many different fronts of Quaker renewal. With the amount of creative experimentation at work among Friends and others today, I sometimes wonder why it does not add up to more of an overall resurgence of Quakerism. It may be that our different horizons of exploration and activity have become digressive, self-seeking and self-serving. Or it may be that we are building toward a renewal that is still beyond our ability to imagine or name.

Perhaps this is a time when Friends must be content to be on the journey rather than being at home in the world. Jesus said, 'foxes have holes, and birds have nests; but the Son of Man has no place to lay his head' (Mt 8:20). 'The Son of Man' was one of the messianic titles that attached to Jesus. Many Jews of his day expected the 'Son of Man' to come as a figure of the end-times, to judge the world for sin. But 'Son of Man' can also mean simply human being. To follow Jesus in authentic humanity *is to escape our comfortable cultural enclaves, to abandon the fenced cities of Canaan, to set out, like Abraham and Sarah, following a God who remains a mysterious, disturbing paradox.*

This nomadic existence does not come naturally for me. By nature, I am a stay-at-home, steady-state personality. I want to share with you just why I have been particularly attuned to the apocalyptic resonances of early Quakerism, and why my course over the past twenty-two years has been so nomadic among Friends.

The sixties experience: crisis and calling

I was once a nice Midwestern boy, growing up in a large pastoral meeting in Indiana. I had a love of nature, an interest in biological science as a possible career, and a soul-mate from my home meeting. We loved each other deeply. But we were growing up in chaotic, apocalyptic times. The civil rights movement, the nuclear arms race, the Vietnam War, new music and art, free love, mind-expanding drugs, new religions, hippies, yippies – all these powerful forces swirled around us. The year 1968 was the culminating moment of all these exploding forces; the best and worst of everything seemed to break loose. Many of these developments were deeply disturbing. The year started with the Tet Offensive in Vietnam and progressed through the assassinations of Martin Luther King and Robert Kennedy, countless urban riots, the disastrous Democratic National Convention, and much more. The world was turned upside-down in 1968 for many Americans, especially those of us coming of age during such confusing times.

It turned upside down for me personally as well, as the bubble of innocence burst between my soul-mate and me, sending us on our separate ways. My world, my sense of a 'happily-ever-after' script for my life, collapsed. In the wreckage of that moment, September 1968, I sat alone in my dorm room one evening. Out of nowhere, apropos of nothing on my mind, words distinctly came to me: 'be a minister'. No flashing lights or ringing bells. Just three words distinctly received.

I pondered that surprising message for the next half-hour. I had been named. 'Minister' (what little I understood of it) named something I realised that I already was, a way of being I already inhabited in some germinal way. But I was also called to become something, to fulfil a vocation I had never before contemplated. I had never thought *of the ministry. Yet I suddenly felt myself pulled into a future I did not understand, but I could begin to trust. A door opened and I passed through. I suppose I could have chosen not to follow. But how could I not? As the prophet Amos said, 'The lion has roared; who will not fear? The Lord God has spoken; who can* but *prophesy?' (3:8). Over the succeeding years, what it means to 'be a minister' has taken on many different casts. My background in pastoral Quakerism led me first to go to seminary and then to work as a Friends pastor. Since then, I have also followed the call in other forms of ministry: teaching, writing, travelling ministry.*

The 1960s meet the 1640s

Along the way, I began to study George Fox and early Friends seriously in the late seventies. I began to familiarise myself with the tumultuous times and colourful groups of England in the 1640s and '50s. Besides Quakers, there were Seekers, Ranters, Diggers, Levellers, Fifth Monarchists – the amazing radicals profiled in Christopher Hill's classic, The World Turned Upside-Down *(Hill 1975). Having lived through the 1960s, I felt I knew people like that, and understood something of the great expectations and crashing disappointments they had experienced. But most importantly, I started reading George Fox's* Journal *and learning of his experience of desolation at age nineteen. When I read of the voice he heard saying, 'there is one, even Christ Jesus, that can speak to thy condition' (Nickalls 1952:11), I felt I knew something of that experience. To be redeemed out of all the confusion and chaos (both inner and outer); to be set upon a path toward some unknown destination, yet somehow given the confidence to take one step at a time; to live by each word that proceeds from the mouth of the Lord, to feed upon the manna as it comes morning by morning in the wilderness: that is the drama of faith. Just as Fox describes those early experiences as if there were no Civil War going on around him, I recall how I walked patiently through the upheavals of the late sixties with a calm that surprises me now.*

'That which people do trample upon must be thy food,' the voice told young George Fox (Nickalls 1952:19). The light that sustained his life was ignored or discounted by most Christians he met. They trampled on it as they ran after doctrines and airy notions of Christ. In a similar way, I have known the truth of those words. I have not exactly had to stand in line to follow the strange path God has set out for me. Life in a wilderness of broken religions is a life of spiritual errantry, wandering a varied terrain, sojourning with various groups, like the life Abraham and Sarah lived. It is to live faithfully in the midst of many questions. It is to be both a Quaker and a Seeker. The life of errantry sometimes means being errant as Abraham sometimes was: off course. I have veered this way and that. I have made my share of mistakes and missteps. But God has helped me get back on course many times, and continues to redeem my life. As a Friends' pastor, a teacher at Pendle Hill, a peace educator with the American Friends Service Committee, a Quaker researcher and writer, my vision has always been clouded by false hopes, idolatrous expectations and fearful compromises. But I can testify that God has been faithful through each phase and has set my feet back on the path.

The great cloud of witnesses

I have been inspired repeatedly over the years by the eleventh chapter of the Letter to the Hebrews. You may know its opening verse, a classic definition of faith: 'Faith is the substance of things hoped for, the evidence of things not seen.' The chapter proceeds to look back over the centuries to the great heroes of faith. Looking back over the patriarchs and matriarchs of Genesis, the writer remarks:

> All of these died in faith without having received the promises, but from a distance they saw and greeted them. They confessed that they were strangers and foreigners on the earth, for people who speak in this way make it clear that they are seeking a homeland. If they had been thinking of the land that they had left behind, they would have had opportunity to return. But as it is, they desire a better country, that is, a heavenly one. Therefore God is not ashamed to be called their God; indeed he has prepared a city for them (Heb 11:13-16).

To seek is to press on toward a 'better country', a place where we can stand with a clear conscience toward both God and our fellow creatures. But we do not make this trek alone. We are part of a great cloud of witnesses through the ages, down to the present, all struggling from their different places to that better place.

What is important about my story is not any uniqueness but whether it might answer something in your story, your experience of God. Take George Fox, for example. He was a truly awesome individual – and he often let people know it, too! But his significance and his lasting contributions lay in putting the power of his experience to the service of others. We may not be on George Fox's level, but we do help make up that cloud of witnesses, the community of faith and the strength of its tradition. That makes a difference in our lives, and makes us together something more than we would be alone.

I think also of Martin Luther King. Just a few hours before his assassination, King preached a sermon in Memphis, saying that he could die happy and content. Like Moses, he had been to the mountain; he had seen the Promised Land of freedom. Like Martin Luther King and like the exemplars of faith remembered in Hebrews 11, I feel I have glimpsed the better country. I have been through the apocalypse. I have known something of the God's wondrous new creation!

> *Therefore, since we are surrounded by so great a cloud of witnesses, let us also lay aside every weight and the sin that clings so closely, and let us run with perseverance the race that is set before us, looking to Jesus the pioneer and perfecter of our faith, who for the sake of the joy that was set before him endured the cross, disregarding its shame, and has taken his seat at the right hand of the throne of God (Heb 12:1f).*

Part Three:

Quakers Through Time

Chapter Thirteen

Reframing Quakerism

Ben Pink Dandelion

'Nothing is nearer to us than heaven, the earth is beneath our feet and we tread upon it, but heaven is within us'
(Kazantzakis 1975:15)

This chapter outlines my understanding of the model which I see emerging from what Tim and Doug have written above, a model I want to use to reframe the context in which we consider the history of Quakerism. The following four chapters revisit the history of Quakerism through this Second Coming model. The title of this part of the book 'Quakers Through Time' plays on the dichotomy of looking at Quaker history: across historical time (i.e. in the three centuries since 1650); and through the lens of thinking about Friends in terms of a religious group believing itself to be working within God's time.

Liberation theology, combining as it does Marxist and Christian insights, has been criticised by rationalist philosophers for failing to understand that Marxism is concerned with the material world, the temporal, while Christianity views 'the kingdom' as resting in the realm of God's time, the eternal. Running through what Tim and Doug have been saying is the idea of these two kinds of time, God's time, and secular human (constructed) historical time: the mythic and the mundane (see Excursus); heaven and earth. In Eden, the two were co-joined. Earth was in heaven, in God's realm, Adam and Eve living in God's time.

At the Fall, heaven and earth part. Humanity, flawed, becomes separated from God, living the struggle between Spirit and flesh, living as children under the word of God, mediated through the law. Humanity lives in this state on the plane of the mundane, in historical time, on earth. T. Canby Jones claims that Fox had a clear view of history in terms of God's interaction with the world. Creation was followed by Fall and the reign of the law. The birth, ministry, death and resurrection of Christ marked the end of the old covenant. However, there was then a second fall, the fall of the church. Luther and Calvin had only achieved partial reformation and it was in this time when Christ had come to teach his people himself that the apostolic age had been restored (Jones 1955:234).

Tim has argued that Paul claims that the life, death and resurrection of Jesus, this intervention of God on earth, this bringing to earth of heaven, offers the potential and reality of human transformation, of the meeting of heaven and earth. The Second Coming, Paul teaches, is contingent with this third (after the Fall and the First Coming) and final intersection of God's time with historical time. It is the endtime, the end of history, the end of earth. The full realisation of the 'kingdom' for all. Early Friends were saying that they were living in the time of this third intersection, that the 'endtime' was now and unfolding. In other words, early Friends were living a realis*ing* eschatology. (See Figure 4 on p. 157)

Kathryn Damiano is clear that living in the endtimes involves a sense of 'eschatological time', that 'life proceeds in God's time rather than humanity's' (1988:118). Time is not about a continuum but an inter-relation of past, present, and future. The emphasis is on the present, not on a future event, nor on the sacralisation of the past (ibid). As William Taber writes, 'The *was* can become the *is*, or the *to be* can become the *now*' (1980:12).

Matthew Fox is more emphatic: 'Now is the time; Now is the place; Now is the occasion; Now is the bringing together of the best of the past and of the future; Now is the moment of divine breakthrough' (1983:105). Ferner Nuhn talks of this Day of the Lord as a 'change in the very mode of experience of time: a change from quantitative to qualitative experience and from linear to eternal time' (1981:38). In this respect, the distinction Quakers were engaging with in their thinking was between *chronos* and *kairos*, between chronological time and significant time in which there is a Divine dimension (Freiday 1981:44).

> Under Christ's teaching, the Christian learns a different sense of timing. The Day of Light and its obedience ends the day of darkness and its obedience. The old order and way do not give way easily, and the believer remains engaged with them. Yet as the Light is kept to, and the cross is taken up, the liberating power of God's time is as inexorable as new wine into old wineskins (Mt 9:17) (Gwyn 1981:92).

Quakers held clear views on the role of historical time in God's plan. Catherine Wilcox suggests that Quakers viewed history in three periods, those of the Creation, the Fall and the Restoration (1991:27), or in two periods, the old dispensation and the new one (1991:28). Doug has written elsewhere of the end of history starting with the end of wordly religion (1986:111) with the beginning of a new world operating in God's realm and God's time, guided by God's direct revelation (1 Cor 3:10). The new life of faith is outside historical time (1986:117), indeed we are freed from it (ibid). Endtime is characterised by the end of human transgression, of the mediated word of God, of living as children under the law. It is a time of humanity's maturation into adulthood, living under direct guidance in an age of faith; of, as Tim suggests, 'the voice of faith sounding within' informing the faithful life.

Doug talks of key moments in history when the sense of the Second Coming appears and feels to be more of a reality. Times of crisis and change, as the 1640s were, as the 1960s have been. Tim describes

Paul as predicting an event, initially expected to happen shortly, in later letters expected to take place at some time in the future. For early Friends, whether with a keen sense of the apocalyptic relevant to their times or because *the* time had come, that 'future' was now. The 'always' was realised in the experience of those first Quakers.

❖ ❖ ❖

> Then I saw an angel coming down from heaven, holding in his hand the key to the bottomless pit and a great chain. He seized the dragon, that ancient serpent, who is the Devil and Satan, and bound him for a thousand years, and threw him in the pit, and locked it and sealed it over him, so that he would deceive the nations no more, until the thousand years were ended. After that he must be let out for a while.
> Then I saw thrones, and those seated on them were given authority to judge. I also saw the souls of those who had been beheaded for their testimony to Jesus and for the word of God. They had not worshipped the beast or its image and had not received its mark on their foreheads or their hands. They came to life and reigned with Christ a thousand years (Rev 20:1-4).

This is the classic millennialist text on how Christ will come again to rescue a depraved world and begin a thousand-year rule accompanied by the Saints. Whilst early Friends were not explicitly millennialist in the sense of believing in a thousand-year rule (Moore 1993:69), their experience was one of realising eschatology, i.e. of a belief that the Second Coming of Christ was happening. 'Christ is come and is coming,' wrote Fox, 'to teach his people himself' (eg. Nickalls 1952:48). Christ had come into the lives and hearts of Friends and was coming to the rest of humanity in a way which would transform the world (cf. 1 Cor 15:51, Rom 8:21, and for a passage much used by Quakers in talking about the kingdom, Is 11:6-9).

Millennialism

This is the theology of the endtimes (see the box on 'Eschatology' on page 106) drawn from the Book of Revelation (see, for example 20:1-4). In pre-millennialism, Christ will come again to rescue a depraved world and then initiate a thousand-year rule accompanied by the Saints. In post-millennialism, the thousand-year rule of the saints precedes the Second Coming. Post-millennialists (such as Modernist Evangelical Friends in the late nineteenth century) tend to be more optimistic about human efforts to prepare for a transformed world and may be involved in social reform movements. Pre-millennialists (such as those Evangelical Friends who saw themselves as part of the Holiness movement) may feel the world's sin is beyond such human endeavour and look only to God and Christ to redeem the fallen state (see Chapter 15, also Hamm 1988). Note: millennialism is often called millenarianism but there appears to be no consensus.

Doug is clear that: (a) Fox's message 'asserted that the vivid apocalyptic expectations of the people were now being fulfilled - Christ was come to lead his faithful in new paths, thus setting up a new order and government'; (b) this age superseded all existing church teaching and structures which could only stand in the way; c) Christ's leadership was inward and immediate in the daily lives of his people as a fusion of Word and Spirit (Gwyn 1986:30). The Light of Christ was the Word which inspired Scripture, a record of the Word's dealings with the world. Critically though, this message was less propositional than experiential (Gwyn 1986:58). It came out of Fox's own experience, and the success of the early Quaker movement was in part due to the fact that it spoke to the experience of so many others.

> And now after the long night of Apostasy and Darkness, which hath been upon the face of the Earth is the Lord appearing, and his Day dawning and his Light breaking forth as the Glory of the Morning; and the Kingdom of God is revealed, and his Dominion is setting up, after the long reign of the Beast... (Burrough 1651).

Doug has commented that 'early Friends gained the nickname "quakers" from the powerful witness of their own bodies, trembling with the birth pangs of a New Age and a New Life' (1981:68). Moore claims that 'for Howgill and Burrough, their immensely successful London mission with its mass meetings must indeed have seemed like the beginning of the Apocalypse' (Moore 1993:75). The passage below from Fox's *Journal* describes his own sense of being reborn into a new intimacy with God and into a state of purity, maturation and clarity beyond that of Adam.

> Now I was come up in spirit through the Flaming Sword, into the paradise of God. All things were new, and all creation gave another smell unto me than before, beyond what words can utter. I knew nothing but pureness and innocency and righteousness, being renewed up into the image of God by Christ Jesus, so that I say I was come up to the state of Adam, which he was in before he fell. The creation was opened to me, and it was shewed me how all things had their names given them, according to their nature and virtue. And I was at a stand in my mind, whether I should practise physic for the good of mankind, seeing the nature and the virtues of the creatures were so opened to me by the Lord. But I was immediately taken up in spirit to see into another or more steadfast state than Adam's innocency, even into a state in Christ Jesus that should never fall (Nickalls 1952: 27).

However, this was not an experience only open to Fox or the other Quaker leaders. It was a universal possibility. Christ is come and is coming (Nickalls 1952:45). Christ had come, inwardly (after Jer 31:31 f), as the Word, to early Friends, and would come to all humanity as they turned to the Light, which was the Light of Christ. Friends were the 'his people' but all could be Friends. This was not an exclusive or limited revelation, as Paul suggests in 1 Corinthians 15:3-9 it had been for him, the apostles, and five hundred others. This was a Christ come again available to everybody.

Tim has argued in this book that Friends were fulfilling the Pauline prophecy of the transformation of the world from childhood to adulthood, from a time of the law, living under external authority with a transcendent God to a time of faith, of inward authority, and of a God in and amongst the community; a time when all would be set free from sin in a new creation united with God. Paul had foretold this, claiming that the first coming of Christ had now made this possible and shown it to be possible. This was to be a new new-covenant or a renewal of the new covenant. Indeed in 1660, the Baptist Joseph Wright complained of early Friends that, 'They boast that Christ is come to them, neither look they for any other coming: That the world is ended with them, neither look they for any other end: That the Judgement is past with them, neither look they for any other Judgement' (Underwood 1970:91).

✣ ✣ ✣

The Quaker belief in operating outside historical time and within a Second Coming framework led to a total rejection of the outward: set-aside priests, places, sacraments (cf. 1 Cor 11:26) and times. Quakers recognised neither the Christian year nor the commonly accepted names of the days and months, coming as they did from pagan sources. Friends redefined the demarcation of time as well as having a unique attitude towards it. All time was equally sacramental. Quaker shops opened on Sundays (Reay 1988:97) and closed on Wednesdays for Meeting.

Quakers protested against 'holy days (so-called)' (Braithwaite 1912:47) and the celebration of times and seasons. When John Luffe went to convert the Pope to the Quaker message in 1658, he told Alexander VII, 'Every day is a sabbath wherein we can serve God' (Braithwaite 1912:424). The Pope asked if there was then nothing to be done 'for the remembrance sake of our Saviour's blessed ascension' (ibid). "No, no," replied Luffe, "I have Christ about me and in me, and therefore cannot choose but remember Him continually" (ibid). The Quaker Christ was inward, not outward in history (Arthur 1995:129). The Lord's Day Act of 1656 was used against Quakers walking on that day (Braithwaite 1912:450). Tensions could run high between conceptions of the Lord's Day and the Quaker experience of the continuous Day of the Lord (Gwyn 1981:80).

Moore makes an interesting comment about Fox and Fell supporting the Government's plan in the mid-1650s to allow Jews back into England on the basis that endtime theology suggests that the Jews need to be converted first as in Romans 11 (1993:117). Quakers in this period held views ranging from the expectation of an imminent Second Coming to the idea that Christ had 'already come in the spirits of believers' (Moore 1993:128). These views were not exclusive, and the tracts of Fox and Parnell in 1655 and 1656 illustrate these positions (ibid). Others saw Quakers as distinctive amongst millennarian groups of the time for claiming the Kingdom had already come (ibid).

✣ ✣ ✣

Other Christians, still waiting for the Second Coming, had instituted all kinds of outward forms to help humanity in its relationship with God *in the meantime* (see Chapter Seven). Churches were established and institutionalised to gather and outwardly signify the waiting faithful, times and seasons to mark key events of the First Coming, all the rites necessary to prompt and remind adherents. The Benedictine None reads:

> Eternal Father, loving God,
> Who made us from the dust of the earth,
> Transform us by the Spirit's grace,
> Give value to our little worth.
>
> Prepare us for that day of days
> When Christ from heaven will come with might
> To call us out of dust again,
> Our bodies glorified in light.
>
> O Godhead, here untouched, unseen,
> All things created bear your trace;
> The seed of glory sown in man
> Will flower when we see your face.

The final vision of humanity's relationship with God is not necessarily distinct in this but the mainstream Christian emphasis on the continued wait is, a waiting which involves the church being structured in a particular way. Priests mediate God's word to an immature humanity, liturgy is required to awaken the sense of the Divine within us. Structured worship gives us a time and a formula to remember eternal truths away from the turmoil of daily life. The sacraments are necessary as the visible outward manifestations of Christ's sacrifice. The Church is a foretaste of what is to come (WCC 1991) and is *only as it is until* the time of the Second Coming. As noted in Chapter Seven:

> ...the pilgrim church, in its sacraments and institutions, which belong to this present age, carries the mark of this world which will pass, and she herself takes her place among the creatures which groan and travail yet and await the revelation of the sons of God [cf. Rom 8:19-22] (Flannery 1975:408).

In the 1996 Papal encyclical *Ut Unum Sint*, the Pope talks about the Roman Catholic Church as a healthy adolescent, not quite yet mature. For Friends, 'adulthood' and the lack of the need to wait had far-reaching consequences on their ecclesiology. In 1 Corinthians 11:26, Paul tells the early Christians to break the bread until the Lord comes again. *The Book of Common Prayer* (1662) reflects this passage almost directly in its section on Holy Communion. The collects for Advent speak of Christ returning 'in his glorious Majesty, to judge both the quick and the dead' and for Epiphany, 'that when he shall appear again with power and great glory, we may be made like unto him in his eternal and glorious kingdom.'

For Friends, this expectation of future change was anachronistic. The Lord *had* come again and all these outward forms pointed backwards to the First Coming and a period of waiting which was now over, rather than forwards to the new universally available present transforming experience.

✣ ✣ ✣

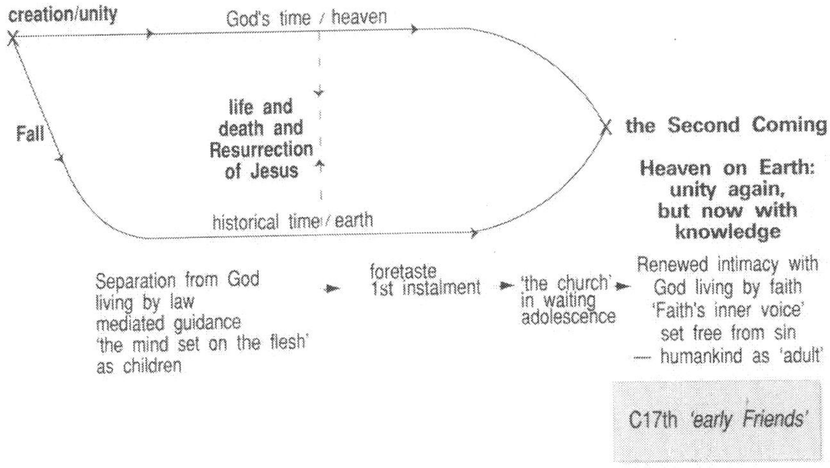

Figure 4

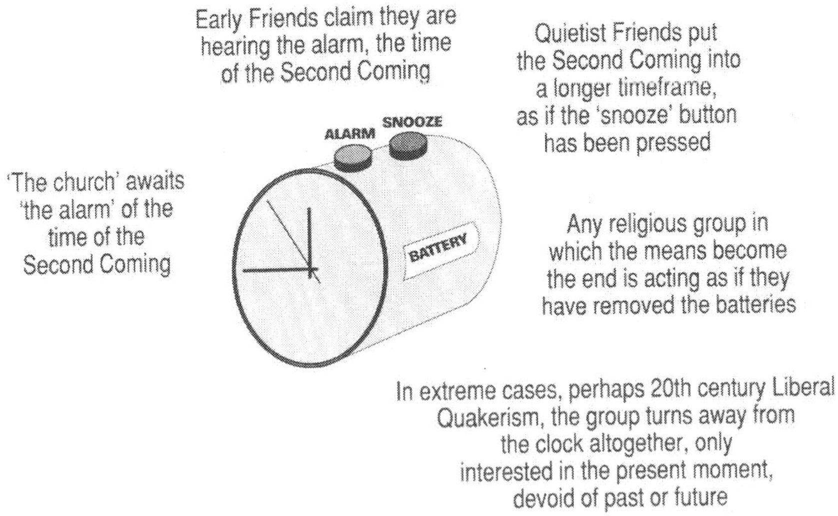

Figure 5

This is my reading of the material in the first two parts of the book. What I want to do in these following four chapters and in the conclusion is to consider what followed on from these early certainties for Friends, and how change amongst different kinds of Quakers both reflects a change of attitudes towards ideas of the Second Coming and today locates Friends in relation to the material presented here.

It is almost as if early Friends heard the corporate or global alarm clock of the Second Coming ringing. Over three centuries, the 'snooze' button has been pressed (Quietism); the clock then rewound so the hands were closer to the First Coming than the Second (Evangelicalism and the pastoral tradition); the batteries taken out (by those for whom the First Coming is more important than the Second Coming); and perhaps the clock itself has even been chucked out (twentieth century Liberal Quakerism, in which people will wake up/ find transformation in their own time!). The next four chapters explore these positions in turn.

Chapter Fourteen

Fresh light, dimmer hopes

Ben Pink Dandelion

After the Nayler incident in 1656 and the Restoration in 1660, Friends began to draw back from some of their earlier claims on perfection. The expectation that Christ was about to restore the whole of creation began to dwindle (Moore 1993:128, Wilcox 1991:132). The tendency was to focus on the present kingdom and to limit the expectation of a final consummation (Moore 1993:131). 1659 proved an exception:

> The fall of the Protectorate in April 1659 and the uncertainties of that year as the Rump Parliament set about to reorganise the nation provided a brief return to the early enthuiasms of 1653, under the political leadership of Burrough. A sense that God was at last going to act runs through the pamphlets of this year (Moore 1993:243).

The Rump did not extend religious toleration and did not abolish tithes. Quakers, such as the prolific Dorothy White, reacted warning parliament of the anger of God:

> Friends, you that are of the Parliament, hear the word of the Lord as it comes to me concerning you . . . how your downfall is near, and this is the word of the Lord God of Hosts unto you all that are now sitting in Parliament, the Lord will overturn you by his Powerful Arm, for the decree of God and his purpose is . . .

> to throw down and break up Parliaments... God himself will rule, and bear rule in the hearts of men, and such as know God ... shall rule for God... for God will throw down and overturn, root up and consume both root and branch of all your parliaments, until he hath brought in the Royal heir, the Prince of Peace, the Everlasting King of Righteousness and he will reign in the destruction of his enemies (White 1659).

Faith in a political solution grew thin and was finally extinguished with the return of a monarchy in 1660.

Barry Reay suggests that the pragmatism of Friends in the Restoration period, possibly seen as a proto-quietism, was eased by a continuing sense of the endtimes:

> I am comeing in Ten Thousands of my saints, yea in thousands of thousands of those poore people wch have been long as trodden downe... fear not their kings nor their Princes, their Parliaments, nor their Rulers, for I will Trample upon kings, & Princes as upon Morters in this ye day of my fury (William Bayly, as in Reay 1985:107).

Reay adds:

> But for most, political defeat reinforced faith in the need for a longer-term, spiritual regeneration of humankind before the millennium could be realized (ibid).

Kathryn Damiano suggests that eighteenth century Friends are a case study of realised eschatology, ie that they lived as if 'God's created order was to be manifested on earth now' (1988:19), on the basis that Friends were involved in the 'living out of Christ's guidance in community' (1988:96). Damiano connects the experience of the Lord's Supper as 'a daily nourishment of the inward person by Christ in those within whom he dwells' (1988:156) with a realised sense of the Second Coming of Christ.

Damiano draws a connection between the realised eschatology of eighteenth century Friends and the thinking of Fox, what I have called above a *realising* eschatology. However, she also states, 'Robert Barclay's theology is foundational for understanding Eighteenth Century Quakerism' (1988:106). Whilst Barclay fails to include eschatology in his systematic theology, Damiano argues that his last chapter on 'vain and empty customs' (Freiday 1967:389) relates to the actuality of living under the guidance of an incarnated Christ. I have reservations about this view, explained below.

Second generation millennialism typically changes form. Within the Shaker movement, in which Mother Ann was considered the female incarnation of the Second Coming of Christ, consequential forms became institutionalised, and sacralised spiritual roles began to appear following her death (Procter-Smith 1993:31). Doug has commented that Penn's eschatological writings lack a real sense of moment and illustrate how pragmatism replaced enthusiasm (Gwyn 1995:297). A sense that Christ had come to a few replaced the vision of unfolding universal transformation. In the eighteenth century, Friends adopted the roles of Elders and Overseers, the institution of membership and disownment, the recording of ministers, and the practices of family visits, to protect the purity of this gathered remnant.

Eighteenth century (Quietist) Friends strove to live under the guidance of the Spirit but Barclay's emphasis on a singular day of visitation (Freiday 1967: 84), rather than living within that single continuous 'day', tempered the vitality of a sense of the Second Coming with an emphasis on waiting and seeking.

> When we talk of the day of visitation which God gives to all, we are not referring to the entire lifetime of a person. For some, it may be extended to the very hour of death, as it was to the thief who was converted on the cross. For some it comes early in life and for others later, as God in his wisdom sees fit. However, many men outlive this day, and after it has passed there is no possibility of salvation for them (Freiday 1967:84).

Friends could no longer choose to turn to the Light, opt and encourage others to opt for the transformation of the world. The universal and open invitation of God to the world had been replaced by a divine selection process, in which humanity could only, and indeed needed to, play a waiting role.

> ...the light and seed of God in man is uncontrollable. It moves, blossoms, and strives with him as the Lord sees fit. Salvation is possible for anyone during the day of his visitation, but there is no way a man can stir up that light and grace at his pleasure or even when he needs it. He must wait for it... (Freiday 1967:93).

Instead of heaven on earth, the separation of the world into natural and supernatural, the mundane and the mythic, became primary in Quietist Friends' conception of society. Their role was to remain pure to their divine role as his people and to avoid the corruption of the world. Richard Shackleton, an Irish Friend, wrote to his daughter Margaret in 1773:

> Mayst thou, dear child, be preserved in simplicity and nothingness of self; in humility and lowliness of mind, seeking diligently after, and waiting steadily for, the inward experience of that which is unmixedly good. This is the way to be helped along, from day to day, through one difficulty and proving after another, to the end of our wearisome pilgrimage (as in Jones 1921:65).

Humanity was no longer a co-agent in the transformation of the world, rather a site of possible corruption and temptation. Bailey has argued that early Friends divinised Fox and raised themselves to the level of apostles in the 1660s, but later de-divinised Fox. Fox became an apostle, the Society believers (1992). In the eighteenth century, an anxiety-ridden spirituality replaced the early eschatological certainties. Self was no longer the vehicle of the will of God in the world but a faculty to be checked and monitored with care. Busy meetings were replaced by silent ones and in Dublin in 1770, twenty-two meetings passed in a row without ministry (Jones 1921:63). Sarah Grubb wrote in 1780:

> I am often afraid lest by indulging my own ideals of what is good, and not labouring after a total resignation of mind,... I should frustrate the divine intention, which may be to humble and reduce self more than flesh and blood would point out (Jones 1921:68).

It thus seems problematical to cite Barclay's last chapter on vain and empty customs, summarised by him below, as a clear signal that Friends still saw that they were living in the endtimes, even though they may have been attempting to live under the direct guidance of the Holy Spirit:

> The chief purpose of all religion is to redeem men from the spirit and vain pursuits of this world, and to lead them into inward communion with God. All vain and empty customs and habits whether of word or deed, should be rejected by those who have come to fear the Lord.
>
> Taking one's hat off to another person, bowing or cringing, and the other similar foolish and superstitious formalities which accompany them, should be foresaken. All of these were invented to feed man's pride through the vain pomp and glory of this world.
>
> Theatrical productions which are not beneficial, frivolous recreation, sports and games which waste precious time and divert the mind from the witness of God in the heart, should be given up. Christians should have a living sense of reverence for God, and should be leavened with the evangelical Spirit which leads into sobriety, gravity, and godly fear. When we abide in these, the blessing of the Lord is felt to attend us in the necessary occupations by which we gain sustenance for the outward man (Freiday 1967:389).

Rather, this appears to be a period of regulating consumption, of maintaining a purity within historical time *in preparation* for when God's time and historical time would next collide. Richard Vann notes that outward appearance was seen to symbolise inward authenticity. He quotes David Hall in 1758:

> Of all the giddy Modes, antick and fantastick Inventions, that ever old Satan or his Agents, with respect to external Dress, have hitherto vampt up, since the Fall of Adam; was there ever any Thing contriv'd so much for the Ruin of Female Modesty, and the Incitement to Sensuality and Corruption, as these immodest, indecent, odious, extravagant Hoops (Vann 1969:194).

In November 1714, even wigs were brought under the care of the Meeting: 'If any Friend wants hair, they should acquaint the men's meeting they belong to, and have approbration and consent, before they get any' (Vann 1969: 192). Luke Howard writes of his life being made anew on becoming a Friend but this is an outward change towards consumption, not an inward revolution prefiguring an immediate global one:

> And then as to my whole Life and Course thereof, I had to learn again the beginning of, both Eating and Drinking, and wearing Apparel, and Talking, and Buying and Selling; yea all to be made new (Vann 1969:194).

Friends were not hearing the alarm clock of the Second Coming ringing, but they could see the hands approaching the endtime moment. At the same time, they were fully aware of the experience of early Friends. Deborah Bell wrote in 1715:

> I saw closely in that Day... that unless I came to be acquainted with the same Power that had Wrought a Change and Alteration in my dear Parents,... I should be miserable and undone forever (as in O'Shea 1993:45).

Whether because the apocalyptic moment had passed or because their religious experience had changed, or been altered by the changing circumstances within which Friends were worshipping (the increased persecution of the 1660s, the toleration of worship after 1689, and the institutionalisation of Quakerism in the Eighteenth century), the Second Coming was on hold. As above, it is as if the snooze button on the alarm clock had been pressed.

In the letter to Titus, quoted by Friends in defence of being a peculiar people, the emphasis is on looking towards the glorious appearing, not of finding the risen Christ within:

> For the grace of God that bringeth salvation hath appeared to all men, Teaching us that, denying ungodliness and worldly lusts, we should live soberly, righteously, and godly, in this present world.
> Looking for that blessed hope, and the glorious appearing of the great God and our Saviour Jesus Christ;
> Who gave himself for us, that he might redeem us from all iniquity, and purify unto himself a peculiar people, zealous of good works (Tit 2:11-14, AV).

Penington's 1660 statement on true Christian unity now appears ironic given the increased regulation of Quakerism within the subsequent 80 years:

> And here is true unity, in the Spirit, in the inward life, and not in outward uniformity... the great error of the ages of apostasy hath been to set up an outward order and uniformity and to make men's consciences bend thereto, either by arguments of wisdom or by force; but the property of the true Church Government is to leave the conscience to its full liberty in the Lord, to preserve it single and entire for the Lord to exercise, and to seek unity in the Light and in the Spirit, walking sweetly and harmoniously together in the midst of different practices (Braithwaite 1919: 640).

Barclay's emphasis on the need to wait for divine visitation and the moderating effect it had on the certainty and vision of Friends was reinforced with his view on Quaker perfection as still incomplete: 'This is not a perfection that has no room for daily growth' (Freiday 1967:156).

Wilcox claims that a Quaker view of three stages of world history (creation, fall, restoration) still held in the eighteenth century but that it was no longer tied to an eschatological theology. The hope for restoration of the world had been modified to the hope for the restoration of primitive Christianity alone (Wilcox 1991:133) and the Light, now longer associated with the Second Coming of Christ, became less and less tied to the historical figure of Jesus (Wilcox 1991:138). The eighteenth century saw, quite logically, the growth of Quaker structure and offices as the experience of the Second Coming became less vital or was displaced to a future time. However, Barclay's critique of 'the Church' ensured that this Quaker reformation was only partial. Friends did not at that stage take up the outward ways of other churches. They simply lent another emphasis to their own traditional practices. At the same time, it is important to recognise that the gospel order of meetings for worship and business and their structure derived directly, in Fox's thinking, from his eschatology. It was an attempt at divine structuring which still gave space to the coming of the Kingdom (Gwyn 1981:87). In other words, the ecclesiology remained rooted in Second Coming thinking, even whilst the experience of that imminent global transformation changed.

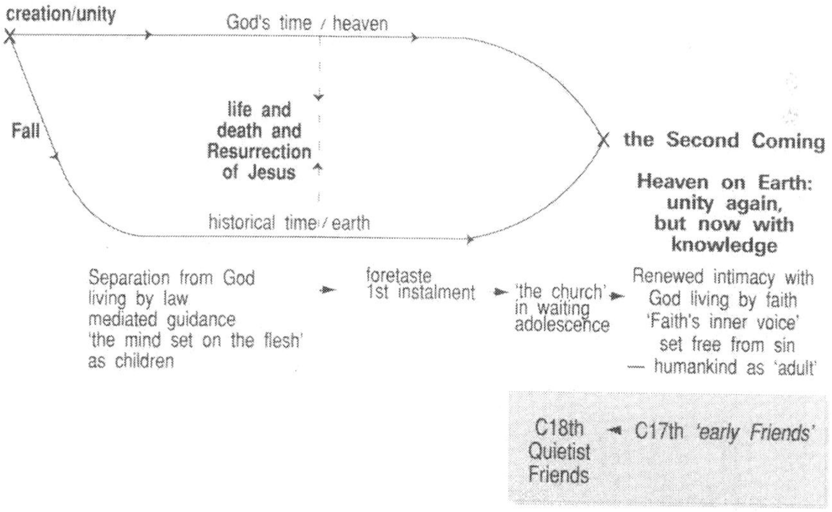

Figure 5

Chapter Fifteen

Why the pastoral system makes sense

Ben Pink Dandelion

If the Quietist Friends of the eighteenth century pressed the snooze button, the move to Evangelicalism and programmed worship in the nineteenth century turned the hands of the alarm clock back explicitly to reach a point where the focus was clearly on the First Coming and the meantime. As the freedoms Evangelical Friends pressed for would later undermine their own enterprise in Britain and in the rest of the unprogrammed Quaker world at the beginning of the twentieth century, it was the move away from a conception of Quakerism as a Second Coming movement among Quietist Friends which accommodated the growth of Evangelicalism within Quakerism.

In Britain, Evangelicalism became ascendant without dividing the Yearly Meeting. In America, the tensions between different perceptions of what was true Quakerism led to the Great Separation of 1827. This separation of 1827 was not the first schism amongst Friends but it was one which divided American Quakerism almost down the middle and which would in turn lead to other divisions. Eventually, five branches of Quakerism (independent evangelical, the Yearly Meetings of Evangelical Friends International (EFI), the Yearly Meetings of Friends United Meeting (FUM), Conservative Yearly Meetings, and the Yearly Meetings of Friends General Conference) would emerge from the after-effects of this critical moment. In the USA, only more recently-formed independent Liberal Yearly Meetings can today claim no direct relation to the incidents of 1827 and the years following.

The 1827 schism produced 'Hicksite' (after Elias Hicks) and 'Orthodox' Yearly Meetings. Hicksite Friends defined themselves around *how* they were Quakers and emphasised the authority of the inward Light even to the point of questioning Scripture. Orthodox Friends looked to the Scripture for authority. Importantly, however, the dispute was not about which incarnation Friends were facing. Both groups were focused on the First Coming and living in the meantime, looking to a future change. Both groups had moved away from the snooze button and were turning the hands back. The question is whether either group expected the alarm of God's time to ring on earth. When and how was the Second Coming? Hicksite Friends had already moved to a position of assuming that they would be building the kingdom themselves through their social witness and their own pathways to human perfection.

As Orthodox Quakerism grew more worldly under the charismatic leadership of Joseph John Gurney, the Orthodox party divided in the 1840s into Gurneyite and Wilburite (later Conservative). Gurney placed the authority of Scripture above any other, including direct revelation, and played down the writings of early Friends as the guides for interpretation of Scripture which earlier Orthodox Friends had held them to be (Hamm 1988:21). Wilburite Friends, under the leadership of the New England Friend, John Wilbur, felt Scripture was being given too great an authority.

Additionally, Gurney separated justification and sanctification, a shift which moved his branch of Quakerism more into the evangelical mainstream of American culture and further from a sense of imminent intimacy with God. Formerly Friends had held that acceptability before God (justification) was contingent with holiness/sinlessness (sanctification). Gurney argued that the former required only faith on the part of the believer, the latter required an act of grace (Hamm 1988:21). It was a two-stage salvation process that gave a pro-active potential to the masses, both to convert and be converted, but which still required the day of visitation and the growth into perfection talked about by Barclay.

Under Gurney's influence, Quakers became Christians first and Quakers second, although the nature of the involvement with 'the world' became a point of division as Gurneyite Quakerism moved in two directions, which Thomas Hamm has labelled Modernist and Holiness. Modernist Friends were eager to work with others in reforming society, Holiness Friends placed their emphasis on revival and salvation.[1]

Before the American Civil War, Gurneyite Quakerism had been post-millennial, ie believing that reform would make the world a better place until the millennium was realised, after which Christ would return. It was progressivism combined with a 'slow-burn' sense of the Second Coming, a combination of Gurney's protestantism and a renewed sense of the Modernist imperative to engage with the world in a meaningful way. The Holiness pre-millennialist Quakers believed the world would degenerate into new depths of depravity at which point Christ would return and establish the thousand year rule of peace. It was a view which precluded any advantages in social reform. True transformation would come with Christ's return to earth (Hamm 1988:108).

Both positions, Modernist (post-millennialism) and Holiness (pre-millennialism), focused on a future event rather than a present sense of the Second Coming. In other terms, they were eschatological in their hopes but not in their experience. In this, they were closer to parts of mainstream Christianity than their Quaker forebears. The increased identification by some of these Friends with the wider

1 This division of tendencies did not cause a schism immediately although it was a precursor to the distinction between FUM and EFI. The introduction of pastors created further Conservative secessions.

Christian church was most fully realised with the advent of the pastoral system and the debates in the 1880s over the possibility of Friends being baptised with water and partaking in the Lord's Supper. Friends of this branch were and are explicitly First Coming in their focus, especially in their explicit references to a *future* Second Coming. Indeed, for the Holiness Friends, pre-millennialism became a central part of their teaching, post-millennialism and reform movements one of their primary targets (Hamm 1988:107). The growth and influence of dispensationalism (a theory of seven periods of stewardship each preceded by new revelation which would culminate in the return of the Lord) amongst Holiness Friends in the 1880s underlined the popular importance of the Second Coming, but also marked it clearly as a future event.

Modernist and Holiness Friends co-operated with other Christians, in either good works for the Modernist Friends, or in revival meetings for the Holiness ones. From this period, a Christian identity has preceeded a Quaker one, highlighting the way in which programmed Friends moved back along the timeline of God's plan for the world. The negotiation of Friends of all traditions onto the ecumenical map was only possible through the loss of the belief in the present Second Coming. The hands of the alarm clock were turned back.[2]

However, it is also true to say that the loss of the Second Coming heritage of early Friends does not appear to have been a conscious one. Friends of this period, like the Quietists before them, had simply lost their awareness of the nature of the message and experience of the first Friends. Given that, some things no longer followed. Within Holiness theology, silence did not make sense when you could be praising the Lord or out saving souls. Other 'peculiarities', including the peace testimony, now belonged to apostate groups of so-called Quakers and could not be considered part of an authentic Quakerism.

---

2 If all sense of the Second Coming or of the interim is lost (when the meantime becomes the endtime), it is as if the clock batteries have been taken out. This does not appear to have happened with programmed and evangelical Friends.

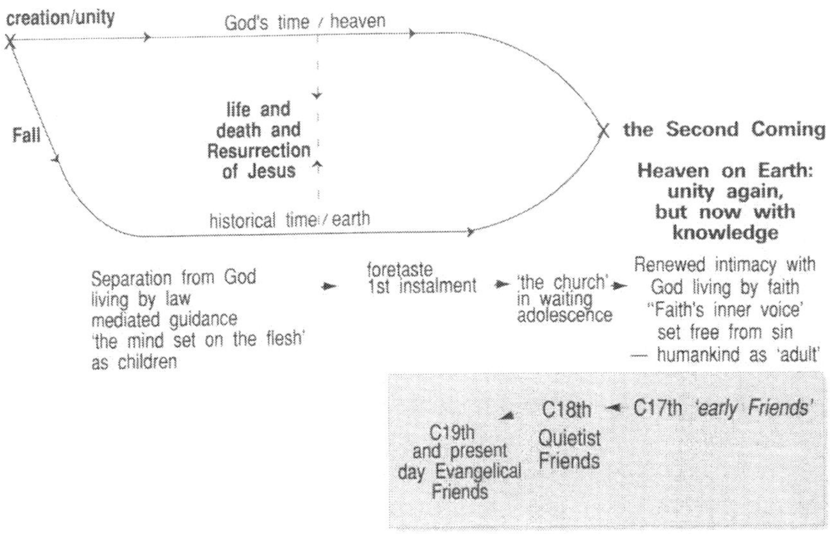

Figure 6

In London Yearly Meeting in 1861, the inward Light was questioned as unscriptural (Isichei 1970:7) - the notion of the inward and present Second Coming was lost on both sides of the Atlantic.

In Britain and in Liberal Quakerism generally, the Second Coming ecclesiology (the lack of mediated guidance and outward forms) would be retained but the liberal reinvention of Quaker theology at the end of the century would not bring back the Risen Christ into their theology (see Chapter 16). In the programmed elements of American Quakerism and elsewhere in the world, the Risen Christ would not be lost but became a future hope rather than a present reality. For example, in 1876, New York Yearly Meeting was the first to insist on doctrinal assent from all its recorded ministers. The eight questions these ministers were required to answer correctly still focused on the inward communion with Christ but also largely focused on the First Coming and a *future* day of judgement (Barbour *et al* 1995:203). As mentioned above, Quietist Quakerism paved the way for these later expressions of Quakerism.[3]

The Evangelical Quaker reinvention was not explicit in giving what was an unconscious surrender of Second Coming experience as a reason for reforming practice. Rather, with the loss of the Second Coming experience, a form-without-reason was open to be filled with fresher and more exciting ideas. The influx of fresh converts to Quakerism - Indiana Yearly Meeting grew by about 50% in the 1880s (Hamm 1988:125) - meant that a teaching ministry was required. In other words, there was an acknowledged need for some form of outward assistance in the sustenance of the faithful life of these fresh Christian Quakers. Pastoral Committees were soon replaced by pastors after 1878 and in those Meetings programmed worship with music replaced the silent Meetings.

If the Roman Catholic church and other Christians are correct that in the interim, humanity requires these forms to help it remain faithful in its relationship with God (see Chapter 7), the adoption of pastors and programmed worship makes sense. In a pro-pastorate article in *Christian Worker*, Elwood Siler argued in 1887 that the church was an agent of God's plan on earth and required leaders to act effectively. Paul is quoted to legitimate deacons and pastors, and the 'valiant sixty' are seen as proto-pastors, Fox at their head. Opponents of the pastoral system were seen as Ranters (individualists) or inheritors of the Wilkinson-Story heresies (congregationalists dissenting from the new Quaker gospel order of the 1670s) (Siler 1887:400).

> Every church must be provided with a living gospel ministry, someone whose business it is to care for the flock; to visit the sick - to look after the newly awakened, and lead them to the

[3] This is not a logical consequence of Quietism. David Willson and the Children of Peace, a group who seceded from New York Yearly Meeting in 1812, became explicitly millennial in the 1830s whilst retaining a Quietist ecclesiology (Schrauwers 1993:130). Willson spoke of an inward Second Coming in much the same way as Fox.

> feet of the Savior; to encourage the new converts, pray with, and for them, and teach them the way of salvation more perfectly; to visit the membership of the church at their homes, socially and religiously; share with them their joys and their sorrows; enter into sympathy with them in their trials and difficulties; see that none stray away from the fold and become prodigals; reprove those who sin, and win them back if possible to the path of duty; if differences arise between brethren, see that the gospel order is followed speedily, that the matter be adjusted and settled in privacy before it be known abroad and the cause suffer loss (Siler 1887:401).

This ecclesiological reform was only partial however. Pastors are not priests. They have a gift of ministry, not the caricature of the monopoly of the mediation of God's word or God's forgiveness. Additionally, not all Gurneyite Meetings became pastoral and those who retained unprogrammed worship found it easier to later re-unite with their Hicksite counterparts in the mid- and late-1950s and beyond.[4]

The bid for greater First Coming church type[5] reforms came in the 1880s and 1890s, particularly under the leadership of David Updegraaf, a Holiness Friend who had become a leading preacher at non-denominational camp revivals. In his Ohio Yearly Meeting

---

[4] Opposition to the pastoral system focused on the idea of a paid ministry and a separated class of Friend, and the consequences of programmed worship. Anti-pastoral Friends were frightened of losing the waiting they saw as so crucial to worship. The arguments centred around notions of Quaker tradition, personal preference, and the need to continue to wait upon the guidance of the Holy Spirit (Hamm 1988:128), not an argument about an intimacy with God as a signifier of the endtime.

[5] I mean by First Coming type that the focus of the life of the church is on the consequences of the first incarnation and the resultant meantime rather than on the present or realised Second Coming.

the move to a revivalist Quakerism brought with it a campaign for the toleration of ordinances, particularly water-baptism, the remaining distinction between Holiness Friends and their Christian neighbours.

Updegraaf asked for the toleration, not the prescription of water baptism, quoting Scripture and Christian charity in his favour. The debate centred on whether ministers could be baptised and retain their ministerial standing. Hamm argues that three strands lay central to the debate: the place of baptism in the Apostolic Church and amongst early Friends; the relationship of the ordinances to 'spiritual worship'; and the balance between individual liberty and corporate discipline. Salvation was not an issue, although integration with the wider Christian world was. Updegraaf felt that if toleration were allowed, thousands of converts might come in (Hamm 1988:135).

The arguments Updegraaf used from the writings of early Friends to show that they had been tolerant of the baptised were easily opposed and on the issue of worship, opponents of the 'water-party' felt on firm ground. Israel Hole, also from Ohio, wrote, in a widely circulated attack on Updegraaf's position, that the duty of the Friends was:

> to call man back from these outward forms and concentrate his thought and attention upon the inward and spiritual life; to call him away from ceremonies, from the . . . outward form, to the inward, to the inward and spiritual worship of God (Hole 1885).

It is difficult to locate any Second Coming emphasis here but the focus on the inward preserves a critique of First Coming Church forms and protects the partialness of the ecclesiological reforms. Hole and his supporters were still open to the direct workings of the Inward Light or Holy Spirit, whilst the Holiness Friends downplayed it, emphasising conversion and sanctification through revival. Neither wing of Gurneyite Quakerism came close to a First Coming church but pre- and post-millennial theology, the pastoral tradition and the debate over ordinances reveal an opening in the experience of Friends able to be filled by reform. This makes sense in terms of mainstream Christianity's ecclesiolology of the interim, and would have been unthinkable for early Friends so filled with the immediacy of the Second Coming.

Updegraaf and others were baptised but the Waterites had little success in their campaign, save in Ohio where, unusually, a vote secured Updegraaf's position, by 198 to183 (Hamm 1988:136). Other Yearly Meetings refused to uphold the ministerial status of those who had been baptised and the Richmond Declaration of Faith of 1887 secured a 'moderate' orthodoxy amongst the Gurneyite Yearly Meetings. This Declaration did not sanction baptism and Ohio never joined the consequent union of Yearly Meetings which subscribed to the Declaration, which became Five Years Meeting in 1902 (later Friends United Meeting). The Richmond Declaration, importantly for this book, explicitly looks forward to the future reappearance of Christ.

The ordinance issue divided the Holiness Friends and weakened their ability to become the dominant wing of Gurneyite Quakerism. Their bid for increasing influence was finally dashed both by the offensive of Rufus Jones and his reinvented Modernist Orthodoxy and also by a further internal division over speaking in tongues. The Azusa Street Revival in California in 1905 gave birth to Pentecostalism. Speaking in tongues was seen by some as a third gift of the Holy Ghost following conversion and sanctification. Holiness Friends were divided on the issue of glossolalia and weakened their resistance to Jones' attacks. (Holiness Friends, including Ohio, are the ancestors of the Evangelical Friends International (EFI) Yearly Meetings today.)

Chapter Sixteen

The Liberal reinvention: the British experience

Ben Pink Dandelion

Liberal Quakerism defies many of the received assumptions about the nature of religion today and in turn many of the sociological professionals who try to define it in terms of traditional religiousness. In Britain at least, and British Quakerism represents the most permissive variant of what was once Orthodox, Quakers behave in all kinds of ways which go against what appears to be happening in other religious groups. They maintain unity without credal statements of faith (Ambler 1989), they maintain numbers without a strict system of discipline (Kanter 1972) and, counting attenders, they are a growing church whilst espousing a permissiveness of belief which appears to be far removed from the conservatism of other increasingly popular churches (Kelley 1972). Within the world of Friends, the Liberal 'tradition' may appear to have lost its Quakerism if not its Christianity. As Liberal Friends challenge assumptions about the nature of religion, they also challenge assumptions about the nature of Quakerism.

In Britain, First-Coming Church influence, coming in through Quaker evangelicals, could be most clearly seen in the adoption of sabbatarianism. Teetotalism also became a creed but was the result of viewing drink as the cause of poverty and crime, rather than a

First Coming focus on Matthew 26:29 ('I tell you, I will never again drink of this fruit of the vine until that day when I drink it new with you in my Father's Kingdom'). However, in a view of time opposite to that of earlier Friends, Victorian Quakers began to proscribe secular activities on the Sabbath (Isichei 1970:157). The early Quaker emphasis on the present and coming Day of the Lord was replaced by the adoption of a sense of the Lord's Day. In some meetings music preceded the worship although a pastoral system was never adopted. Mission meetings were not combined with regular Quaker worship. British evangelical Quaker activity was compartmentalised and stratified in a way its American counterpart never was, a legacy of the sectarian heritage of British Quakerism. This continuing inheritance later accommodated the Liberal Quaker shift away from mainstream Christianity.

From the 1870s, the domination of evangelical thinking began to diminish and 'progressivism' became explicit within British Quakerism (Isichei 1970:34). This theory held that new truths legitimately and naturally replaced old ones. In this way, parts of the Bible which challenged Friends in the 1880s could be explained away as having been true for another age. History, and God's plan for the world, were unfolding in a progressive sense. Continuing revelation was one of the key concepts of later nineteenth century British Quaker theology (ibid). It fitted with Darwinian explanations of evolution and the ability to accept these new ideas. Moreover, it validated and accommodated not only the search for a new new-dispensation with which the Evangelical and Liberal Friends so eagerly sought to rescue their beleaguered Quakerism but also ran directly counter to any sense of realised eschatology with its sense of *the Now*. The claims of Damiano in relation to eighteenth century Friends cannot be made of the nineteenth century. The endtimes was not to be corporately *realised* (only awaited) after 1830 on either side of the Atlantic.

In Britain, the separation of Quakers from 'the world', initially mutually desirable, had been worn away by the State conceding rights to the Quaker movement over the centuries and by an increasing tolerance of, and identification with, worldly customs and ways. Unlike the

Amish and their struggle to remain separate (Kraybill and Olshan 1994), Friends sided with the State in the 1890s (Phillips 1989). Quaker progressivism became linked with a liberal sense of progressive history.

Rufus Jones wrote in 1895:

> There is a kingdom of the Spirit, for the Spirit of God is in his world, shaping history, . . . putting down evil, and making for righteousness, silently guiding the forces in this great battle of Armageddon (Hamm 1988:157).

At the turn of the century, the key Quakers in the Liberal Friends', reinvention of Quakerism claimed that Quakerism needed to be a faith relevant to its times; ever-open to new Light under a fresh theology of continuing and progressive revelation; rooted in the authority of personal experience (Davie 1997:112). The 1922 Book of Discipline for London Yearly Meeting dropped its section on 'Christian Doctrine' in favour of 'Illustrative Spiritual Experiences of Friends'. It is a short step from this combination of theological parameters to the possibility of diversity and, critically, a diversity which can include the non-Christian (and, in a secularised society, the non-theist). Quakers in Britain, and elsewhere in Liberal Quakerism, today hold a wide range of 'belief-stories', stories which help them make sense of their *experience*, which is primary. Belief can be a story as it is only 'towards' Truth and cannot hope adequately to convey a religious experience and set of truths which are ultimately beyond words. Even if expression were adequate, truth is partial and provisional under the remodelled theology of the Light and the progressive sense of human understanding. What may be true today, as far as anything can be, may be modified tomorrow.

The aims of the Quaker reformers widened to embrace the whole of society. Within post-millennialism, Christ would not come again to transform humanity but would come again after humanity had transformed itself. This was a middle position between God working in God's time, and humanity working in historical time: God would work in God's time after humanity had worked in historical time. The Socialist Quaker Society, formed in 1898, three years after the Manchester Conference (which has come to symbolise the ascendancy of the Liberal enterprise) can be seen to symbolise this post-millennialism. The SQS claimed a 'burning desire for significant social and economic change' (Adams, undated:1). However, when explicit religion began to disappear from Liberal Quakerism in the latter years of the twentieth century, these Friends were left with only a sense of humanity working in historical time in an amillennial way.

With the move to a partial sense of working in God's time and then a loss of this altogether, it is not surprising that Liberal Friends so enthusiastically revived Quaker historical studies. Lewis Benson claims early Friends were interested in history too but 'holy history' (1961:30), a history of a people of God attempting to be faithful as a way of understanding their present experience. As Jones and Braithwaite rewrote Quaker history to fit their new modernist interpretation of the Quaker faith, as essentially and primarily mystical with an emphasis on Christian citizenship (Phillips 1989:60), their massive academic project was about as sacred as the new perceptions of God and time would allow. It also remodelled Quakerism to fit the new vision of a Quakerism in tune with its age and open to fresh thought and revelation (Davie 1997:67, Gwyn 1995:350). Experience was elevated above Scripture to a position of ultimate authority (Davie 1997:112). Early Quaker history was reinterpeted in terms of historical time and Christian citizenship instead of the apocalyptic movement later scholarship offers as an alternative interpretation. Divine origins of Quakerism were replaced with theories of human influences on Fox (Hamm 1994:18). These shifts accommodated and nurtured the later shift to post-Christian Quakerism (Dandelion 1996a, Davie 1997).

It is an interesting shift in belief. First, this shift is largely invisible, cloaked under a culture of silence in which the value given to silence frames a reluctance and inability to share beliefs (Dandelion 1996a).

Second, it is a shift which marginalises belief and places it as secondary within a Liberal (or now liberal-Liberal given the present celebration of plurality) Quakerism rooted in and legitimated through the *experience* of its members (ibid).

In talking to Liberal Friends about credal statements of belief, it is possible to locate at least eleven reasons why these Friends are opposed to their adoption (Ambler 1989, Dandelion 1996a). For example, words demean or cannot fully express religious experience, credal statements may give rise to a false sense of surety and in turn complacency, credal statements operate to exclude those who cannot agree with them and may give non-Quakers a false impression; credal statements are unnecessary.

Listening to these reasons, typically thrown out thick and fast in amongst an excited exchange, it becomes clear that there is a certainty around the opposition to credal statements of belief which is in paradoxical opposition to the freedoms these defences are designed to protect. In effect, there is an almost credal attitude to the fact that the group does not have creeds. In other words, there is a credal attachment to the way in which Liberal Friends are a religious group, whilst there is a great permissiveness about the belief-content of that religious life. If we insert the practice of unprogrammed worship into the eleven reasons against creeds, it soon becomes clear that Liberal Friends do not judge it in the same way they would a belief statement. In other words, Friends appear to maintain a credal attachment to this form of worship maintained over three centuries even though, for example, it may then appear to be true for all time, or give rise to surety and complacency, and even though it excludes all those who find it inappropriate or inaccessible.

It is this clarity concerning a conformist and conservative way of *being* a religious people that forms the behavioural creed (Dandelion 1996a). Liberal Quakers maintain unity and protect their theological freedom through cohesion in the way in which Friends are to be Friends. Liberal Friends can question or disbelieve the divinity of

The behavioural creed

This is the term used to describe the position within Liberal Quakerism where there is a credal attachment to the way in which Friends are a religious group even whilst there is a strong opposition to credal statements of belief. In other words, there is a paradoxical credal attitude, for example, to the opposition to creeds. All of eleven reasons against the adoption of credal statements of belief (Ambler 1989, Dandelion 1996a) are ignored in terms of the adoption of fairly constant ways of worship and of business, ways of *being* a Quaker. Ben argues that it is the behavioural creed which maintains unity within a Liberal Quakerism where belief is secondary, marginal, and individual (1996a).

Jesus but not the sacralisation of silence. They do not have to believe in God but they need to follow the set of implicit and explicit rules about if, when, and how to break the silence. Discipline is maintained around the *form* of Quakerism, through Elders and Clerks, but not over its content in the Liberal Quaker tradition. Form is prescribed: interpretation of the experience, that the form is designed to produce and protect, is individual.

When Liberal and Evangelical Friends meet, tensions are typically assigned to theological difference. This is not necessarily the case. There is a prior and major difference in the very understanding of what it is to be a Friend. It is the Great Separation revisited. For one group, the definitional boundaries of what it is to be a Friend lie in the form (how the group is to be in its religious life); for the other in its certainty on beliefs (what the group believes in its religious life). These two groups are not even speaking the same language in their understanding of the term 'Friend'. When groups focused on the behavioural creed meet groups focused on the centrality of belief, understandably, the two cannot easily communicate. These different emphases tie directly back to the different positions the two groups have taken over how to interpret and respond to changes in their sense of an imminent Second Coming. One group has emphasised experience, retaining Second Coming structures as paramount, the other has placed primacy on the gospel and the First Coming. (It is similar to the tension over whether Quaker or Christian is primary in the adherent's faith identity.)

In the way they talk of their religious experience and in their diffidence about explicit religion, Liberal Friends appear to have lost the experience of the Second Coming. However, they have also chosen not to reform their structures. They chose instead the behavioural creed as a way of maintaining an explicit religiousness. In a way this makes sense. It safeguards *the experience of God* which is fundamental to that Friendly persuasion, and in its lack if explicit belief-talk, it can defend itself against the rationalist philosophers' attacks on the meaninglessness of religious concepts. Only Liberal Quakers indeed can understand the non-language-game of unprogrammed Friends and, consistent with this, do nothing to try and convert others to what cannot make any sense.

In a sense all Christians are focused on the Second Coming even if their emphasis is on the First. It is a question of experience and emphasis. What happened in this radical reinvention of Liberal Quakerism was that the way was opened for the Second Coming to become irrelevant.

Chapter Seventeen

From God's time to historical time: secular amillennialism

Ben Pink Dandelion

Without the shock of the realities of the 'Great War', the total shift from a sense of working in God's time to historical time may have come sooner. Friends could no longer sustain the sense of being 'the spiritual vanguard of a new social and political order' (Phillips 1989:319) and of co-operating with the State. Instead, Wilfred Littleboy's 1917 Swarthmore Lecture was explicitly eschatological, almost a call to return from a social programme to a religious one. As for American Friends with the experience of the Civil War, in Britain the Great War gave rise to eschatological fears as well as hopes. (The Cold War and the nuclear threat in the sixties and seventies also renewed an interest in endtime theology.)

However, overall, the experience of the 1914-18 war shifted attention away in the post-war years from theology to witness (Kennedy 1989), a diversion which ironically later helped mask the increasing theological pluralism of Britain Yearly Meeting[1].

---

[1]Only later did the diversity threaten this mask of witness which had allowed it to develop, as the meaning and necessity of the peace Testimony itself came under question.

The growth of the observance of Christmas amongst Friends (Carrdus 1993) underlines the loss of the former attitude to times and seasons. God's time has been levelled into historical time in which Friends celebrate Thanksgiving and Christmas. The sacralisation of all of life was initially underpinned and finally destroyed by a permissiveness which increasingly tolerated, and was then taken over by, the secular. At the same time, it is recognised by some Friends that such festivals may now hold the same importance for those Quakers who have lost the sense of an imminent Second Coming as they do for those in mainstream churches:

> The theory that every day is holy, that every day should be a Christmas when Christ is born in our hearts, every day an Easter when resurrection is to be celebrated, is admirable. It is, though, beyond most people to give due attention every day to all the significant events of the religious life. We need to make special opportunities, though these times need not coincide with particular dates (White 1996:24).

The 'intentional sacramentality' of Quaker worship becomes confined in this present-day reading on the need for rite, rather than taking its place amongst a wider implicit sacramentality of the everyday. It is almost as if Friends can only hope to reach the sense of the sacraments, given the pressures of today's world, at these pre-assigned moments, specially designed to heighten our awareness of the Presence in the Midst. Denominationalisation (the move away from a sectarian spirituality wary of the world's ways) precedes and accompanies secularisation. Thus, from a sense of the endtime, Friends moved to the meantime, as the church had done beforehand (Gwyn 1986:xx) and finally entirely to increasingly intrusive secular time (Fenn 1995), in which God was not extant except by invitation. Liberal Quakerism was gradually de-eschatologised and later de-divinised.

Initially, the new form of a Liberal Quaker millennium was to be social, not spiritual, salvation achieved through the reformation of conscience (Wilson 1970). Then, millennial hope disappeared. The end of the cold war ('human eschatology' - Ricca 1994) also meant

The basis and place of pessimism

The treatment of twentieth century Liberal Quakerism in this chapter is not an optimistic one. It talks negatively of the dominance of seeking above finding and of the culture of 'the now' over and above some sense of major future transformation. This pessimism about where Liberal Quakerism finds itself at the end of this century is a personal value judgement and the same reading of the nature of this form of Quakerism could be taken by other writers as a sign of strength and renewal. In Chapter 18, Ben makes it clear that his own distress around the future of Quakerism firstly says far more about his feelings about Quakerism than about the will of God, and in the end far more about himself than about the authenticity of various forms of Quaker life.

Having said this, there is evidence that Liberal Quakerism has changed considerably in the last fifty years. The work of Punshon (1990), Davie (1992), Heron (1992, 1995), Redfern (1993), and Dandelion (1996a, 1996b) all points to a shift away from a clear and mutual sense of a distinctive Quaker-Christianity to a supermarket Quakerism where adherents pick and choose their spiritual diet on an individual basis. Ben's statistical work shows a reaction against Christian language. Unity is fostered on the basis of a 'behavioural creed', not in terms of shared beliefs. Also, moves away from notions of 'the will of God' cause pain for those whose lives have been based around finding and following that will.

It may be that these writers are indeed 'prophets of doom' (Hetherington 1998:14) but it does not discount the model we are presenting here. It may indeed only affect the conclusions one draws about where the acceptance of the model leaves Liberal Quakers today.

the end of a pessimistic millennialism which had led many to reconsider ideas about end-times (Cooper 1981:6, McCandless 1974). Friends came to live not even in historical time but in present-time, the self and its relation to the-now-moment elevated to a congruity with God, 'God', or 'not-God' (he, she or it). An ahistorical atemporal mysticism and the means to 'God' became more important than the end (Benson 1961:25). The psychological easily replaced extreme immanentist positions on the Divine. The loss of sin from the Liberal Quaker vocabulary made salvation redundant and with that shift God became unnecessary, an optional extra which Liberal Friends could define in their own best interests.

✣ ✣ ✣

At London Yearly Meeting in 1993, reflections on the phrase 'Be Still and Know that I am God' led some Friends to a position of personal identification with the Divine. Modern psychology has rewritten religious discourse and placed the personal and individual 'I' into the Divine 'I Am'. Some Liberal Friends have become their own gods with their own benign agendas. They, not the Light, are to reform the consciences of those around them, economic and social power buying the luxury of a life of reflection and protection from the harsher realities of life they may seek to soothe. Even a personal sense of millennium is inappropriate in a culture which seeks to control the present. When Tony Blair, the leader of the British Labour Party, spoke at his party's convention prior to his election landslide of 1997 of having 'a thousand days to prepare for a thousand years', he was not necessarily taking his party into a Christian Socialist viewpoint. Rather, his comments reflected just how far a previously religious agenda has been co-opted into secular ways and secular time.

Whilst, as Downing claims, eschatological theology 'knows the present as a *time-for*, a time for response for what is on the way' (1969:16), the common present-day Quaker view that politics and religion are inseparable says more about the politicisation (secularisation) of the Quaker agenda than about a God-led political agenda as practised by the early Friends (Gwyn 1981:69). As Doug has laid before us in such detail in *The Covenant Crucified*, Quakers today are operating a contractual system, not one of covenant (Gwyn 1995).

✣ ✣ ✣

Doug has been exploring the connections between the phenomenon of seeking in the 1640s, which proved such fertile ground for converts to Quakerism in the 1650s, and its present-day counterpart. Relating to the work of Wade Clark Roof on twentieth century seeking (1993), Doug suggests that there were two types of Seekers amongst the first Friends, Seeker A and Seeker B types (1997). Seeker As looked to reclaim primitive Christianity, to resurrect an original and true vision of religious authenticity. Seeker Bs felt that such a vision was backward-looking and that God was leading his people into a new age and a new way of being. After the age of the law came the age of gospel. Now was the age of the Spirit. The past had been corrupted easily enough before, God would not take his people backwards to expose such a fragile faith to apostasy once again.

These different perspectives can be found across the writings of early Friends and it might be possible to delineate two kinds of Quakerism. Indeed, the first decades of Quakerism might be explored as an interplay of these two influences, a north/south, Fox/Nayler, male/female divide with different interpretations of history and of the Quaker role within it, held together by a common belief in the Second Coming.

As millennial hopes dwindled, and the Nayler incident exposed the fragility of Seeker-B theology, Fox tried to draw the two strands together. Fox was a Seeker-A type but also Seeker-A theology copes better with the postponement of the transformation of humanity and the pragmatic moves by Barclay to a contractual theology (away from a sense of covenant) and a slow-burn regeneration of the individual and of the world. Debates could not help but get personal and there were splits off both ends of the broad Seeker AB composite church Fox was attempting to hold together, Perrot as a Seeker-B type with a progressive sense of history and of revelation, and Wilkinson, Story and later Keith as Seeker-A types. Later still, it is possible to view Wilburites and Holiness Friends as Seeker-A types, Hicksites, Gurneyites, Modernist Friends and the founders of Liberal Quakerism as Seeker-B.

Roof describes these two kinds of Seekers in today's religious world, neo-pentecostalists as A types seeking to revive family values, and

New Age thinking as B types looking for a new new-dispensation (1993). It is also fruitful to look at present-day religious/Quaker tensions in terms of this typology.

Indeed, these Seeker types still reflect different kinds of Friends today. Perhaps in all the traditions, but within Liberal Quakerism especially, there has been an increased shift to a third kind of seeking. I want to define *Seeker-C* types as those who prefer to travel rather than arrive. Seeking is all. Legitimated through a theology of partiality and provisionality, the search is ongoing and forever. Seeker-Cs can seek everywhere where they will not find final truths. The behavioural creed accommodates their theology and reflects it. Process is more important than result. The means to the end becomes the end. How Friends are to be religious is more important than what religion consists of in terms of beliefs or certainties. As early as the disownment of George Keith in the 1690s by Philadelphia Yearly Meeting, and through Quietist times to the Great Separation of 1827, we can find a strand of Quakerism emphasising the primacy of right

Seeker C

Building on the work done by Roof (1993) and Doug (Gwyn 1997) on Seeker A and B types (see Chapters 1, 8, and the box on Seekers A and B on page 97), Seeker C typology has been developed by Ben to describe those for whom seeking is more important than finding. That is, that authenticity is to be found in process, not outcome, or that the desired outcome or truth is already manifest in the search, not in further fruits. It fits the popular saying 'to travel hopefully is better than to arrive' and reflects the now-dominant strand of Liberal Quakerism where certainty, other than in the process, is problematical. In Chapter 17, Ben jests that Seeker C types can seek everywhere where they will not find final truths. There are Friends who are neither A, B, or C types or who are amalgam-types, but it is possible to see different dominant positions in the history of Quakerism fitting mainly into one of these categories. From the disownment of George Keith in the 1690s through the Great Separation of 1827 to today's emphasis on the means as the end, we can locate a strand of Quakerism where the primary emphasis has been on right form (see the box on 'the Behavioural Creed' on page 181) over and above right belief.

behaviour over and above right belief. The growth of emphasis on form, which was to sustain and nurture the spiritual life of Friends 'in the meantime', continues the increasing emphasis on orthopraxis (where unity is founded on behaviour and procedure). This orthopraxis was used to disown Keith and was given new status by Liberal theology to emerge as a fully fledged Seeker C ideology in which an amillennial praxis is all.

In Liberal Quakerism today worldwide, Seeker C seeking is predominant. To be on the edge of truth has replaced the former ideas of being on the edge of the endtimes. Seeker B progressivism and continuing revelation have a currency which has all but destroyed a clear sense of living in a particular God-given point in human history, or even, as Seeker B thinking has been replaced by Seeker C tendencies, of expecting that time to come at any time in the future. As with the behavioural creed in general, of which it is now a legitimated part, this form of seeking accommodates and encourages diversity of belief. Conservatism in one area underpins a permissiveness in another. Except that, in an ironic and perhaps fateful way, this permissiveness is itself part of a fundamentalism. Certainty in the Liberal tradition is not allowed. A lack of certainty is part of the behavioural creed. Nearly a quarter of British Friends are agnostic (Dandelion 1996a).

The 'silent revolution' in the nature of Quaker theology away from a normative Quaker-Christianity to a pluralistic post-Christianity contributes to the potential for secularisation as Quakers cease to talk explicitly of religious experience, cease to need to be religious in order to participate fully in the life of unprogrammed Liberal Quaker Yearly Meetings, and cease to believe in any major future societal change, negative or positive. Now, the 'religious life' is only about serving itself in a cycle of perpetual seeking. Praxis becomes more important than doxy and indeed all. Spirituality is personal, amillennial, and focused on 'present-time', and all sense of history (including the Jesus story) is non-essential. Liberal Friends have moved from a sense of working within God's time to historical time to an atemporality concerned with the self and the now. The Second Coming is inappropriate and irrelevant.

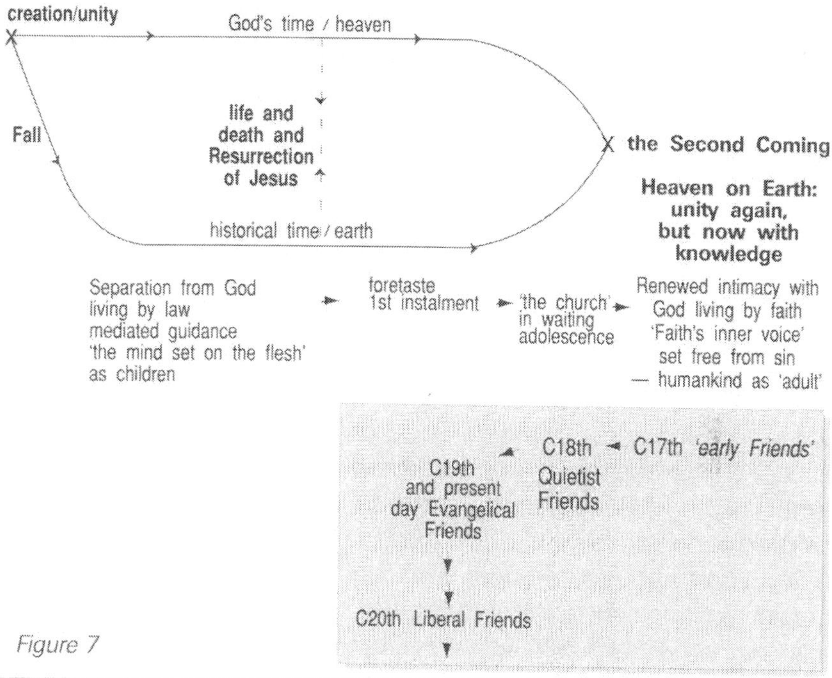

Figure 7

Another strand to the arguments about the shift from being a Second-Coming 'church' to a secularised non-coming co-operative of consensus rests on an analysis of the role of theology in the spiritual life, and of what Friends were doing as regards theologising across the three centuries.

Doug has described to me the interplay in the 1650s and 1660s between Seeker-A and Seeker-B theologies as an experience of atonement. Underwood claims that it is not surprising that systematic Quaker theology did not appear until the second generation given the first's focus on religious experience itself (1970:91). However, by the 1690s, Friends were theologising about the atonement instead of experiencing it[2].

[2] The Keith controversy began with theological disputes about this, disputes settled by recourse to notions of orthopraxis, failing to clarify the Quaker position on the atonement, a dispute later to surface with the Great Separation of 1827, and forewarning of times ahead when belief would be marginalised and the definitional boundaries around liberal Quakerism constructed within ideas about form.

Evangelical Quakerism accommodated the growth of Liberal theology in its increased worldliness and liberalisation of the old peculiarities. Liberal Friends were Seeker-B types reviving a sense of progressive history and believing that a new new-dispensation would be ushered in by their influence combined with the benign paternalism of the Empire (Phillips 1989). By the 1890s, they were reflecting on this theologising, their increasing sense of working only in God's time underpinned by, and encouraging, a renewed interest in historical studies (Davie 1997).

By the 1990s, some Friends are not even bothered with thinking about what others once wrote about the atonement. Like those who were experiencing this act of God's grace firsthand, they are text-less, but now indifference and a lack of interest have replaced living in the Life and Power. Praxis has also replaced experience. Janey O'Shea, former Quaker Studies Tutor at Woodbrooke, used to say that you cannot begin to pray until you have put down the book on praying. In a reverse pattern, Quakers have taken up the book on the religious life. They have initially indulged in this religious life but, on the path to secularisation, have later realised that the content of the text is no longer appropriate to the needs of a life of seeking. As the Doug Gwyn song satirises, 'where there's a way there's a will' - the search for meaning has been replaced by having the means.

✣ ✣ ✣

The emphasis on the behavioural creed does serve to enthuse those many converts who come either from the unchurched or as refugees from credal churches (Heron 1992). Quakers in Britain are a growing group, in terms of attendance, because they represent a stepping stone into the religious enterprise which requires nothing of the enquirer (Dandelion 1996a:330). They appear to be serious about their religious life (eg: the behavioural creed) and it is perception of seriousness, not conservatism as was first thought (Kelley 1972), which dictates church growth (Perrin and Mauss 1991). However these very Attenders are not becoming Members because it is not clear to them what it is they would be committing themselves to (Heron 1992).

The problem with this emphasis on the behavioural creed is that there is nothing in the Quaker form which is itself explicitly religious. Silence, and absence of religious forms, are not in themselves religious. When this is coupled with individualism and an experience-based authority system, it is not surprising that a certain degree of ethical humanism seems to sit alongside what is already a post-Christian religious tradition[3]. Agnostic seeking, however optimistic, has no language other than that of searching.

The irony and the danger is that this radical new Quakerism looks like the original thing. The dismissal of text, the emphasis on living in the moment, have all the hallmarks of a Second Coming church. The whole structure continues to reflect this and for some, the possibility of refinding the Life and Power remains whilst Meetings continue to use a method which encodes three centuries of experience. However, Second Coming and amillennial Quakerisms are radically different in a way best characterised by their differing understandings of their relationship to God's time.

Programmed Friends appear at least to have sensed the dangers of operating a Second Coming structure without a parallel experience and, in adopting some of the waiting strategies of other parts of Christianity, have retained a more explicit religiousness. If programmed Friends appear to turned the clock back in terms of the culmination of God's plan for the world with the Second Coming, Liberal Friends appear to have dropped out of the plan altogether.

In terms of the Second Coming, the whole story is far too biblically Christian and rationally unthinkable to help make any sense of a religiousness espousing personal growth and individual transformation. So, it no longer matters to these Friends where they are, if at all, in God's plan for the world, especially if their God is not the kind of God who would have such a plan in the first place. An amillennial emphasis on 'the now', eternal in its present-tense, has

[3] In that so many Friends no longer use a Christian language as part of their belief-story.

taken over from ideas of any major future global or societal transformation. Some Liberal Friends now only have historical time in which to work, devoid of a sense of God's time and of a way of remembering it, and even, in their extreme immanentist and implicit theologies, of a God who could have a time. Ethics have replaced witness, mission has now metamorphosed into 'outreach'. A hedge once built to maintain purity of the Truth around a peculiar people lingers to now allow an ecumenical and permissive religious group to minister only to its own sort, preferring those of a different race and class to find their truths elsewhere.

Yet, there is also an arrogance to much of the Liberal Quaker pro-ecumenical lobby. The other churches need Friends ('we seem to be the sort of people other people want to be represented by' one Friend commented in Britain Yearly Meeting) and therefore Quakers appear to feel the need to join them. Little is said about a Quaker need for the other churches. It is an arrogance underpinned by a continuing sense of difference but one which is submerged under the desire to collaborate with new-found fans in the other churches. Quakers are no longer *the* true church, but one amongst many and it is equally valid for the religious person to become a Friend and/or a Methodist. Liberal Quakerism is the right way merely for the self-selected, for those who believe the claims. Liberal Quakerism is both different and the same. It is only partially true and yet, for those within it, more right than others.

Within this complex of similarity, difference, partial truth and superior truth, and within a sense of now working only in historical time, the whole of Liberal Quakerism can come to represent the Second Coming. Quakerism becomes the kingdom (Parkinson 1996), again obtusely paralleling the early Quaker need to publish Truth to bring the world away from its apostasy. No longer concerned with the endtimes for themselves, Liberal Friends represent it for the whole of Christianity once those believers have got over the delusion of a transcendent God.

In other ways though, Liberal Quakerism simply seems to be following the other churches into observances of the outward, denominationalisation and secularisation. If Liberal Quakerism is a vanguard for anything, it may be the dangers of permissiveness, an increased tolerance vainly hoping for an increased appeal but one which may only be suicidal in the end. This is especially true given an inability to recognise that these Friends live by, and structure their religious group around, a series of claims relating to the sacramental nature of all life (*Quaker Faith and Practice* 27.39, 27.42, 27.43) which experience appears to no longer support. Liberal Friends are a Second-Coming Church without a Second Coming. A priesthood of all believers (*Quaker Faith and Practice* 11.01, 19.31) without a common belief, even in a priesthood.

Chapter Eighteen

Face to faith: turned inside out

Ben Pink Dandelion

The title of this chapter, written from a more personal perspective, plays on the sociological concepts of being either an insider or an outsider, in terms of the researcher's relationship to the group being studied. Social researchers who are going into the field are depicted as either insiders or outsiders. Either they are familiar with the area they are researching (they are perhaps part of the group that they are looking at) or they are total outsiders (the traditional sociological role supposedly providing the objective academic distance that is required to do the research and to analyse the situation). As my research has been in Quakerism I am an insider, and I will come back to this. I will also be using the term insider and outsider in terms of the religious life and the various changes that have happened to me through the process of becoming a Friend and being involved with Friends.

Unlike Tim and Doug I don't have a period to look back to, to displace myself into and to romanticise about. I can't go back to Paul and say, 'these were the good old days', or go back to early Friends and be inspired and say, 'well maybe if we had a little bit of this now who knows what might happen.' My work has been on the present day so I romanticise us now, or not, as the case may be. I am dealing with the present day, in particular with Quakers in Britain today. I am not a theologian. I am, by accident, a sociologist. The people who are my heroes, highly respected sociologists, are not people we talk a lot about in Friends.

Like Tim and Doug I have feet in two camps. Not Catholicism and Quakerism as in Tim's case, and not Quakerism and Quakerism as in Doug's case. But I have feet in the camps of rationalism and rational enquiry and of Quakerism and, alongside that divide, from my upbringing, feet in the contrasting notions of hedonism and contract, between freedom and obedience: these are the tensions that I want to consider. I think probably that many Liberal Friends find themselves in that place today: living these tensions between freedom and faithfulness (if you prefer that word to obedience); but also between rationalism and a kind of common-sense view of the world, and a totally extra-rational, non-rational religious view. These worlds are not compatible in my opinion. I really do feel I live in two different worlds and that I jump between the two of them and I may even be doing that in this chapter. They are different explanation systems for how the world operates. One involves God, in a philosophical sense a meaningless concept. We can't say anything about God because we have nothing to go on. We cannot explain even the word God in rational terms. In a sense, as a religious person, I live within a belief story, a language game, a way of explaining the world and explaining, trying to explain, my experience. But then I also live in a world which looks at the people who makes these kinds of claims. My PhD dissertation talks about 'they', the group. 'The Quakers claim that...' etc. I will return to that process of needing to get on the outside of something I am also on the inside of.

First, a little bit of background. I was brought up in a very strict atheist household. The vicar was not allowed through the door when we moved into a new village. There was no Bible or any other religious text in the house, and if anything at all religious came on the television, the television went off. This was quite something. The television was usually on, but it would at those points go off. My father was a rationalist atheist. Religion made no sense. My mother had an 'illegitimate' child when she was 17, in 1939, and had such a bad experience of 'religious morality' (ending up with her child being sent to Australia as 'from a broken home with an unfit mother'), that she, understandably, had a gut reaction against religion. They sent me to a Quaker school 'to do me the least harm'. They believed in private fee-paying education and where we lived the choice was the Catholic school or the nearby Friends' school. My father and my mother had worked for Friends Provident and knew a little bit about Friends and so they thought that this was the least harmful option. Of course, just because I went to a Quaker school didn't mean I learnt very much about Quakerism. It was ironic and disappointing for my mother when I later became a Quaker.

I then went travelling for about a year on my bicycle to India. When I came back I started a course in hotel management and then dropped out in a series of political shifts which took me further and further to the left and then off the edge. So I went from being a Liberal to being a Trotskyist (thrown out because of my pacifism), and then into an anarchist world for about a couple of years (which is where my name comes from). I became burnt-out as an anarchist. I was arrested eight times in as many months and given that anarchists aren't known for their organisation (being anarchists), there wasn't a great sense of support. I also found myself rather on the edge of the anarchist movement as a pacifist. I had been writing about anti-sexism and I was then invited to a Quaker Conference on Anti-Sexism so I found a way back into Friends and realised, or re-realised, that here was a pacifist group with an anarchistic structure. No leaders, no votes. It seemed like the group for me and I started going to Meeting regularly. It was also a stabilising influence, a sense of home, and I applied to join after six months and was admitted. I question this now. I often say 'they should never have let me in'.

I became a member as a non-religious Friend. I had no problem with my parents' atheism. It seemed utterly sensible to me, though I was an optimistic agnostic, prepared to believe that there might be something and that silence seemed a good way to find out. But it was a full year after I became a member that I would actually admit to any explicit religious experience: whilst some Friends may not like the term 'conversion experience', I think that's what I had on a Greyhound bus travelling in America.

I was crossing from coast-to-coast, a three day journey. I had run out of money totally. I had begged off an English student travelling in America for him to buy me a ticket to get back home, and as a sign of my goodwill and honesty I gave him every cent I had which then meant I had nothing to buy any food with for that three days. That may be by-the-by, or it may be that the heightened sensitivity which comes through lack of food and, on those bus journeys, a lack of sleep, allowed me to be more vulnerable and open to the Spirit. But certainly half way across America I suddenly and unexpectedly, and unwantedly in a sense, felt 'held'. Held by God. Picked up and just looked after, an experience which has stayed with me every day since 5 September 1986. I feel continually accompanied by God. Continually held and looked after by God. I became a religious Quaker. However, I was still a religious Quaker without any investment in what that kind of religion should consist of. So two weeks after I finished my degree in Philosophy and Cinema I started the PhD in Quaker Belief and had the luxury of four years looking at what Friends in Britain believe today.

I thought it was going to be a kind of text enquiry. That I would look at lots of books; talk about philosophy and get a bit of cultural studies in there. However I also wanted to use a questionnaire and I wanted to interview people and I wanted to interview groups so I picked supervisors who were experts in those kinds of techniques. In short, they were sociologists and I became a sociologist because they kept saying, 'no no we're not interested in that, we want you to do this.' They were interested in relations between claims and sociological readings of reality and so we return to this sense of being both an insider and an outsider. Often in the early days my supervisors would say to me, 'you're sounding too much like a Quaker. You're writing this stuff and you're not doubting your informants,' i.e. the Quakers I was talking to. So I would interview a Quaker and then say, 'well, this happened in Meeting and this happened, and in business meeting we seek to know the will of God and...' and I would write this down: 'Quakers seek to know the will of God and find it in their business meetings.'

'No, no, no,' my supervisors would respond. That's not sociology. That's just Quakerism. Doubt your informants.' I was asked to step back and say 'ok, you are telling me, you are claiming, that you are seeking the will of God in your business meetings' so I could write 'Quakers claim that they are seeking the will of God in a business meeting.' Then you can bring in a rather harsh or cynical sociological rider: 'this is a voteless decision making process in which the minority exercise a veto.' That's the reading of my supervisors on the Quaker business method. If there is not unity in the group, even if it's only one or two people against the way the sense of the Meeting seems to be going, then the matter may be deferred or put off. So it appears that the minority is exercising a veto, and in pure social relation terms that's what happens - although Quakers wouldn't see it like that of course. And this is why the two worlds in a sense are incompatible. They are totally different readings of what's going on, although the cynical sociological one may come into play, and I believe it does when we lose the theology. When Friends are not following the discipline then maybe they are in a process where the minority have a veto. So I defend the sociological technique as giving us clues as to what can happen, and to what may happen.

One of the problems about being an insider is that you may know too much. You may think you know it all already. There is a quote in Pennterra, *a Quaker science fiction novel, where a character comments, 'having lived in an isolated community of Friends for so long it wasn't obvious what an outsider would find strange' (Moffett 1988:91). There is the question again of stepping outside the group and trying to view it from a non-Quaker perspective. Quakers may believe that business meetings are seeking the will of God, but how does it appear to the non-Quaker? And of course we all have our biases - every researcher has a bias and that's something to be careful of as well.*

The other problem is actually affecting what you're researching. I was an insider, and I was an insider in different ways as the study went on. When I began I was involved locally. I was unemployed but I was active in various committees at a local level. In the middle of the study I had become a part-time Quaker employee on the Bradford Summer Gathering and I was becoming more involved nationally. By the end I had a full-time job at Friends House and was fairly involved in Yearly Meeting work. The way in which I was an insider changed over the years.

So I would be sitting in business meeting maybe taking a couple of notes, and I'd be asked for an opinion, for example. Or my silence would be conspicuous. So, one of the things that happened was that about three quarters of the way through my research I said, '40% of my interviewees expressed a belief in reincarnation and yet we don't talk about it. We never mention it, and many of them said they couldn't mention it in their own Meetings. They felt awkward about it.' Well by the time I was at the Friends House job they said 'Ben, that's very interesting. Why don't you go and organise a weekend on reincarnation?' So then of course the whole conspiracy of silence broke down because I'd mentioned it, then I'd been asked to run a weekend on it, and then in fact Quakers were talking about reincarnation so I could no longer say '40% of Quakers believe in reincarnation and yet never talk about it'!

There's a problem in moving between these worlds of Quakerism and academia. There's a practical problem and there's an ethical problem. The practical problem is who you are at any one time. And this is also the ethical problem. Am I the researcher or the Quaker? I gave a couple of papers at the University of Brighton and a lot of Friends came along. This was chaired by a Professor and it was chaired in a worldly secular (academic) way. When one Friend said, 'could we have some silence beforehand?', the reply was that it wouldn't be appropriate in the University setting. However, at the end when the Professor asked for questions, there were some questions from Friends and a final comment from an Elder, 'Well perhaps we could end in some silence.' The Professor was helpless in the face of this majority of Quakers then bowing their heads and going into silence. He didn't know what to do. So at the end of the silence, I said, 'thank you Friends,' and shook hands with the Quaker next to me. There had been a whole shift in the definition of setting. My role had gone from being an academic, to being, in a sense, an Elder closing the Meeting.

It's a question perhaps of split allegiances as well. Do I care more that we continue to say that we seek the will of God than that I write all this sociology about minority vetos and weighty Friends being leaders? In the end I moved Meeting and I think that's partly because I had so dissected the Meeting I had been involved with that it became almost impossible to re-engage with it. Sociologists typically disengage. They leave the field and go back to their nice cosy academic departments. I had to re-engage. I had to go back into Meeting and stop, try to stop, being a sociologist. Part of my strategy for that was to go to a different Meeting. In my viva my examiner said, 'can you ever be a Quaker again?' a question that's lived with me since.

✣ ✣ ✣

Something happened to me towards the end of the research period and this was the death of my mother, and in that the death of the last person who knew my father, who had died 18 years earlier. It was almost another rebirth experience. Not her death but this awful sense afterwards, of now having to be an adult. I was 29 and I had to be an adult. I couldn't be as irresponsible as I had been because now the buck stopped with me. I am my family. I am my last resource financially. I had a motorcycle accident about four months after she died, and as I lay there in hospital I remember feeling terrible that I had had an accident, although it wasn't directly my fault, because I hadn't been faithful *to this new responsibility. This wasn't right living. What happened in that period was that God changed for me. The God of the Greyhound bus had been my friend. 'Welcome aboard, Ben. You know I'm with you now. Anything you decide to do I'm with you.' Co-workers, friend, arm on my shoulder. Now I had to be responsible and I had to be obedient.*

There's a piece in Quaker Faith and Practice *from John Punshon about how he was at an interfaith gathering in Birmingham and he said:*

> *On one occasion at a big interfaith gathering I was being very Quakerly and very enlightened. The discussion was about prayer, and I confessed it was my habit to pray anywhere and that I could do so sitting comfortably in a chair. A Muslim woman in the conference was shocked at what she saw as my easy-going familiarity with God. A lack of respect. My denial of my own human dignity. 'When you think of God', she said 'there is only one possible response. It is to go down on your knees' (1995:27.08).*

Now, like John, I still don't do that in Meeting. But that's certainly the feeling inside for me now.

Doug has talked about agonised Puritans, about people who weren't sure if they were part of the elect or not and agonised. I don't understand why they were agonised because either they were part of the elect or they were not and there was nothing they could do about it. (They should have just enjoyed themselves!) I had not had an agonised life. The other side to that kind of rationalist atheist existence at home had been a hedonistic philosophy. How did you measure whether something was good? Well, was it fun? And if it's fun you do it. 'Don't read books, that's boring. Watch TV. Don't practise the violin. Why do you want to play that piece over and over again? Come and watch TV, it's more fun.' I don't read books. And I don't now play the violin. So I grew up in a world which was both hedonistic, value being placed on pleasure, and also with a strong emphasis on contract. 'You are your mother's son, therefore you will do this. This is your role.' What comes back into play as I discover a God to whom I have to be obedient is a very real tension between these two forces. Because basically, once I'd left home, I'd done pretty much what I wanted. I'd gone cycling, I'd dropped out of college when I wanted to drop out, I'd started college when I wanted to start college, I'd bought and sold cars and motorbikes when I wanted to. I hadn't worked for a long time when I was an anarchist because it was against my political beliefs to do paid work. Suddenly though, I can no longer do what is just pleasurable and there is a very clear sense of contract re-emerging in my life. Contract to God. As well as a contract to Quakerism. And the unrelenting question, 'Who am I?' which may have been asked as a sociological researcher, takes on incredible new significance. 'Who are you to decide what you might like to do?'

I have become an agonised Quaker. There are two reasons for that. Partly because of the Quaker bit - what I'd discovered in my research - but partly because I can no longer ever be sure whether I am doing the right thing. I am not automatically part of the elect, I have to work at my salvation. There's a wonderful quotation in Quaker Faith and Practice *from Violet Holdsworth about giving ministry in Meeting:*

> *Each Friend who feels called upon to rise and deliver a lengthy discourse might question himself and herself most searchingly as to whether the message could not be more lastingly given in the fewest possible words, or even through his or her personality alone in entire and trustful silence. Cream must always rise to the surface. True. But other substances rise to the surface besides cream. Substances which may have to be skimmed off and thrown away before bodies and souls can be duly nourished. Is my message cream or scum? It may be an unusual and it may be a very homely query, still it's one that every speaker, in a crowded gathering especially, should honestly face. Some of the dangers of silent worship can best be guarded against by its courtesy (1995:2.64).*

So I need to ask of everything I do or say - is it cream or scum? Is it the will of God or not? Is it just the hedonism creeping back in? In The Last Temptation of Christ *by Nikos Kazantzakis, translated into*

English by the Quaker Pieter Bien, there are two bits that really spoke to me. Not that I read books, but I just happened to be looking through! Here is the first:

> *The son of Mary has gone to a monastery in a desert. He gets there after a long journey. 'The Abbot is dying' said the monk. 'You've arrived too late my Brother. Go back.' 'God commanded me to come' the son of Mary replied. 'Is he capable of hoaxing his children?' The monk cackled. He'd seen a good deal in his lifetime and had no confidence in God. 'He's the Lord isn't he? So he does whatever comes into his head. If he wasn't able to inflict injustice, what kind of an omnipotent would he be?' (Kazantzakis 1987:141)*

I'm not sure about the injustice bit. I like to remodel God as benign. But there is that sense that there's always the possibility of being tricked or hoaxed, if not by ourselves, then perhaps because we're being tested. I know this isn't language that Liberal Friends commonly use, but this is the way I see it. The second piece is where the Rabbi, who is dying, is having a dream:

> *Everything is of God he reflected. Everything has two meanings. One manifest, one hidden. The people comprehend mainly what is manifest. They say this is a snake and their minds go no further, but the mind which dwells in God sees what lies behind the visible and sees the hidden meaning (Kazantzakis 1987:155).*

I feel I live that idea that everything has two meanings. Nothing is an accident. Nothing is a coincidence.

I am a distressed Quaker, as well as an agonised one, because of Quakerism. My study shows that Quakers in Britain are increasingly diverse, that there is little to check the shift to pluralism, and of more concern to me than pluralism, having not been brought up a Christian (I tend to work with a theocentric rather than a Christian language), that we face the loss of explicit religion amongst British Friends. I have been told I sound too certain about God and that is distressing to others. But I have decided not to censor myself, but to just hope people can translate or ignore. So I am a Quaker and I also have a strong sense of contract. So then I have an idea of what it is *to be a Quaker. And then I have an idea of what other Quakers perhaps should be doing in order to be Quakers. For example, I am very clear that Quakers should not be celebrating Christmas. Having times and seasons is all part of the decline, the secularisation of our belief. I probably have difficulties with dual membership. I don't think we should be members of the national ecumenical bodies because Liberal Friends are such different kinds of believers to mainstream Christians.*

However, I also have two problems with all this certainty. One is that human beings are wonderful people whom I generally trust and love unless proven otherwise. If someone is a dual member then who am I to question that? I'm not questioning if their choice is helpful to them, even if intellectually I find the concept difficult. I am not going to stand outside the church and say, 'why are you going in here to listen to a priest? That priest is impeding your relationship with God.' I'm not going to do that because that's about human lives and human experience, even if I may be critical of a church which continues to have a structure which I think gets in the way of humanity's relationship with God. So the first thing is that my certainty is at a particular level. I have to be so clear. There are so many little sub-clauses. I am certain, but in this way, and of course bearing in mind that...

I had a commentary in The Friend *early in 1997 saying that I felt we needed four things if we were going to increase our spiritual state. Four things. One was becoming more serious, so giving religion more weight in our lives. I want us to be explicit about the fact that we are a religious Society. Surely there should be something we can say to each other, if not to the world, coming out of worship? Secondly, that we should have more fun. If we are no longer going around trying to be pious and do the right thing and if we actually 'own' the religious enterprise, then we can have more fun. Thirdly we need to be more honest with each other and honest with each other as quickly as possible. For too long we have been paralysed by the fear of causing offence. Let us at least maintain the standards of honesty between ourselves that we campaign for between governments. And let us say it quickly - not hold onto it and wait for the right moment. I live on the edge of doom. Anyone may die at any time. I suppose because that's been my experience. So we need to say it today. Not wait for tomorrow. And then finally, I said I want to ask that we never doubt the will of God, that there is a way which God is willing us to follow in all aspects of our daily lives. I know this is foreign language to many Friends, but I believe it passionately and I see it at the heart of the Quaker belief in direct revelation. Also, however, we must not doubt the will of God once it has been revealed.*

Now this is a large debate. I have had numerous letters about it. One letter in The Friend *said, 'What Ben Pink Dandelion writes is largely nonsense', which I think is a great accolade. Others are worried about a lack of free will but I am not necessarily, in logical terms, talking about an omnipotent God. I am not talking about everything being predetermined. But I'm saying there is a will of God. I'm saying that because that's the way I explain my experience.*

Which brings me back to theology and my conundrum. What can I say about God? How do I know God has a will? Well I don't. I have this experience which I describe in this language within this belief story. And maybe theology is purely an invention. It is the way in which we make sense of our experience. And if someone makes sense of their experience through a particular kind of God, so their God is not the kind of God who can have a will, who am I to say then, 'you shouldn't doubt the will of God.' I cannot say it! I cannot say it to the world. I cannot say it to any believer and I certainly cannot say it to any non-believer because its a meaningless statement. So actually what I'm saying is more about the nature of Quakerism than about the nature of God. I'm saying that if folk call themselves Quaker then I believe these are basic, fundamental steps for renewal, part of which is to own the concept of the will of God. So that needs to be made clear. I am talking about Quakerism. Not about God.

The second problem with my certainty is that, because of my view of theology, I am really only talking about myself. One of the things about living in a group that places so much emphasis on continuing revelation is that I myself may be an old fashioned kind of Quaker. The group has passed me by. The group now has a God which is not the kind of God which can have a will. 'Ben, you're back there 50 years, a 100 years. I mean "not celebrating Christmas"? Please. We started getting into that earlier in the century.'

In this book, we are looking at a picture of, in a sense, God's plan for the world. The beginning is in the garden of Eden, going into the Fall, and then through a sequence of events where God intervenes in human history to bring us to a point of the Second Coming. Through the First Coming of Christ we are given the possibility of a Second Coming and a foretaste of what this renewed intimacy with God will be like. And we end up looking at Paul, looking at Revelation, looking at George Fox, looking at early Friends, and living in a world in which the Second Coming may have come, or didn't come, but may come at any point. It's a big bang Second Coming theory. Trumpets will sound. Christ will come again and the whole of humanity will be transformed. This is what the early Friends thought. We shall be set free from sin. We shall be united with God through Christ. As before we have been living under the Law, we shall be living under Faith. We shall be in the age of the Spirit. As before we have been living as children under the Law we shall now be living as adults.

It's a fantastical picture, and right the way through teaching the material at Woodbrooke, students have expressed their great difficulty in wrestling with this...'What do you mean, Second Coming?' 'God's time?' 'I mean what's it going to be like...?' 'Is it still going to happen?' 'NOW?' 'Do we really believe that this can happen now?' It stretches us. In this book, I have asked you to suspend your disbelief. To treat it as if you're at the movies and you're watching this picture unfold, to suspend your disbelief or counter-belief. And that's been happening. The book is coming to the end now and in the next chapter, we are stepping outside the picture and asking, 'what do we make of this?' But what was interesting to me is that it is just so fantastical and that's why it is so difficult to go along with. How can Friends talk about a Second Coming which is going to transform the whole of humanity in this kind of a way?

I went to a seminar the other day and there were people there from the Raelians, which is a small new religious movement who feel they've made contact with the people from another planet who set off creation on earth as an experiment so many thousands of years ago. The Raelians are now preparing for a meeting with these people from another planet who will come to a specially prepared embassy on earth, to which we are all being asked to give money. Humanity was an experiment, but we are now getting up to the level of intelligence which they had when they set the experiment off and now it's the time to talk to us. Well what do you make of that? Other planets, and landing strips. It's fantastical and we laugh. We say 'No, no, no. We don't believe that. Other planets? No.' And yet we are saying, some of us are saying, maybe there is a God. 'A what?' 'A God.' 'Where?' 'Well...up there somewhere. It set off humanity. Maybe not an experiment but a plan. A process. We come through the other end to the Second Coming where we are reunited with God with knowledge. We will not take the apple again. Because now we have knowledge.'

It's a short step from one fantastical story to another fantastical story. To then be saying, well what are we even to make of God? 'God' is a fantastical concept. What are we to do with it?

The danger is that we can argue ourselves out of Quakerism. We can see it as an explicitly and necessarily Christian Second Coming church and that is too much to swallow, maybe for Friends everywhere. For me, then, it would be a short hop back into my rationalist world and out of religion altogether. My problem as a distressed Quaker, passionate, about certain things, is that I can argue myself out of Quakerism. But in doing so I also argue myself right of Woodbrooke, probably, and right out of my other world, this academic world that looks at Quakers. I am turned inside out, but also my whole world is turned upside down.

Even though then it will be as if I have no existence because the whole of my world is framed by Quakerism or the study of Quakerism, maybe that doesn't matter. However, that's not easy because I love my colleagues and I love working in a place like Woodbrooke. And I love Friends. But the most annoying thing at the end of it all, is that I've realised that from some deep place, it's not even a possibility. Not a possibility to give all this up, because, at the end of the day, and in and through every moment of it, God is not an option. I continually return to that. I just can't give it up. Because with all its tensions of living in two worlds, and its distresses and its confusions, I live an accompanied life.

Part Four:

Conclusions

Chapter Nineteen

Consequences and possibilities

Ben Pink Dandelion

Chapter 17 presented Liberal Quakerism from a critical viewpoint but whether that pessimistic outlook on the future of that part of the Quaker world is shared or not by the reader, laying the model of the Second Coming over the history of Friends raises fundamental questions as to what kind of religious body Friends in all parts of the tradition are today.

For example, is it sufficient to designate programmed Friends as Christians in the same way as other First Coming groups or does the partial reform that branch of Quakerism undertook still suggest a Second Coming legacy which may produce unexpected consequences? As one workshop participant questioned me, 'If you are saying that programmed Friends were sensible in adopting a pastoral system given the loss of the Second Coming experience (if we take it that outward forms can be helpful in sustaining faithfulness in the period between the first and second incarnations of Christ), what are we to say about the fact that they did not adopt ordinances, a priesthood, etc.?'

My solution to this obvious and logical question is that the partial reform reflects the maintenance of some aspects of the experience of the 'Kingdom', ie: the continued openness amongst programmed Friends to the direct unmediated guidance of the Spirit, alongside their recognition of the authority of Scripture. If the two are in balance, as Gayle Beebe suggests they are for Evangelical Friends (1997), then perhaps partial reform is all that is necessary to help sustain a faithful community. Their focus is on the First Coming and the meantime but they are aware that they live a partial and random experience of heaven on earth.

✣ ✣ ✣

Liberal Friends are generally not focused on the First Coming and they have not adopted those outward forms chosen by other religious groups to help them sustain a waiting faithfulness. They are a diverse group, whose adherents represent many positions on the chart (page 190). Many have come in from other religious groups. Most of these prior commitments will have been focused on the First Coming (there are few other Second Coming churches) or none: some will have been Buddhists or members of new religious movements prior to, or alongside, their Quaker involvement and there are the 47% of converts previously unchurched immediately prior to entry.

These Friends may be unaware of the Second Coming origins of Quakerism and lay their First Coming theology or amillennial perspectives over the Quaker structures. For other Liberal Friends, the Second Coming origins and the consequential theological distinctiveness of the Quaker movement remains foundational.

The issue of membership of the international ecumenical body, the Council of Churches for Britain and Ireland (CCBI), highlights this divide. In the most controversial decision in the last decade of British Quakerism, London Yearly Meeting decided to apply to join under 'Clause 2b' for non-credal churches in 1989 and reaffirmed that membership as Britain Yearly Meeting in 1997. There are numerous causes for concern voiced amongst Friends but work done by Tim and I with a Woodbrooke student group suggests that beneath the plethora of reasons for comfort and discomfort lies an ambiguity towards the Quaker response to the importance placed on the externals of faith (for example the creeds, sacraments, priests, church buildings and Christian calendar), the symbols and reality of their First Coming/meantime focus, by the other churches:

> The basis for membership of CCBI affirms this external expression of faith, an external which along with other externals, such as sacraments, Bible, and separated priesthood, is seen to be central for some other churches.
>
> One Quaker response to this is to say that because externals are irrelevant, the basis is not where our real interest lies; we are concerned to affirm and develop the unity that we have found with other churches in work in the world. The basis is a secondary matter and ways should be found for us to remain in membership and be full participants in the work for the kingdom of God along with the churches.
>
> A second Quaker response is to say that externals are not simply irrelevant but are part of what is contrary to Truth and true unity. While we can joyfully do work in common with those of other churches, we cannot compromise our position on the outward forms of religion - the very forms through which the churches seek their unity - without losing something fundamental to our Quaker witness, a witness that the churches seem to value. (From 'A Contribution from the Woodbrooke Module "Reluctant partners? Quakers and the Churches" to the group reviewing ecumenical experience in Britain Yearly Meeting 1996.')

Ecumenical involvement is a function of Friends having turned the clock back on the Second Coming, as is the possibility of dual membership. Only by moving away from the immediacy and transformation of the Second Coming experience have Friends been able to get so close to believers whose focus is the First Coming. Quaker debates about whether or not to take the bread and wine at ecumenical worship (eg: Jones 1996) highlights how far Quaker inclinations have changed. In the Churches Together in England 'Called to be One' exercise, the Quaker response acknowledged being 'this side of the kingdom'.

Plotting the theological tendencies of different traditions of Friends across 'God's plan for the world' (page 190) is useful as we honestly face up to what kind of religious group we are. Even as the Universalist and Christocentric division is revealed as illusory (*Quaker Faith and Practice* 1995:27.04), there are other typologies.

- Sheeran divides Friends between those who have experienced a gathered Meeting and those who have not (1983).
- I have described Friends in three types according to where they place authority for the shape and work of the Society: corporatists, congregationalists, and individualists (Dandelion 1996b). Corporatists and congregationalists still hold to some kind of collective decision-making and in this could be tied to Sheeran's notion of those Friends who have experienced a gathered Meeting. Individualists may have done so too but place no greater authority in it than their own personal revelation. None of these types appears to have a direct connection to whether or not any Friends maintain a belief in an imminent Second Coming or live in the realised or partially-realised experience of the Kingdom. Corporatists may look back to early Friends for inspiration and authority as they continue to practise gospel order but this is not necessarily the case. Congregationalists may be more interested in the lived tradition and individualists in none, but the evidence for such links as contiguous is slim.
- Similarly, the three Seeker types listed in Chapter 17 do not obviously or easily fit into such an analysis. Rather, they help identify different kinds of reformers. Where are those Friends looking for their visions? Backwards, forwards or solely within a process?
- I have also argued that such is the nature of continuing revelation that there is always a portion of, say, Britain Yearly Meeting, grieving the loss of the former ways and beliefs (Dandelion 1996b). However, the degree of grief felt may be independent of views on the Second Coming.

- The will of God is variously described and defined by Quakers today and may be another measure of diversity. Birgit Felleisen's unpublished work in this area highlights the differences. For some, God has an answer to every question. For others, God only gives broadbrush answers and we are to work out the detail: God is only specific about important matters and leaves us the mundane. For another group, the will of God is to follow a particular process. The answers are not of God, just the method Friends have adopted and maintained. For some, their God is not the kind of God who can have a will, and for atheist Friends 'the will of God' is best thought of as 'the best way forward'. The personal view of what it is Friends are seeking in the silence of business meetings affects the interpretation of the silence and of the outcome. Again, however, it is not dependent on a view of the Second Coming, save for those who deny any possibility of a Divine Other, as the maintenance of the method across three centuries of change highlights. So it is with views of what happens in the silence of unprogrammed worship.

In this way, the Second Coming model does not produce an all-encompassing framework into which all other differences can be accommodated and explained. It does however uproot these typologies and rightly marginalises differences over what can be secular constructions of ecclesiology and the nature of the will of God.

Unfortunately, the model gives an emphasis that is challenging and one which will require change. It seems to me that there is something in Quaker attitudes to their self-definition, in whichever branch of Quakerism, which is protective ('we are not like those other Quakers') and minimalistic. Our spiritual lives can all too easily lack urgency or excitement. Quakers are part of a tradition now, still apart from 'the world' in some ways but comfortably within it in others. The contrast with millennial thinking is stark:

> 'Christ has come to teach his people himself' is not a matter of time-honoured tradition, but a time-shattering crisis in which the future has suddenly cascaded upon our present. It is the

> ultimate 'future-shock' that forces us to make our next step as if it were our last one. For as we are in Christ, we are in the End of the world, the purpose and goal of all creation, the Alpha and the Omega (Gwyn 1981:93).

Whilst all the branches of Friends can lay a partial claim to the legacy and teaching of early Friends, none of them is the sole inheritor of the Second Coming emphasis of the first Friends. Evangelicalism is true to the Valiant Sixty but the message is a different one. Unprogrammed worship may have a direct lineage back to the Westmorland Seekers and early Quakers but the purpose and focus of waiting in the silence has changed. Conservative Friends may be the closest in outward form to early Friends with the combination of unprogrammed worship and an interconnected revelation of Spirit and Scripture, but this tradition too is de-eschatologised, coming as it does out of the Orthodox and Gurneyite parties.

Critically, there is also something in where Friends find themselves on the time-line for God's plan that necessarily informs the way they relate to where other Friends and other Christians are on that same map, as evidenced in the passage above on reactions to ecumenical membership.

❖ ❖ ❖

Towards the end of courses based on this material, I have asked the students where they would put themselves in terms of their understanding of Quakerism and the Second Coming.

I see thirteen options:

A) the model is essentially nonsensical or wrong;

B) the model is sound but that early Friends were wrong (either in their sense of timing or in the misinterpretation of foretaste for Second Coming) and the Second Coming hasn't happened yet;

C) Friends have lost the Second Coming experience and it is not important, either:

i) because being a First Coming Church is equally valid and perhaps more appropriate;

ii) because different kinds of ecclesiology, including the unprogrammed Quaker one, are appropriate in the meantime;

iii) because there will be other apocalyptic moments; or

iv) because Christianity is not important now/because we have new ways of thinking about the world and/or our relationship to God;

D) Friends have lost the Second Coming experience and need to reclaim it in order to retain an authentic and distinctive witness;

E) Friends have lost the Second Coming experience and need to reform the structures in order to retain an authentic and distinctive witness;

F) Friends have maintained a Second Coming experience but it has changed over the centuries; and from that, either:

i) Friends have maintained a Second Coming experience and others could have it too; or

ii) Friends have maintained a Second Coming experience and have it given in trust, as it were, for the future of the whole church;

G) we are not clear about the model but are open to some kind of Second Coming experience even if we don't know what it will be like;

H) none of the above and/or we cannot know for certain;

l) all or combinations of the above and/or we cannot know for certain.

As Friends worldwide may be able to pick one of these options, students distribute themselves among all of the options.

Debates over the nature of endtime and whether there is more than one Second Coming moment differentiate some Friends. Were early Friends wrong in their sense of an unfolding Second Coming or just ahead of their time, their experience mirroring the foretaste Paul and others had experienced centuries before? Was there an eschatological potential which Friends saw and the rest of humanity ignored? Do we, or does God, choose the time of the Second Coming?

Option F) was noticeably the most popular amongst Liberal groupings. This is an option which remodels Scripture in its understanding of what the Second Coming will be like and in itself has no authority with which to support its claims. It is not about trumpets and critical moments of the sudden transformation of the whole of humanity but is a slow-burn Second Coming unfolding through the ages, which Friends are still experiencing, albeit in a less intense way than their predecessors.

Unprogrammed Friends reclaim their heritage in choosing this option. They retain their identity as a Second Coming Church but also an optimism about the present day health of silent-tradition Quakerism. They take the model outlined above without the pessimism of Chapter 17. For these Friends, Quakerism is a Second Coming Church *with* a Second Coming! Most of the Liberal Friends presented with the model outlined in this book have accepted the model and rejected my commentary. This optimistic view of present day Second Coming experienced by Friends but easing itself upon the whole world is caught well in the 1996 epistle of Ohio Yearly Meeting (Conservative). This reads in part:

> As the Jews waited hopefully for a messiah, the carpenter's son came proclaiming the acceptable year of the Lord. To many it was blasphemous, but some believed and set about establishing the kingdom of heaven.
>
> As seventeenth century England was mired in deadly controversy over issues of church doctrine and government, the man in leather breeches [George Fox] came proclaiming that Jesus Christ had come to teach his people himself. To many it was blasphemous, but some believed and set about establishing the Society of Friends.
>
> Today, at a time when the world is in great need of spiritual healing, we again proclaim the acceptable year of the Lord, testify to our experience that Jesus Christ is come to teach us himself, and affirm his promise that when two or three are gathered in his name, Jesus Christ is present in the midst of us. To many this is still blasphemous, but some believe and know the joy God offers everyone.
>
> Come and see what our eyes have seen, hear what our ears have heard, taste what our mouths have tasted. For the Lord is good, and his mercies continue forever. Now is the time to begin anew on this beautiful morning of the Gospel Day. Begin deep down inside, where each of us stands, guard over the gate of change in our hearts. Are we willing to surrender all to receive all? Then we may join together in that great stream of living water. Now it reaches out - to our families, our meetings and churches, our communities and our workplaces until soon old things have passed away and behold, all things are created anew!

The Friends who would claim option F) as best describing their position see the partial reform of the programmed Quaker tradition as surprising and 'full-blown' First Coming churches either as wrong-headed, as in Fi), or in waiting, Fii).

Either option is problematical for ecumenical relations. In Fi), the rest of humanity could equally experience this transforming experience and the bringing of heaven on earth but, presumably, choose not to, or are misled by their institutions into believing they still need the word of God mediated by a priest and into believing that they cannot experience an inward communion now. In other words, the church is impeding the spiritual growth of its members by continuing to promote apostate notions.

In Fii), the church and all other religious paths are validated as fulfilling a function for all those who are not yet experiencing this renewed intimacy with God, an intimacy given to some but not to all. In this scenario, Quakers are as a vanguard for the rest of Christianity, a vanguard of the true church (Parkinson 1996). Similarly:

> The Society has a sense of aspiring to be a particularly 'pure' manifestation of the universal church through its repudiation of creed, liturgy and separated priesthood ('One in the Spirit' as in *Who We Are* 1995:159).

This complex starting point for ecumenical relations, which underlines the idea that some Friends, if Christian, are not Christian in the sense that others claim to be, also problematises relations between different kinds of Friends, both within one branch and between branches, given that Friends find themselves at a whole range of places on the time-line between the First and Second Coming events and even, as suggested in Chapter 17, off the map altogether.

If the Second Coming experience is fundamental to our understanding of our past, present, and future, then this is where Friends need to be dialoguing. This is the issue Friends need to be honest about, even if it is to say that 'the model' (or this Truth) no longer has life for us. In doing this, the old divisions of Liberal and Evangelical and programmed and unprogrammed break down. As with Michael Sheeran's typology of Friends who have and who have not experienced a gathered Meeting (1983), Friends will gather around their experience, not by geography or Yearly Meeting type.

More and more Friends are happy to worship in a programmed Friends' church or an unprogrammed Quaker Meeting. What is important is the authenticity of the worship, the room for some silent waiting and an explicit religiousness. In what has been called a 'centrist' position crossing anachronistic labels, Friends can find a renewed sense of heritage, vision, and experience.

At the very end of the Woodbrooke course, I asked our student group three questions:

a) What have you made of the picture we have been exploring?

b) Is there any part of it you will want to share with your Meeting?

c) What, if any, are the consequences of this course for Friends in general?

Here are some of their answers.

a) What have you made of the picture we have been exploring?

- Fascinating. A model to understand Friends in a new way, to see our history in a wider Christian perspective, and to help understand some of our present divisions and dilemmas .

- I have been interested in the changes which have taken place in Quaker thought and practice consequent to changes in history and customs and in religious thinking. I have been especially interested in the dramatic expectations of early Friends with regard to the Second Coming.

- It continues to fascinate and inspire, providing a way to understand early Friends and why Friends are as they are today. It continues to feel difficult to communicate this vision. Very few people have the time or inclination to 'suspend disbelief' while the whole picture is presented, and yet that is what is required for it to have an impact.

- The possibility of the whole of humankind liberated from sin and reconciled with God and each other can be reduced to a much more limited and personal idea of transformation... [but] this is a different picture and should not be confused with the one we have been looking at.

- End time, God's time and historical time, all new concepts which made the understanding of apocalypse so much easier. Very refreshing; I was able to translate the experience of early Friends into a modern dimension for the first time. It was a revelation!

- ...the 'end time' is not affected or accomplished with our believing it has come, or is going to come, but with what we do in the 'meantime' to fulfil God's purposes. This is the corporate (or cosmic) aspect of the individual's story. We tend to think that we wait for time but in fact it is time, God's time, that waits for us. We say 'the time has not yet come' but in God's view, as it were, it is we who have not come to the time. Coming from a certain Christian belief system, the dead also await the 'Second Coming' when they will experience with the living the final resurrection and the transfiguration of all things. Those who are fully alive, ie. come to full union with God, in this life are already *there*, already at the moment they die while those who are not at one with God wait like us. The saints have to wait for everyone else. The Christ (like the Bodhisattva) though at one with God is both at the end of time, there, and also with us now during his atoning work while we catch up, as it were. So the end-time is not a matter of waiting only or belief or even realising it in our individual lives or partial corporate manifestations (though it might include those) but a time for working through and accomplishing the work of reconciliation which must be done to bring the whole world to at-onement: the end of time accomplished by humankind in and with Christ. Christ cannot come again (without violence towards his people) unless all of us are together - with Him.

- Since coming to Friends I have not given more than a passing thought to a future Second Coming. I have believed with early Friends that 'Christ *has* come', but have not discussed some kind of end to time as we know it.

  Thus the picture we have been exploring has been of great interest to me, and has given me a new understanding of where Friends once were and now are and why. I shall read Paul with renewed interest, and, I hope, new insight.

  However, I am not prepared to consign the return to Paradise (through the flaming sword) completely to the future and accept an interim time, in which aids to guidance from God and outward means to express experience are validated because it is a time of waiting. If we believe in the unmediated Word of God, we must live and worship in expectancy that it will change us, set us free from sin, guide and order us. How the end comes, I am prepared to leave it in the hands of God.

- I do think that Fox's sense of the Second Coming - God appearing in individual hearts and minds where the 'Inner Light' was seen and acted upon - already happening, has much truth in it. But it is difficult to see how the later falling away of Quakers from understanding and acting on this, could have been avoided in the face of all the punishment and long imprisonments that they were having to endure. We are nowadays a 'sect' in the whole Christian church, no longer raising our voices to condemn the Church for outmoded practices, special times for worship, special people trained to act as intermediaries between other people's souls and God, but agreeing with these practices to help keep the Church's faith going *until* the Second Coming (Some Quakers - my father was one - still believe that the Kingdom of God *has* arrived, and can go on arriving, little by little, but most agree with other Christians that it is yet to come.)

b) Is there any part of it you will want to share with your Meeting?

- I want the whole of the Quaker world to engage with this model and to renew its understanding of itself.

- I believe all our Meetings should be faced with some of the questions we have had before us these last three weeks. I hope we can take Tim's knot with us and feel all we have learnt is valuable and belongs together even if we can only use parts of it at any one time.

- I will continue to share this thinking as part of my teaching at Woodbrooke. Despite the difficulties of presenting it adequately, it does communicate something with life in it. At the least, it throws light on the biblical picture in a way which at the same time confirms Quaker faith and practice.

c) What, if any, are the consequences of this course for Friends in general?

- It has the potential for spiritual renewal, to a revived sense of purpose and meaning, to a vivid way of exploring Quaker ecumenicism. Equally it may underpin an explicit reinvention of ourselves out of this picture, which would also be healthy in its engagement with the concepts, and for its honesty.

- The consequences for Friends are enormous... I think it is important to keep telling the story of Quakerism and keep trying to find ourselves in it - ie. to find ourselves in the picture. We are a 'community of memory'. 'Tradition is democracy extended through time.' Yes, we are free to rewrite *Faith and Practice*, but are we *willing* to listen to our tradition? It has been the failing of Liberal Quakerism that 'pure experience' has no ideological presupposition and framing, and that openness to the *future* is about living totally *in the present*. But the *past* plays a role too - the more *conscious* and *intentional* we can be in relation to the past, the more *free* we can be in the *present* and for the *future*.

- We may not now be able to say what the consequences will be for Friends but this material could give help to being sure we are clear about our origins and to connect them with the future. It may also help to make us less fearful when words like God, Christ, or Jesus are used and the essence is carried forward into the future even if the words used (or not used) have changed.

- It provides fresh support for distinctive Quaker faith and practice: it strengthens an understanding of Spirit which combines the individual and the corporate; it affirms a commitment to and confidence in the Quaker Business Method; it encourages honest and faithful ministry which is not afraid of the uncomfortable word.

- The most important consequences of this course are that it shows the strength of our roots in the primacy of direct revelation from God focused through the lens of our understanding of Paul and of George Fox. Both of them point to Christ as the source of the spirit that guides us and the source of the teaching that helps us understand our experience.

✣ ✣ ✣

I list these not to blow a trumpet but to emphasise how I have seen the material affect a group of Friends who engaged with it over a three week period. Not all the comments were positive; one Friend commented:

> I cannot think of any quantifiable benefit which Friends in general could derive from this particular course.

However, I continue to feel, not only that it was not an accident that Tim, Doug, and I found ourselves teaching this course together, but that the life it has given me may have wider consequences for Friends in general. Quakers may feel they do not need renewal but I believe this can and needs to be a key component in a revitalisation of Quaker faith.

It is a complex picture and a controversial one. Readers will disagree with the view of Paul, of George Fox and the early Friends, and of the analysis of the succeeding three centuries. It is also a picture which places Quakerism firmly within Christianity and that will be problematical for some (although some Liberal Friends are able to conceptualise a Second Coming in its inward form without threatening their universalism). As you can see from the above responses, not all the students were of one mind. All the options can be compelling. (Amillennialism, for example, may make Christian-Jewish relations more straightforward.) However Friends find it, though, it is a picture Friends need to explore further.

Why Quaker history now needs revisiting

Lewis Benson (1961), Mervyn Endy (1981) and Thomas Hamm (1994) have been amongst those historiographers who have laid bare some of the prevailing agendas of previous Quaker historians. As Quakers themselves, their own histories may not be without prejudice. This book looks at Quaker history in a new way, that is through the lens of Second Coming thinking, a way which we believe is critically important to a more appropriate understanding of Quakerism. It is also possible, within the model presented here, to locate most Quaker ideas and theologies somewhere on the time-line between First Coming and Second Coming (see the figure on p. 190.) Thus, in our schema, each history of Friends has its own relationship to a particular point in the story of the separation and fusion of the mythic and the mundane.

In this sense, all earlier Quaker history needs revisiting to see where it relates to the model presented here. This model aside, the Seeker typology described in various places in the book (see the box on Seekers A and B on page 97, and the box on Seeker C on page 188 undermines those accounts of Quakerism which see early Quaker thought as homogeneous (if contradictory) and changes in the nature of Quaker theology as devoid of other shifts (for example the shift between seeker positions such a change in theology may reflect).

The anti-Judaism of Christian models

The model we describe here is problematical in relation to its treatment of Judaism. Whilst Christian culture talks easily about a Judeo-Christian tradition, it can also be seen as a political fiction: a) for Jews, the 'tradition' is Judaic, not Judeo-Christian - Christianity is an off-shoot, not a development, b) Christianity can use this sense of evolution to mask an anti-Judaism innate in Christian supercessionary teachings and centuries of anti-semitism.

We are extremely uncomfortable with this but need to acknowledge that anti-Judaism is part of this model. What we do with the model is another matter. We are aware how this model takes faith/life *beyond* Christianity (albeit in Christian terms), and also how other faiths have their own models for the fulfilment of humanity's purposes. We are also aware that the rejection of the Christian triumphalism of this model by some Friends facilitates a more mutual approach to Christian-Jewish relationships. Similarly, for those Friends who take the Second Coming model *without* the preceding chronology, or source teaching, talk of 'tradition' is less compelling and therefore less problematical.

Epilogues

Ben Pink Dandelion

One year on from the end of the course which began this book, what do I have to say now?

I have been living with this model for some eighteen months now. It is no longer an option, as I said at the end of Chapter 18. It informs my view of Quaker history, of the Quaker place in the ecumenical world, and my sociological work on the extent to which different branches of Quakerism are sectarian or denominational. I have taught the material in Britain and in two American Quaker colleges and even run an outreach day using the Second Coming as its basis. By all accounts and through my own experience, I am convinced that it is an essential lens with which to view three and a half centuries of Quaker experience.

Personally, I continue to straddle (at least) two worlds (see Chapter 18). The fantastical and explicitly Christian nature of the model challenges me and pushes me close to flipping back to my adolescent atheism. Only by reclaiming a theocentricism do I avoid the possible consequences of returning to atheism such a challenge promotes.

In that sense, I am amongst the group of Liberal Friends who fall off the chart on page 190. I have realised that I am a Liberal Friend in other ways too: in my view that theology is constructed rather than true; in my view that such construction is partial and provisional, and that, in turn, that I am a seeker too, possibly even a Seeker C, preferring the journey to the destination and clear that any statement can only be a 'perhaps' one.

In a recent book chapter entitled 'The Absolute Perhaps' (Dandelion 1998), I locate the boundary of Liberal Quaker belief around the issue of certainty. I argue that it is certainty, and claimed truth of theological statements, which presents Liberal Friends with the greatest difficulty. Theology can only be partial, provisional, and personal. If there is an absolute in Liberal Quakerism, it is this absolute perhapsness that bounds belief. Indeed I would now go so far as to argue that this is a defining characteristic of a Liberal Friend. Liberal Friends are those unprogrammed Quakers who do not believe theology is wholly and completely true. Other unprogrammed Friends, or those 'Centrist' Friends happy in unprogrammed worship as well as programmed, may hold a different view and I would then hesitate to call them Liberal.

In this sense, Liberal Friends will not be able to accept the certainty of the model presented in this book even if they were open to its intrinsic Christianity. They have no choice but to perhaps-ualise the model and its premises. Christian Friends who feel they are eldered because of their Christianity may well ask themselves if it was not rather for their certainty that they were censored. Non-Liberal Friends may be able not only to work with the model in a way not open to their Liberal counterparts but to believe it in a way that Liberals could never do, however far their sympathies may rest with the material.

This insight and clarity has ironically led me to greater sympathy with Liberal Quakerism. I can now see what it would take, ie. theological certainty, for me to be thrown out of the group and I can lose my Groucho-Marxian frustration about being part of a club which would have me as a member.

However, the certainty about the, perhaps, which forms the boundaries is also only a 'perhaps' for me as I operate a meta-perhapsness, even about this Liberal truth claim. Certainty *and* its critics are all potentially only 'towards', in that the game operates for all religious truth claims which cannot be verified or falsified. I live in a world of religious perhapsness, accommodated and validated and observed by my rationalist sociological method in which the meaninglessness of religious truth claims can only be taken as optimistic expressions of agnosticism at best. Accidentally but truthfully, when asked if I was then a follower of 'the absolute perhaps', I answered '*Probably*, yes.'

Asked about the Second Coming, I herald its interpretative importance above its theological truth. Liberal Friends, however distant their relationship to the material and to believing in it, need to know their Quakerism through this lens. The model, whether metaphor or reality (see 'Excursus'), remains vital in both the senses of that word.

Douglas Gwyn

Really now, do the apocalyptic spirituality and prophetic witness of early Friends have anything to do with us today? As I suggested in Chapter 12, speaking from my own experience, there are some compelling parallels between England in the 1640s and the United States in the 1960s. The wide-open, earth-shaking sense of the counter-culture was definitely moving through many American Friends meetings in the latter sixties and early seventies. I gather that similar currents animated British Quakerism during the same period. But even in the wild and woolly United States, things have cooled down a lot since then.

The sixties were apocalyptic times when deep, tectonic shifts in the culture were afoot and a sense of utopian possibility abounded. But these days, after the long cold shower of the Thatcher-Reagan era, certainly have a *post-apocalyptic* feel. Films like *Blade-Runner* have helped define that sensibility for us. Posed in futuristic situations, such films nevertheless portray a context much like our own: masses of people captivated by the vast corporate and military forces that have emerged victorious over the fitful eruptions of counter-cultural insurgency, foreclosing the future within a seamless, almost timeless present.

This is the cultural experience often labelled *postmodern*. The modern era, with its giant strides of scientific and technological advancement, its sense of history as inevitable progress, and its confident, heroic valorisation of the New, came to its *dénouement* in the 1960s, as the full impact of the Bomb and the ecological degradation of global industrialisation deconstructed our confidence in scientific progress. As we began to enter a global economy through multinational capitalism, we reached a moment in which the New was everywhere. In a moment of stunning dialectical reversal, the New disappeared. Everywhere victorious, it has become a static reality. In this situation, the *temporal* is eclipsed and the *spatial* becomes the dominant mode of sensibility. Thus, *multiculturalism*, the effort to come to terms with the vast map of human identities and differences, becomes our new political logic, the noncompetitive 'new game' of interplay upon the wall-to-wall carpet of our multinational capitalist world. (For a larger development of this cultural situation, see the 'Conclusion' to Gwyn 1995.)

Well, we may not like the carpet of multinational capitalism, but it is hard to change it while we are standing on it and there seems to be no other place left to stand. Setting fire to it seems ill-advised. In this situation, multiculturalism seems like an impotent parlour game much of the time. The celebration of our diversity feels like a glib and hollow exercise as we watch the wheels of economic and political power continue to grind notwithstanding. But as these movements mature, they may be transformed in their meaning and potential.

Our cultural situation may be dissimilar to that of the earliest Friends, and seemingly unsuited to their apocalyptic faith, but it has strong affinities to the Greco-Roman cultural world of the Apostle Paul. In that situation, the Roman Empire circumscribed the entire Mediterranean world and beyond. And while considerable military and political power still centred in Rome, the Empire was rapidly decentralising economically, turning a number of cities around the Mediterranean into bustling hubs of trade and multicultural interchange. Ethnic groups, cultures and religions had never before been so intermixed. Greco-Roman culture was a religiously seeking culture *par excellence*. Endless combinations of syncretistic, mix-and-match religion grew in that situation. Much of it was at least diverting, and some of it was personally transformative, but rarely did syncretistic religion pose any serious challenge to the dominant paradigm of Roman power.

Amid that garish pastiche of religious plaids, stripes and polka-dots emerged the early Christian movement. At first glance, it looked like one more mutation on the religious market: an ethnic religion from an obscure corner of the Empire (Judaism) dressed up in some Stoic and other popular Greek ideas, appealing to some Diaspora Jews and other assorted individuals, often cultural misfits of one kind or another. (For more information on the social profile of the earliest Christians, see Meeks 1983.) The movement spread rapidly, particularly in the growing commercial centres of the Eastern Mediterranean.

The rough-and-ready mixture of people from various ethnic, religious and class backgrounds made the Christian movement seem even a bit more cheaply synthetic than most new religions, a tad more polyester in feel, we might say. That made Christianity all the more odious to the cultural elites of the Empire. But this was not simply another mix-and-match spirituality, a synthetic religion; it was *a synthesis of faith.* It was more than Jews and Greeks, men and women, slaves and masters learning how to be nice to each other and eat at the same table. It was these same people becoming *something profoundly new together in Christ.* The synthesis did not emerge from the sum total of their parts. It was something that came to them from the future, redefining the meaning of their differences. It was the Presence of the Risen Lord, the Crucified Messiah, the radical Other, who relativised all their differences, who transfigured all their identities into a new way of being. People didn't enter this new reality alone. They became the body of Christ together, with all their differences intact. Yet their identities and differences were recontextualised in the light of Christ. (See my reflections on Paul's apocalyptic consciousness in the 'Excursus' of this book.

As Friends today, we find ourselves cheek-by-jowl with many others: Christians, Jews, Muslims, Hindus, Buddhists as well as various proliferating new religions. It is vitally important that we come to terms with our many forms of otherness. Interfaith, ecumenical, multicultural and other cross-group dialogues are not only unavoidable but crucially important. But these efforts are only *preparatory*, I believe. Moving among all the others we must come to know, and from whom we must learn, there is a radical Other. Lurking among all the identities and differences, there is One who has identified to the death with us, yet whose true, transcendent identity is more alien than anything we can encounter on the human plane. This One emerges among the many. This unmapped Identity crops up in the awkward gap between us, an embarrassing and abiding lump under the wall-to-wall carpet. By all means, let universal understanding, tolerance and collaboration proceed apace. But the truly transformative experiences and politics will occur at the limits of our understanding, the failures of our tolerance and defeats of our collaborative efforts. In the postmodern situation, the truly New will be rediscovered in the radical Other. The apocalyptic/revelatory New, which is 'the same yesterday, today and forever' (Heb 13:8) will emerge not as we run hither and thither, proclaiming 'lo, here', and 'lo, there' (Mk 13:21), but as we 'stand still in the light that shows you where you are' (Fox 1831:7:20).

The *Book of Revelation* spoke to the situation of the church at the end of the first century, when Roman persecutions were becoming more systematic and vicious. Though its dense thicket of symbolism and monstrous apparitions is off-putting to many today, Revelation is a powerful document of political resistance. It poses an early Christian community in solidarity with the many oppressed and captivated peoples of the Roman Empire. Its visions are a set of static tableaux, portraying the Caesar establishment as an increasingly demonic power enslaving the earth. The Christian community, moving into escalating conflict with the cult of Caesar worship, has become the vanguard of resistance on behalf of the many peoples of the Empire. Though the *Book of Revelation* is ostensibly about the end of the world, its successive visions are less a time-line for Armageddon than a series of schematic portrayals that lay bare the fundamental contradiction, the lethal conflict at work below the surface of daily life.

Early Friends forged a compelling interpretation of the Book of Revelation as they saw themselves locked in a seventeenth-century instalment of the same fundamental conflict: between the Lamb of God and the demonic forces of a coercive state church. The Quaker movement was a gathering of the Lamb's followers, resisting the power of the Dragon, Antichrist and Babylon. This 'Lamb's War' campaign found them moving all over England, challenging the State-church alliance parish by parish. But as much as they moved all over the countryside, they were paradoxically standing still all the time, holding their ground on 'spiritual Mount Sion' against the onslaught of persecuting clergy, constables and magistrates. Wherever Friends received Christ in his return 'to teach his people himself', and were gathered together under him, they saw Babylon falling and an unjust world ending. (For a larger treatment of the early Quaker Lamb's War and Fox's interpretation of *Revelation*, see Gwyn 1986:179-207.)

In our times, we modern Friends are finding ourselves in solidarity with the peoples of the earth, facing another instalment of the same ancient conflict. We confront systemic powers of exploitation, violence and environmental degradation that deny and oppress the peaceful community of God's creatures. Is there a place where we can gather together, where we can see the powers for what they are and stand still for the timeless truth of God's *shalom* on earth? I can only conclude by repeating the closing words of John on the island of Patmos: 'Amen. Come, Lord Jesus!' (Rev 22:20).

Timothy Peat

> Without an understanding of the Christian tradition, there is a whole depth of understanding missing from Quakerism.

This was the note on which my personal chapter, 'Face to faith: tied up in knots', ended. There I said that I need to be in touch with those roots in order fully to appreciate Quakerism. What has been offered in the first part of this book is a fresh interpretation of those Christian roots, in particular, a new understanding of the Second Coming. Emphasis is given to this aspect of the Christian tradition that in much Christian dialogue recedes into the background. But taking seriously the doctrine of the Second Coming makes possible an important shift in understanding: it points to the incompleteness of present Christian life and practice. As such, it is an antidote to a simplistic exclusivity that can be attached to the Christian gospel. To acknowledge that the Christian story is still awaiting its final and most important scene is to guard against a triumphalist Christian message which finds no room for God's work outside traditional Christianity. In Rosemary Radford Ruether's influential work, *Faith and Fratricide* (Ruether 1974), she argues that when claims are made by Christians that what is hoped for at the Second Coming is already a present reality this has catastrophic consequences:

> The ultimate eschatological event, the ultimate 'coming' of the Messiah, must still signify that final future when 'every tear will be wiped away.' *This clearly has not taken place,* nor has Christianity appropriated its message in a way that has been a very convincing means to this 'end'. *The attribution of an absolute finality to the heightened expectations surrounding*

> *the life and death of Jesus must be regarded as a flawed way of appropriating the real meaning of eschatological encounter.* This historicizing of the eschatological has most serious consequences. Both Christian anti-Semitism and the patterns of totalitarianism and imperialism that have appeared in Christendom (and its secular revolutionary stepchildren) find their root in this error (Ruether 1974:248) [italics added].

Making teaching about the Second Coming more central may illuminate Quaker history; what Ruether suggests is that it may do much more than that: it may bring to the Christian community a sense of humility in relation to its claims with a consequent openness to change and to signs of God's work outside traditional Christianity. The consistent Jewish refusal to countenance Christian claims that the messianic age has come while suffering and misery prevail can be a constant check on Christians making absolute claims about the present reality of truth and salvation (Ruether 1974:20).

Given this possibility that a reappraisal of the Second Coming may be significant for understanding Quakerism and have significance for the wider Christian world, what is also offered in this book is a fresh look at what kind of event the Second Coming might be. The fresh interpretation proposes that Paul's view of the Second Coming of Christ was not of an individual returning but of an incarnation of God in all humanity. This, on the one hand, may be more accessible to us now because it does not depend upon a kind of magical return of Jesus. On the other, faced with the state of the world, it seems an impossibly idealistic picture. One thing that helps to make it conceivable is the glimpse of this kind of possibility being realised in the lives of the early Friends. Their claim that among them there was no sin, no separation from God, has been given serious weight in this work. It has been suggested that among them this possibility of a human community in which God was incarnate was realised, if only for a short time. Reflecting on the experience of the early Friends at the end of *Apocalypse of the Word*, Doug Gwyn makes this observation:

> Just as Christ is incarnated within the individual in the raising of the seed (the new will in that person) the gospel gathers individuals into a unity of common experience, understanding, and obedience which corporately incarnates Christ... History, as the vast realm of human activity carried out by men and women in alienation from God and from one another, is *ended* as they hear and obey the voice of Christ, who reconciles them to God and to one another (Gwyn 1986:209).

Although the expectation they had that their shared experience would spread rapidly to all was not fulfilled, in considering the early days of Friends, there is a glimpse of the corporate incarnation of God conceived of by Paul.

It should be acknowledged that making the Second Coming a central issue evokes an obvious criticism. Is this not a teaching which is necessarily disempowering? If humanity has to wait upon God to act to bring about a radical transformation in human kind what is the point of any effort for social change? My own appreciation of this doctrine takes me in a different direction. The challenge it gives me is one which every Quaker is called to meet each time she or he sits in Meeting for Worship. The understanding that God may speak in the Meeting for Worship involves a focused and faithful waiting, a vital part of which is a letting go of personal effort to say something clever or appropriate. This may give an indication of what taking the Second Coming seriously points us to now. It *is* personally disempowering, but only in the sense that it is through letting go of our own power that the power of God can be released in us to bring real change. Mike Nellis was Joseph Rowntree Fellow in 1997 and used the year to travel round Meetings with the aim of revitalising Penal Reform as a concern among Friends. As the fellowship year proceeded he found himself drawn to the works of Meister Eckhart.

Before quoting from Eckhart he describes his sense of alienation in the midst of his normal working life:

> I, like others around me, was becoming a minion in a bureaucracy, the servant of an alien purpose, stifled, corroded, deadened. Authenticity and even honesty were being progressively disparaged. Such a climate is anathema to spiritual growth, and I have found Eckhart, with whom I finally began to get to grips last year, most useful in understanding the dangers of such external pressure, and the nature of the malaise they engender: 'In the just, nothing shall work but God alone. For if it happens that anything outside impels you to work, then the works are certainly dead. Even if God were to impel you to work from outside, such works would be dead. For if your works are to live, God must move you in the inner most of the soul, if they are really to live, and there is your life and there you live' (Eckhart) (Nellis 1998:3).

'Nothing shall work except God alone.' This is a description of how things will be according to Paul's description of the Second Coming; it describes too the sense that empowered the early Friends who believed the Second Coming was happening among them. It is truly outside our power to effect a transformation for all, but we can give ourselves to a focused and faithful waiting upon God, with a readiness to act decisively when called, not just in Meeting but in every effort for social change.

> Beware, keep alert; for you do not know when the time will come (Mk 13:33).

Excursus
Biblical understandings of time, history, and the end

Douglas Gwyn

Even to *speak* of the end of the world *is* the end of the world. Just *raising the subject* of Christ's return is to imply that he *indeed was raised* from the dead. There is an unsettling effect when one utilises these biblical categories of thought. It jars the predominant worldview, our modern, scientific understanding of the cosmos and of time. Thus, speaking of the end of the world threatens to end the 'world' we have constructed together, to subvert the sense of reality that 'makes the world go around'. It becomes important, therefore, that we explore the biblical worldview that undergirds concepts like the end of the world and the return of Christ. How did the ancient Hebrew mind contemplate time, history and ending? What was the particular sense of ending that emerged in the apocalyptic preaching of Jesus and Paul? The answers we find to these questions will provide the framework for understanding the earth-shaking power of early Quaker witness.

Every worldview defines ultimate reality in some way. What is the 'big picture' of our existence? Every worldview also defines the intimate realm by which the individual may know what is ultimate. How do we know the truth? To put it another way, there is some objective reality and some subjective way of living, knowing, and acting within that objective world, however imperfectly. In visual terms, we could say that a worldview poses a cosmic, or universal, *frame* of reference. That frame is viewed from a certain *point* of reference. A certain viewpoint frames reality. At the same time, once established, a certain frame of reality imposes a given viewpoint. These two components of any worldview thus interact and define each other.

Metaphysics, for example, frames reality in terms of *being*, of the first principles that underpin existence. One's individual being, or spirit, is one's point of reference for knowing the universe. By contrast, the biblical worldview unfolds in terms of *time* rather than being. In other words, reality is revealed in terms of temporality. The Bible offers a metahistorical sense of reality, rather than a metaphysical one. It deals with the divine dimension that includes but also transcends history as we know it, just as metaphysics deals with the ground of being, undergirding particular beings as we know them. In the biblical worldview, there are divine undercurrents underpinning human events, no matter how obliquely. The events or experiences of one's life are a key to understanding what God is doing in the larger realms of history. All reality is historical, from the most intimately personal to the ultimate realms of human social, political, cultural and biological development. Even Genesis 1, though certainly poetic and prescientific, offers a boldly developmental model of cosmological origins.

Thus, in the biblical worldview, the largest frame of reference spans the origin and destiny of the cosmos, including everything in between. The intimate point of reference is the individual spiritual journey, one's relationship with God through time. God's *faithfulness* becomes a key term; it is the steadfast, reliable, benign work of God amid the vast, confusing stream of circumstances, both personal and cosmic. So one's relationship with God is comprised of some complementary form of human faithfulness, played out in the concrete circumstances one faces.

But between the ultimate frame of reference (the totality) and the intimate point of reference (the particular) is posed a key mediating term, the community of faith, the historic people (or peoples) of God.

This corporate entity of people discerning and enacting God's purposes together brings individual spiritual experience into the social realm. The faithful community not only helps sharpen individual faithfulness to God's purposes by nurturing personal faith; it also poses a model of faithful community to the larger human society, which is generally estranged from understanding or following God. In a world where such alienation leads to widespread violence, oppression, and exploitation, the faithful community must demonstrate an alternative model; it must stand as a city set upon a hill, a light to the world. It is this vocation, not any claim to favoured status, that underlies any true understanding of a people chosen by God.

The defining quality of God's people is *covenant*, a lived relationship of faithfulness and loving-kindness that plays out in all directions – toward God, toward community members, toward strangers and toward all God's creation. Covenantal faithfulness is a dialogical, accountable relationship with God and all God's creatures. In the concreteness of actual circumstances and over time, covenantal faith generates within a community particular definitions, shared understandings of who God is and what God's will requires in lived situations. That means that every covenantal understanding is time-bound according to the historic situations of its faithful community. Thus, while covenant in the purest sense is lived relationship itself, it comes to expression over time through particular doctrines and behavioural codes. These explicitly defined understandings are absolutely necessary to any sustained attempt to live faithfully with one another. At the same time, however, the same definitions tend to become rigidly doctrinaire and legalistic. As circumstances change, the community of faith struggles to adapt old definitions to new situations. Sometimes that struggle is successful, sometimes it is not.

To put it another way, covenant incarnates the living Word, it embodies the transcendent, timeless Word of God in concrete situations of time and place. If it didn't 'come down to earth', it would hover vaguely in the air. But as it comes to earth somewhere in particular, through concrete acts of faithfulness, it will be limited by its time and place. Just as Christ was embodied as a certain human being with certain characteristics in a particular time and place, so covenantal communities must embody the historical circumstances from which they emerge. We might imagine our ideal Christ to believe in, or we might imagine our ideal faith community to believe in, or mate to marry. But by entering into the particularity of who Jesus was, or the actual tradition a faith community upholds, or the uniqueness that a particular love offers, we engage in a real faith. And through that engagement, a real history unfolds; not merely names and dates, but a saga of struggle and transformation. Over time, God's active purposes in the world generate multiple covenants, multiple communities of faith, multiple realms and seasons of faithful action in the world. Each in its own way struggles to be faithful in its own circumstances. Ultimately, each faith tradition is a unique actor in the universal drama of faith. Unfortunately, these different actors do not always recognise one another's faithfulness in the overall drama. Thus, participants in churches, synagogues, ashrams and sanghas are seldom able to see beyond the idiomatic truth of their own faiths to recognise the complementary quality of one another's traditions.

The beginnings of Israelite historical consciousness

The Bible's distinctly temporal worldview has its deepest foundation in Israel's experience of liberation from slavery in Egypt. In that event, a people encountered a strange god who was not a force of nature or the patron deity of a national state. This god (or perhaps more accurately, antigod), *Yahweh*, was revealed through *a sequence of events* experienced by Hebrew slaves. Yahweh's name encoded a temporal understanding of God: the Hebrew behind 'I am that I am', just as easily translates 'I will be as I will be'. Yahweh called Moses to be a prophetic interpreter of events and a mediator of divine will, both to the Hebrew people and to Pharaoh. The slaves were called to follow Moses out of bondage, while Pharaoh was commanded to 'let my people go'.

Through the drama of the Exodus, a new sense of reality began to unfold. This new Hebrew faith never discounted the universalist, pre-philosophical 'wisdom' tradition of the ancient Near East. Israel remained with one foot planted in that view of reality, where careful observation and reflection upon natural and social phenomena could lead individuals and societies into divine harmony. But intertwined with and extending beyond that standard ancient outlook was a belief that the most crucial reality was not something observed but *revealed*. God spoke and things happened. God enlisted human cooperation, especially on the part of Israel, a people chosen and set apart to demonstrate divine harmony in the world. But God would ultimately find a way to work out divine purpose in the cosmos either with or without Israel. The role of the prophetic mediator began with Moses and extended through Israel's subsequent history. Because covenant is a dialogical relationship, the Hebrew prophets not only communicated God's word to the people; the people's concerns and welfare were also presented through the prophets' intercession before God.

Over the course of the Exodus, the wilderness years, the deliverance into Canaan, the Tribal period, and the rise of Israelite monarchy, a *narrative understanding* developed, defining who God was, what God did, and what kind of society God willed. This was a vast interpretive enterprise, spanning centuries, engaging the entire community of faith, but facilitated by the prophetic mediators of Israel's covenant with Yahweh. Each new circumstance demanded fresh prophetic discernment of God's will. It also added layers of interpretation to the meaning of the past. And on occasion, it even projected forward into prophetic oracles of future divine action. But the Hebrew prophetic vocation always centred on the present situation of God's people in their concrete spiritual, social, and political circumstances.

The Day of the Lord

The 'Day of the Lord' is a crucial term to understand here. The term probably goes back to the tribal period, when Israel's peasant army attacked Canaanite strongholds or responded to invasions by Canaanite or Philistine forces. In Hebrew usage, the 'Day of the Lord' conveyed a sense of crisis, a decisive event that tested the people's faith and demonstrated God's power on their behalf. It was a 'Judgment Day' when God decided against the aggressor, the exploiter, and for the oppressed, the victimised.

But in later years, after the Davidic monarchy established national security and prosperity through institutionalised militarism, the 'Day of the Lord' was relegated to liturgical observations, relating to the steady-state cycles of time. It was associated with the New Year's celebration, when autumnal rains signalled that Yahweh was recreating life, ensuring a new cycle of fertility. During the New Year festival, prophets employed by the royal court and the temple priesthood also prophesied the Day of the Lord as a time when Yahweh would deal vengefully with hostile nations and redouble Israel's national fortunes. Thus, the alien Yahweh was 'naturalised' as a guarantor of fertility, and 'nationalised' as tool of Israelite foreign policy.

The *Book of Amos* records a decisive moment when that inversion of liberationist history was confronted. By the mid eighth century BCE, the royal-military-cultic establishment had exploited Israel's peasantry to such an extent that serious socio-economic polarisation was everywhere evident. Sometime during that period, an obscure prophet from Judah made an appearance at a New Year's celebration in Samaria. Amos began with the usual divine invectives against Israel's neighbours, promising divine retribution for their ruthless violence and oppression. But then he turned the same divine plumbline of justice against Judah and Israel, prophesying divine punishment and the national disenfranchisement of both Hebrew states (see Amos 1-2). Thus, Amos 'liberated' Yahweh from the national interests of Israel. He also posed a new universalism in Israel's sense of divine history: what was just for Israel's neighbours was just for Israel. Chosenness must not be reduced to 'most favoured nation' status, but must serve God's purposes of just and peaceful relations among all peoples.

The painful riddle of history

Over succeeding centuries, as first Israel in the north and then Judah in the south fell to foreign conquests, the biblical sense of history became increasingly painful and problematical. Acting as God's representatives, the prophets had brought covenantal lawsuit against Israel, a charge of 'bad faith', citing systematic breaches of God's demands for social justice and cultic purity. In that light, the reversal of Israel's *national* fortunes could be accepted as just. But where did that leave the *people* of Israel? Where did that leave God's *purposes* in the world? After some fifty years of captivity in Babylon, the Jewish exiles were allowed by the new Persian overlords to return to Canaan/Palestine. But not only did they lack their former autonomy; they also struggled to rebuild Jerusalem and to defend themselves against hostile neighbours.

So the post-exilic period only deepened the ambiguities of history. Heaven and earth seemed much further apart than during the classical period of prophecy, during Israel's national life. The Yahweh that had liberated Israel from Egypt and delivered them into the Promised Land, even the Yahweh that threatened Israel with judgment, seemed far off now. The *mythic* realm of Yahweh, holding court in heaven and issuing divine decrees over human events, seemed hopelessly distant from the *mundane* realm where a long succession of imperial overlords determined the fortunes of a small, weak Jewish people in Palestine (see Hanson 1975).

Over time, this situation encouraged the influence of Persian dualism in Jewish thought. Strong separations of good and evil, light and darkness accompanied the widening gulf between mythic beliefs and mundane realities. A pessimistic outlook overcame late Old Testament prophecy. The entire realm of social and political relations was viewed as irreparable. Only radical intervention by God would redeem the world. But as pessimistic as the worldview became, the grandeur of future salvation also expanded. God's future liberation would redeem not only Israel but all peoples, even the creation itself. Thus, the universalistic, even cosmic overtones of history continued to grow during those discouraging times.

The apocalyptic outlook

Here we witness the advent of the *apocalyptic* literature in some late Old Testament texts: the late chapters of Isaiah and the books of Zechariah and Daniel. Apocalyptic literature deals in cataclysmic images of destruction and transformation, final reckonings between cosmic good and evil, the restoration of social harmony and natural goodness. It utilises highly mythic, dream-like symbolisms, far removed from the engaged politics of Israel's classical prophets. The unfathomable distance between the golden future and the tawdry present matches the cosmological gap between the heavenly realm of myth and the earthly plane of the mundane. History has become so problematical that the apocalyptic prophet or seer often must have visions given or interpreted through a mediating angel. Sometimes the meaning of history is locked in a sealed scroll. At other times, the meaning is spoken, but only in the form of oblique riddles, parables, allegories, and dreams.

When it moves into bizarre, disjointed visions of terrible monsters and mass destruction, the apocalyptic literature of the Bible is off-putting to many. But it is crucial to the on-going development of biblical metahistory. With apocalyptic literature, the biblical sense of history becomes truly universal, embracing all humanity and all creation. Despite its alienation from lived circumstances, the apocalyptic outlook provides the basis for the later ministries of Jesus and Paul, as well as the early Quaker movement.

The New Testament

John the Baptist and Jesus entered the scene of biblical history after four centuries of discouraging times for the Jewish people. Palestine had been subjected to wave after wave of foreign domination (represented as four beasts in Daniel 7), the Roman occupation proving to be the most systematic and ruinous over time. Into this deteriorating situation came John the Baptist preaching repentance, the imminent coming of the Messiah, the advent of the kingdom (realm or community) of heaven. He prophesied not sweet relief but a coming crisis, a baptism of fire. He invited his fellow Jews to be baptised as converts to a new Israel worthy of the Messiah. Thus, his baptism in the Jordan River was not only a cultic washing from moral sin and the taint of Gentile occupation; it was also a rite of initiation into an imminent new age.

Jesus of Nazareth continued several of John's themes, particularly that of radical repentance. But a definite shift of emphasis was quickly evident. Whereas John preached the *imminence* of the kingdom, Jesus proclaimed its sudden, subtle *presence* within and among his hearers. Both prophets preached in apocalyptic terms: dire warnings of coming crisis, and harsh rebukes to those who rejected or doubted the message. However illiberal their words may sound to us today, there was political realism behind their rhetoric: the Jewish people were on a collision course with the Roman occupation; God might be merciful, but the Romans would be ruthless.

But most of all, Jesus' ministry was apocalyptic in the basic sense of the word's Greek root. *Apokalypsis* means 'revelation', a tearing away of the veil. Apocalyptic language at its best is language that unmasks the apparently self-evident reality of our mundane existence and makes clear the underlying mythic dimension. Through apocalyptic consciousness, God's presence and activity, the 'kingdom' or realm of God, are laid bare in ordinary circumstances.

Jesus' use of parables was central to his apocalyptic message. He used homely comparisons and stories from everyday life as little apocalypses, unexpected keys that opened to human awareness the mystery of God at work. His images and metaphors ranged mostly through agrarian and domestic life: seeds, light, yeast, housekeeping. It was with great irony that he compared the kingdom of God – a realm of grandeur, science-fiction-type fantasy, and elaborate speculations – to such commonplaces. But when these figures communicated to people, it shook them loose from the captivity that normally held their minds, making them see the power of God in their lowly circumstances.

The grassroots movement Jesus generated over a short period of time was a surprising groundswell of hope, reconciliation, and communal sharing. It began to fulfil his proclamation of the kingdom of God on earth. His ministry bridged many realms: economic, gender-based, ethnic, social, and political. When he arrived in Jerusalem for the Passover celebration, a tidal wave of agitation and expectation accompanied him. Through some kind of collaboration, temple officials and Roman administrators combined to arrest and execute Jesus during Passover. Yet what seemed to be the end was actually a new beginning. Through his terrible death and mysterious appearance to his followers, the teller of parables became the parable. The story of Jesus' life, teaching, death, and resurrection itself became the metastory, unlocking the power of God in all kinds of people. Like the mustard seed that Jesus used to exemplify the realm of heaven, this Galilean carpenter's son was the utterly mundane figure that unlocked and fulfilled the sublime mythic hope of the Messiah, the Christ.

Paul was the key figure in communicating this powerful new parable not only to his fellow Jews but to the larger Gentile world. Rabbinically trained and conversant in Hellenistic thought, Paul translated the events that had unfolded completely within the realm of Palestinian Judaism into a message not only intelligible but transformative within the Greco-Roman culture of his day. It is important to recognize that many early Christians participated in articulating the gospel message, many of whom are not known to us. But Paul seems to be the most central, synthesising figure in that process.

Apokalypsis, 'revelation', is a key word in Paul's surviving letters to early churches. Recalling Galatians 1:12, we remember that Paul based his apostolic authority not upon an ability to transmit the story of Jesus from those who knew him, but upon a direct revelation, an '*apokalypsis* of Jesus Christ'. Let us think what that meant in terms of the temporal worldview of Paul's Jewish heritage. The risen Christ had been revealed and was revealing to Paul and others. Where did this risen Christ come from? From the resurrection which, according to Jewish expectation, was not to occur until the end of time. So something mind-blowing, earth-shaking, time-exploding occurred when Jesus rose from the dead and began to reveal himself to his friends. The revelation/apocalypse of Jesus Christ was ultimate future bursting into the present moment, the mythic rupturing the mundane. To live faithfully to that experience is to live in the end of the world right now. You may or may not believe the world is about to end in some larger historical sense, but to live according to the light or revelation of Christ is to live according to the end now.

All of Paul's language about walking according to the Spirit rather than the flesh, of thinking according to the mind of Christ, according to the wisdom of God, rather than human wisdom – all these ideas took form within an apocalyptic worldview. Paul was working out what it meant to live in the end of the world. To be in Christ is to be a 'new creation', neither male nor female, Jew nor Greek, slave nor free (Gal 3:28). The predominant categories of social status – gender, economic class, ethnic identity, etc. – no longer bind us absolutely. We must continue to deal with them out there in a world that is still spellbound by them, but we will not be defined by them any longer. Again, within the Jewish apocalyptic worldview, the new creation was an end-time, eschatological reality. But Paul proclaimed the new creation as *an unfolding present reality*. As Christ is present with us, the future becomes the present now.

To be baptised in the Spirit, into Christ's death, is to identify with the one who died at Jerusalem, who rose from the dead, who invades our present from the future, and who beckons and pulls us into the End. The End is the goal or purpose of our lives and of everything around us. Thus, Christ as the *eschatos Adam*, the 'last Adam' (1 Cor 15:45), stands before us as not only our *eschatological destiny* (our end in time) but also the *teleological purpose* of our existence (the end as goal of individual life and world history).

The Bible presents the first Adam as the *original* of human existence. All humans are Adam's type. Though Adam's fall into alienated consciousness and behaviour is not *inevitable*, it is *universal*. By contrast, the risen Christ, the eschatological Adam, coming from the future, is the *terminal* of human existence. The last Adam terminates our existence in the first Adam. This transformation is not inevitable; we can resist it. But it is offered to all and is universal in its implications; Christ is the end of the world. This redemptive power coming at us from the future utterly upends and confounds our sense of cause and effect. We are used to analysing how present realities are generated out of the past. That is, present effects arise from prior causes. But where Christ is received and followed as Lord, the future redefines the meaning and redirects the destiny of present realities.

It is not that cause and effect no longer apply. The Omega does not negate the Alpha. They are the same. But a mysterious, paradoxical *freedom* emerges from the invasion of the future into the present. For all its undiminished force of causation, the past loses something of its binding effect upon us in Christ, the last Adam.

This situation can be roughly figured visually thus:

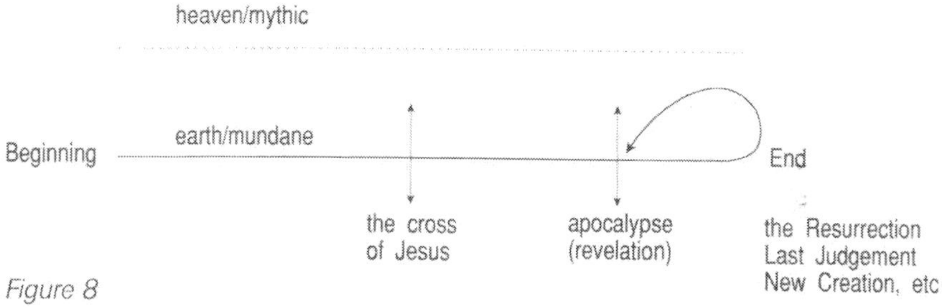

Figure 8

The horizontal plane of social interaction, or the time-line of personal and world history, is intersected by the apocalypse/revelation of Jesus Christ as it breaks in from the End, the ultimate future. This has a rupturing effect, like Jesus' image of the new wine in old wineskins. The vertical dimension, linking the mythic and mundane levels of existence, opens. There are no limits to the heights or depths that Christ unlocks. In Christ, we descend to the form of a servant, having no more dominion over anyone. Like Paul, we may suffer dearly for our witness to Christ as Lord. But we also rise in Christ to the highest vistas. Like Paul, we may feel ourselves lifted up in ecstasy to 'third heaven'. Thus, where the apocalyptic *mystery* of Christ drops into our life-line, our *history*, the cross is revealed in its awful/awesome coordinates. Standing there, Paul could witness that 'the present form of this world is passing away' (1 Cor 7:31).

Paul's experience of liberation from sin and law took place within this apocalyptic horizon. No longer defined by sin or by law, Paul found a new freedom to act as a new creation in Christ. Thus, he was still very much a Jew and proud of it; yet he was also free to be an apostle of Jesus Christ among all peoples. How could Paul feel so ultimately 'justified' and reborn? Because he had already been to Judgment Day, the end of the world. On the Damascus Road, he was literally knocked down by Christ's apocalyptic revelation. The light blinded him from seeing himself and his world as he had before. That self and that world *passed away* in that experience. Saul became Paul. As he continued to live in and according to that continuing revelation, his new identity and life came into focus.

It seems clear that Paul expected the world to end soon, in some total fashion. Obviously, things did not turn out quite that way. If we think of that 'Germanic sentence', we might say that there were many more dependent clauses to be added to the enormous 'sentence' of history before that final verb will come and transform the meaning of everything. But Paul had heard that 'last word' pronounced. His

The Germanic Sentence

The meaning of the End can be compared to the structure of a Germanic sentence. In German, the verb of the independent clause of a sentence is typically saved for the end. So, as the sentence goes on, many different ingredients may be assembled – nouns, adjectives, articles, dependent clauses – all waiting to receive their full and final meaning from the final verb. When that last word comes, it defines the meaning of the entire sentence, sometimes in a way that the hearer or reader does not expect, but often with compelling power.

Christ, the living Word of God, is present everywhere in the world, at all times in our lives, just as the final verb of the sentence pervades the sentence at large, even though it is not yet spoken explicitly until the end. Whenever Christ is revealed to us, however obliquely, we gain some sense of that final, full meaning of our lives, of all reality. Our lives contain many disparate and seemingly unrelated facets and phases, like the dependent clauses of a very complex sentence. Yet Christ, the living Word, insinuates himself throughout the whole, in a way that can be fully understood only at the end – indeed, *after* the end.

When we've been there ten thousand years,
Bright shining as the sun,
We've no less days to sing God's praise
Than when we first begun.

('Amazing Grace').

beautiful poetry in 1 Corinthians 13 suggests that that verb is *agape*, 'love'. Paul affirmed that after everything else has passed away (after every dependent clause has had its say), love will remain. Love will redefine every previous verb, modify every dependent clause, every episode of personal and world history, redeem the hopeless shambles of this wonderful and terrible run-on sentence we are helping to write. When that final, ultimately defining verb is revealed to us, we can only try to play our part faithfully and lovingly, knowing where the sentence is going, even though we cannot see the entire structure.

Epilogue

Jesus came to his people at a moment when their world was falling apart. The grinding oppression of the Roman occupation was forcing Palestinian Jewish society to fall apart at the seams. Exorbitant taxation, collaborationist political leadership, and religious conflict at all levels of Jewish life created unbearable pressures. Insurgent politics were on the rise. The Jesus movement began to generate a nonviolent alternative to self-destructive rebellion. But it was abruptly terminated through pre-emptive action by priestly and Roman authorities. Finally, some forty years after Jesus' death, the holocaust he prophesied was induced by armed Zealot rebellion and a crushing Roman response. A world ended with the destruction of Jerusalem and its temple. The symbolic centre of international Jewish identity disappeared from the face of the earth. Out of the ashes, a new, gentile-dominated church and a Diaspora-oriented rabbinic Judaism emerged.

The apocalyptic vision comes into acute focus at times when the world is coming apart and there are no evident solutions. It is extreme in its dualistic, either/or imageries and imperatives. Yet it looks to an ultimate coherence and unity of world history. It is witheringly pessimistic about the ability of individuals or societies to become healthy and self-sustaining. But it is ultimately optimistic about God's ability to transform the most hopeless situations.

The apocalyptic worldview is always in danger of running into passive speculation and prediction, sitting back and waiting for God to 'fix' everything. This is the alienated consciousness that looks for solutions 'out there' somewhere. Certainly, the apocalyptic worldview has no monopoly on alienated consciousness. But at its best, when the power of God is revealed 'in here' instead of imagined 'out there', a presence-centred apocalyptic outlook can combine the intimacy of personal spiritual experience with the ultimacy of the world, the creation, and history itself. It deals in powerful oppositions between despair and ecstasy, between grandiose visions and very practical responses to concrete situations. But it requires the mediating element of covenantal communities to ground the interplay between the intimacy of personal experience and the ultimacy of the cosmic whole.

With an apocalyptic outlook, it is always possible to see that 'the present form of this world is passing away', that the apparently self-evident and self-justifying structures of our world are fragile and all-too-humanly devised. But apocalyptic awareness is particularly apt to certain historical situations, moments of crisis and transition in a culture. In our chapters on the rise of the early Quaker movement, we saw a renewed Christian apocalyptic vision develop in response to just such a moment in seventeenth century England. Could it be that now, at the turn of the millennium, we are again faced with a culture in crisis? Could it be that the Christian revelation, long tamed in our culture, may regain its original apocalyptic meaning and power, like new wine bursting out of old wineskins? 'Can these bones live?' the Lord quizzed Ezekiel. The prophet answered, 'O Lord God, you know' (Eze 37:3).

Model: metaphor or reality?

The Second Coming outlook of the early church and early Friends is rooted in a historical sense of reality. It is based on the belief that the world has some overarching, meaningful history, one with a coherent beginning, middle and end. It is premised on the conviction that there is a God who has a benign plan for the world and its people. Such an outlook is by no means standard among Friends and many others today. In the face of modern, scientific understandings of the universe, its nature and origins, such beliefs may seem primitive at best. Isn't it ludicrous for modern people to continue to hold to such ideas?

(Continued overleaf)

Well, maybe. But consider two parallels. You could pick up a novel and look at it in several different ways. You could examine its physical production – its paper, printing, binding, etc. Or you could read it with an eye toward its grammar. You could parse every sentence, showing the magnificent regularity of its complete sentences throughout. The laws of grammar grind out their truth in a well-written novel, like the laws of physics in a well-ordered universe. But on these levels, most pulp fiction could be set alongside great novels. But at the level of story, there is a great deal separating them. While a writer must produce good sentences, the artistic success of a novel resides at other levels, some of them perhaps beyond analysis.

Or consider an individual human life. It is a marvel of physiological processes. Just on that level, every human life is a miracle, and the physical development of each individual is a great drama. But that drama would be considered a tragedy, and the individual life a failure, if judged by the final outcome. Something gives out sooner or later and death ensues. Yet on the level of an individual's spiritual life history, the end is by no means necessarily a failure. It is the end that often bestows the final, lasting meaning on a life. Earlier generations of Friends were so convinced of the final victory of a good death that they published volumes of last words and noble Quaker ends in the series *Piety Promoted*.

Could it not be possible that the same dynamics apply to the world as a whole? Just as we look for meaning in the stories of our lives, so we search for some sense of coherence and justice in the enormous saga of the world. And one does not have to be exclusivistic in Christian faith to believe that the destiny of the world has *something* to do with Christ, the object of faith, hope, and devotion among many millions of people around the world. To believe in the *Parousia*, the return of Christ in glory, is to believe that, however else God may work in the world, God was working through the Jesus Christ of the gospels and continues to work through Christ toward some good End. Metaphor or reality? A metaphor is only a metaphor to someone standing outside it.

[This excursus has drawn from a fuller statement on the biblical sense of history and the apocalyptic spirituality, *Unmasking the Idols* (Gwyn 1989).]

References

Adams, T. *A Far-Seeing Vision: the Socialist Quaker Society, 1898-1924.* Bedford: Quaker Socialist Society, undated.

Ambler, R. *Creeds and the Search for Unity.* London: Quaker Home Service, 1989.

Bauer, W.; Arndt, W.F.; Gingrich, F.W.; and Danker, F.W. *A Greek-English Lexicon of the New Testament and Other Early Christian Literature.* Chicago: University of Chicago Press, 1979.

Arthur, J. 'Britain Yearly Meeting's Relationship with the Christian Churches.' In *Who We Are: questions of Quaker identity.* London: Quaker Resources for Learning, 1995:129-34.

Bailey, R. *New Light on George Fox and Early Quakerism: the making and unmaking of a God.* San Fransisco: Mellen Research University Press, 1992.

Barbour, H.; Densmore, C.; Moger, E.H.; Sorel, N.C.; and Van Wagner, A.D., eds., *Quaker Crosscurrents: three hundred years of Friends in New York Yearly Meetings.* Syracuse: Syracuse University Press, 1995.

Beebe, G. 'Evangelical Quakerism and the Future of Friends.' Paper delivered at the Quaker Hill Consultation, Richmond, Indiana, 1997.

Beker, J. C. *Paul the Apostle.* Philadelphia: Fortress Press, 1980; Edinburgh: T. & T. Clark, 1980.

Benson, L. 'The Relation of Quakerism to its own History.' *Quaker Religious Thought* 3/2 (1961):25-40.

-- *Catholic Quakerism: a vision for all men.* Philadelphia: Philadelphia Yearly Meeting, 1968.

Braithwaite, W.C. *The Beginnings of Quakerism.* London: Macmillan, 1912.

-- *The Second Period of Quakerism.* London: Macmillan, 1919.

Buber, M. *Moses*. Oxford: East and West, 1946.

Burrough, E. *A Measure of the Times*. 1651.

-- *The Trumpet of the Lord Sounded in Sion*. 1656.

Cadbury, H.J. *Quakerism and Early Christianity*. London: George Allen and Unwin, 1957.

Carrdus, A. 'The Quaker Unchristmas.' *The Friend* 151 (1993):1659-60.

Cooper, W. 'Introduction' to Freiday, D., ed., *The Day of the Lord: eschatology in Quaker perspective*. Newberg: Barclay Press, 1981:5-9.

Damiano, K. *On Earth as it is in Heaven: eighteenth century Quakerism as realised eschatology*. PhD dissertation, Union of Experimenting Colleges and Universities, 1988.

Dandelion, P. *A Sociological Analysis of the Theology of Quakers: the silent revolution*. Lampeter and Lewiston: Edwin Mellen Press, 1996a.

-- 'From Lymbo to Bymbo' *Friends' Quarterly* 30/3 (1996b):163-70.

-- 'The Absolute Perhaps: towards an understanding of Liberal Quaker theology.' In Scott, J., ed., on the Identity, Authority, Community Consultation 1997, Forthcoming 1998.

Davie, M.D. *British Quaker Theology Since 1895*. Lampeter and Lewiston: Edwin Mellen Press, 1997.

Downing, C. 'An Eschatological Theology.' *Quaker Religious Thought* 10/1 (1969):15-27.

Dunn, J.D.G. *The Epistle to the Galatians*. London: A. & C. Black, 1993.

-- *The Partings of the Ways*. London: SCM Press; Philadelphia: Trinity Press International, 1991.

Endy, M.B., Jr. 'The Interpretation of Quakerism: Rufus Jones and his critics.' *Quaker History* (Spring 1981):3-21.

Fenn, R.K. *The Persistence of Purgatory.* Cambridge: Cambridge University Press, 1995.

Fox, G. *Works.* Philadelphia: Gould, 1831.

-- *Newes Coming Out of the North, Sounding Towards the South.* London: Giles Calvert, 1654.

Fox, M. *Original Blessing.* Santa Fe: Bear and Co., 1983.

Flannery, A. ed., *Vatican Council II: the Conciliar and post Conciliar documents.* Dublin: Dominican Publications, 1975.

Freiday, D. ed., *Barclay's Apology in Modern English.* Privately published, 1967.

Freiday, D. 'Life in the New Era: apocalyptic eschatology in scripture.' In Freiday, D., ed., *The Day of the Lord: eschatology in Quaker perspective.* Newberg: Barclay Press, 1981:41-60.

Gadamer, H.-G. *Truth and Method* trans. Weinsheimer J., and Marshall, D. G., London: Sheed & Ward, 1989 (second revised edition).

Gwyn, D. ' "Into That Which Cannot be Shaken": The Apocalyptic Gospel Preached by George Fox.' In Freiday, D., ed., *The Day of the Lord: eschatology in Quaker perspective.* Newberg: Barclay Press, 1981:61-96.

-- *Apocalypse of the Word: the life and message of George Fox (1624-1691).* Richmond: Friends United Press, 1986.

-- *Unmasking the Idols: a journey among Friends.* Richmond, Indiana: Friends United Press, 1989.

-- *The Covenant Crucified: Quakers and the rise of capitalism.* Philadelphia: Pendle Hill, 1995.

-- *Words in Time: essays and addresses.* Philadelphia: Kimo, 1997a.

-- 'Early Quakers: when seekers became finders.' Paper presented at Manchester College, Oxford, May 12, 1997b.

Hamm, T.D. *The Transformation of American Quakerism: Orthodox Friends, 1800 - 1907*. Bloomington: Indiana University Press, 1988.

-- 'George Fox and the Politics of Late Nineteenth-Century Quakerism.' In Mullett, M., ed., *New Light on George Fox, 1624-1691*. York: Sessions, 1994: 15-21.

Hanson, D. *The Dawn of Apocalyptic*. Philadelphia: Fortress, 1975.

Hays, R.B. *The Faith of Jesus Christ: an investigation of the narrative substructure of Galatians iii.1-iv.11*. Chico: Scholars, 1983.

Heron, A. *Caring Conviction and Commitment*. London and Birmingham: Quaker Home Service and Woodbrooke, 1992.

-- *A Century of Change: Quakers in Britain, 1895-1995*. Kelso: Curlew, 1995.

Hetherington, R. 'The Defining Marks of British Quakerism' *Friends' Quarterly* 32/1 (1998):10-19

Hill, C. *The World Turned Upside Down: radical ideas during the English revolution*. London: Penguin, 1975.

-- *The Experience of Defeat: Milton and some contemporaries*. London: Penguin, 1985.

Hole, I.P. *A Discourse, Delivered in Ohio Yearly Meeting of Friends, 9th Mo., 1st, in Answer to Arguments by D.B. Updegraaf, in Favor of the Ordinances*. Columbus: William G. Hubbard, 1885.

Hooker, M.D. *From Adam to Christ: essays on Paul*. Cambridge: Cambridge University Press, 1990.

Isichei, E. *Victorian Quakers*. Oxford: Oxford University Press, 1970.

Jameson, F. *The Ideologies of Theory: essays 1971-1986*, vol. II. Minneapolis: University of Minnesota, 1988.

Jeremias, J. *New Testament Theology*. London: SCM Press, 1971.

Johnson, L.T. *The Writings of the New Testament.* Philadelphia: Fortress Press, 1986; London: SCM Press, 1986.

Jones, R. *The Later Periods of Quakerism.* London: Macmillan, 1921.

Jones, T. C. *George Fox's Teaching on Redemption and Salvation.* PhD dissertation. Yale University, 1955.

--. 'A Quaker Interpretation of the Lord's Supper.' *Friends Journal* March 1996:19-21.

Kanter, R.M. *Commitment and Community.* Cambridge, Massachusetts: Harvard University Press, 1972.

Kazantzakis, N. *God's Pauper: St Francis of Assisi.* trans. Bien, P. London: Faber, 1975.

-- *The Last Temptation of Christ.* trans. Bien, P. London: Faber, 1987.

Kelley, D.M. *Why Conservative Churches are Growing.* New York: Harper and Row, 1972.

Kennedy, T. 'Why did Friends Resist?: the war, peace testimony, and the All-Friends Conference of 1920.' *Peace and Change* 14 (1989):355-71.

Kraybill, D.B., and Olshan, M.A. *The Amish Struggle with Modernity.* Hanover: University Press of New England, 1994.

Levy, B. *Quakers and the American Family.* Oxford: Oxford University Press, 1988.

Littleboy, W. *The Day of Our Visitation.* Swarthmore Lecture. London: Headley Bros., 1917.

Mack, P. *Visionary Women: ecstatic prophecy in seventeenth-century England.* Berkeley: University of California Press, 1992.

McCandless, J.H. 'The Life of the Cross and the Coming of the Kingdom' *Quaker Religious Thought* 15/4 (1974):3-25.

Meeks, W. *The First Urban Christians: the social world of the apostle Paul.* New Haven/London: Yale University Press, 1983.

Moffett, J. *Pennterra.* Sevenoaks: Hodder and Stoughton, 1988.

Moore, R. *The Faith of the First Quakers: the development of their beliefs and practices beforethe Restoration.* PhD dissertation, University of Birmingham, 1993.

Murphy O'Connor, J. *Paul: a critical life.* Oxford: Clarendon Press, 1996.

Nellis, M. 'Quakers and Education for Community Justice.' Unpublished paper presented at Woodbrooke College, January 1998.

Nickalls, J., ed. *The Journal of George Fox.* Cambridge: Cambridge University Press, 1952

Nuhn, F. 'The Peaceable Kingdom: the Quaker witness and the Judeo-Christian hope.' In Freiday, D., ed. *The Day of the Lord: eschatology in Quaker perspective.* Newberg: Barclay Press, 1981:30-40.

Onions, C.T., ed., *The Shorter Oxford English Dictionary.* 2nd edition. Oxford: Oxford University Press, 1972.

O'Shea, U.J. *Living the Way: Quaker spirituality and community.* The Religious Society of Friends (Quakers) in Australia Incorporated, 1993.

Parkinson, F. *Evolutionary Christianity: a new vision for Quakerism.* Privately Published, 1996.

Penn, W. *One Project for the Good of England.* 1679.

Perrin, R.D. and Mauss, A.L. 'Saints and Seekers: sources of recruitment to the Vineyard Christian Fellowship.' *Review of Religious Research* 33/2 (1991):97-111.

Phillips, B.D. *Friendly Patriotism: British Quakerism and the imperial nation, 1890-1910.* PhD dissertation, University of Cambridge, 1989.

Procter-Smith, M. ' "In the Line of the Female": Shakerism and Feminism.' In Wessinger, C., ed., *Women's Leadership in Marginal Religions*. Urbana: University of Illinois Press, 1993:23-40.

Punshon. J. *Testimony and Tradition*. London: Quaker Home Service, 1990.

Quaker Faith and Practice: the book of Christian discipline of the Yearly Meeting of the Religious Society of Friends (Quakers) in Britain. London: Britain Yearly Meeting, 1995.

Reay, B. *The Quakers and the English Revolution*. London: Temple Smith, 1985.

Redfern. K. *What are our Monthly Meetings Doing? a concern for revitalization of Meetings for Business 1992-93*. London: Quaker Home Service, 1993.

Ricca, P. 'Towards a Theology of Peace.' Paper given at ecumenical gathering, Budapest 1984.

Roberts, J.M. *The Hutchinson History of the World*. London: Hutchinson, 1987.

The Roman Missal. Alcester and Dublin: C. Goodliffe Neale Ltd., 1975.

Roof, W.C. *A Generation of Seekers: the spiritual journeys of the baby boom generation*. San Francisco: Harper Collins, 1993.

Ruether, R.R. *Faith and Fratricide*. New York: Seabury Press, 1974.

Sanders, E.P. *Paul and Palestinian Judaism*. London: SCM Press, 1977.

-- *Paul, the Law and the Jewish People*. Philadelphia: Fortress Press, 1983

-- *Paul*. Oxford: Oxford University Press, 1991.

Schrauwers, A. *Awaiting the Millennium: the Children of Peace and the village of Hope, 1812-1889*. Toronto: University of Toronto Press, 1993.

Schweitzer, A. *The Quest for the Historical Jesus*. New York: Macmillan, 1968.

Sheeran, M. J. *Beyond Majority Rule: Voteless decisions in the Society of Friends*. Philadelphia: Philadelphia Yearly Meeting, 1983.

Siler, E.C. 'The Pastoral Question.' *Christian Worker* 17 (1887):397-401.

Spears, J., and Spears, L. *Friendly Bible Study*. Philadelphia: Friends General Conference, 1990.

Stern, G. *Meaning and Change of Meaning. with special reference to the English language*. Goteborgs Hogskolas Arsskrift, 38, Gothenburg, 1931.

Swāmi, Shri Purohit, trans.,*The Geeta*. London: Faber and Faber, 1935.

Taber, W. 'The Theology of the Inward Imperative.' *Quaker Religious Thought* 18/4 (1980):3-19.

Thiselton, A. C. 'Semantics and New Testament Interpretation.' In Marshall, I.H., ed., *New Testament Interpretation*. Exeter: Paternoster Press, 1979:75-104.

Underwood, T.L. 'Early Quaker Eschatology.' In Toon, P., ed., *Puritans, the Millennium and the Future of Israel*. Cambridge: James Clarke & Co., 1970:91-103.

Vann, R.T. *The Social Development of English Quakerism 1655-1755*. Cambridge, Masachusetts: Harvard University Press, 1969.

Wenham, J. W. *The Elements of New Testament Greek*. Cambridge: Cambridge University Press, 1965.

WCC. *Statement of Unity*, Canberra. 1991.

White, D. *Friends, you that are of the Parliament, hear the word of the Lord*. 1659.

White, W. 'Keeping Christmas.' *The Friend* (December 24, 1996):24.

Who We Are: Questions of Quaker Identity London: Quaker Resources for Learning, 1995.

Wilcox, C.M. *The Theology of the Early Friends and its Implications for the Ministry of Women in Seventeenth Century English Quakerism.* PhD dissertation, London University, 1991.

Williams, S. K. The Hearing of Faith: ΑΚΟΗ ΠΙΣΤΕΩΣ in Galatians 3.' *New Testament Studies* 35 (1989):82-93.

Wilson, B.R. *Patterns of Sectarianism.* London: Heinemann, 1970.

Ziesler, J. *Pauline Christianity.* Oxford: Oxford University Press, 1990 (revised edition).

Index

D

E

F

G

H

I

J

K

L

M

N

O

P

- Entries in *italics* are concepts that are examined in the book.